INSIDER SECRETS

THOUSANDS OF LIFE-IMPROVING, MONEY-SAVING TIPS FROM INDUSTRY EXPERTS

A **PLUMBER** SAYS

" Soap can gum up the pipes, so use as little as you can. "

A **DOCTOR** SAYS

" Try to avoid scheduling surgery for a Friday. "

A **MECHANIC** SAYS

" Your car doesn't need fluid flushes. "

INSIDER SECRETS

THOUSANDS OF LIFE-IMPROVING, MONEY-SAVING TIPS FROM INDUSTRY EXPERTS

BY THE EDITORS OF READER'S DIGEST

Reader's
digest

New York, NY / Montreal

A READER'S DIGEST BOOK

Copyright © 2012, 2014, 2017 Trusted Media Brands, Inc.

ISBN 978–1–62145–349–9

Previously published as *13 Things They Won't Tell You*

Library of Congress catalogued the original edition of this book as follows:
13 Things They Won't Tell You : 375+ Experts Confess the Secrets They Keep to Themselves / Liz Vaccariello and the editors of Reader's Digest.
    p. cm.
 Summary: "Behind-the-scenes advice from hundreds of service professionals that will shock you—and save you time and money.OVER 1,300 EYE-OPENING MONEY-SAVING TIPS! Our experts reveal how to avoid being scammed, what services you don't need to pay for, behind-the-scenes deals (but you have to know how to ask), and how to get the best value for your money"— Provided by publisher.
 ISBN 978-1-60652-499-2 (hardcover) — ISBN 978-1-60652-503-6 (adobe) — ISBN 978-1-60652-502-9 (epub)
1. Consumer education. I. Vaccariello, Liz. II. Reader's Digest Association. III. Title: Thirteen things they won't tell you.
TX335.A13 2012
640.73--dc23
                        2012008838

We are committed to both the quality of our products and the service we provide to our customers.
We value your comments, so please feel free to contact us.

    Trusted Media Brands, Inc.
    Reader's Digest Books/Adult Trade Publishing
    44 South Broadway
    White Plains, NY 10601

For more Reader's Digest products and information, visit our website:
    www.rd.com (in the United States)
    www.rd.ca (in Canada)

Printed in the United States of America

3 5 7 9 10 8 6 4 2

CONTENTS

1   What You Don't Know About Your Home

2   *Plumber*
5   *Handyman*
9   *Gas and Electric Company*
13   *Exterminator*
16   *Locksmith*
19   *Burglars*
22   *Contractors*
25   *Real Estate Agent*
29   *Mover*
33   *Housecleaner*
37   *Professional Organizers*
41   *Yard Sale Fanatics*

47   What You Don't Know About Your Food

48   *Waiter*
52   *Fast Food Worker*
54   *Barista*
57   *Bartender*
60   *Pizza Delivery Guy*
62   *Grocer*
66   *Butcher*
68   *Farmers' Market*
71   *Food Manufacturers*

79   What You Don't Know About Your Health

80   *Nurse*
84   *Doctor*
88   *Urgent Care Centers*
90   *ER Staff*
93   *Pediatrician*
98   *Dentist*
102 *Eye Doctor*
105 *Dermatologist*
107 *Podiatrist*
110 *Sleep Doctor*
115 *Surgeon*
118 *Pharmacist*
121 *Therapist*
123 *Personal Trainer*
126 *Dietitian*

133 What You Don't Know About Your Family

134 *Wedding Planner*
139 *Happily Married People*
142 *Marriage Counselor*
146 *Mother-in-law*
149 *Parents*
152 *Nanny*
154 *Kid's Teacher*
157 *Kid's Camp Counselor*
160 *Mall Santa*
163 *Vet*

173 What You Don't Know About Your Local Businesses

174 *Car Dealer*
177 *Gas Station*
181 *Car Mechanic*
184 *Car Detailer*
188 *Dry Cleaner*
192 *Hairstylist*
196 *Makeup Counter*
200 *Gym*
202 *Computer Tech*
204 *Baby Store*
207 *Shoe Salesman*
212 *Florist*
215 *Jeweler*
218 *Funeral Director*

225 What You Don't Know About The Media

226 *TV Weatherman*
229 *LinkedIn*
232 *Facebook*
236 *Reality TV Show Producers*
239 *TV Chefs*
243 *Deal Sites*

255 What You Don't Know About Your Money

256 Banker
260 Credit Card Companies
262 Identity Thieves
267 Financial Advisor
271 Tax Accountant
274 IRS
279 People with Money
283 Cell Phone Sales Rep
286 Sales Clerk
290 Debt Collector

303 What You Don't Know About Your Job

304 Headhunter
308 Hiring Manager
311 HR Person
314 IT Department
317 Coworkers
320 Payroll Manager
323 Productivity Experts

329 What You Don't Know About Your Vacation

330 Travel Agents
335 Pilot
340 Flight Attendant
343 Airlines
345 Hotel Desk Clerk
348 World Travelers
352 Cruise Lines
354 Amusement Parks
359 Park Rangers

365 Index

Part One

WHAT YOU DON'T KNOW ABOUT
YOUR HOME

Is your home a well-oiled machine or a money pit? When you know the tricks shady contractors try to pull, what turns a quick plumbing fix into a pricey project, and how movers will try to overcharge you, you'll get the house you want minus the overspending and stress.

Beyond the remodelers, the plumbers, the exterminators, and the power companies, we didn't rest until we got you the complete story. Real estate brokers, housecleaners, and sketchy locksmiths showed us their cards. But the info that's worth its weight in gold? Convicted burglars told us what makes them pick your place over the neighbor's.

To keep your home safe and saleable, and keep your stress level at an all-time low, check out—and heed—the top secrets we got insiders to reveal.

WHAT **YOUR PLUMBER** WON'T TELL YOU

Here are the smartest ways to avoid costly plumbing mistakes.

1. Monday is our busiest day. That's the day wives call us to correct the "work" their husbands did over the weekend.

2. Know where the main turnoff source is. I can't tell you how many calls I get from people screaming and crying that their house is flooding and they don't know what to do.

3. Pay me by the job, not by the hour.

4. Don't get wrapped up in how much I'm charging for the materials. Sure, my material cost is different than the guy's who runs his business out of his garage. But it's not the copper you're paying for—it's the experience. At the end of the day, my material cost is between 25 and 30 percent of the cost of the job.

5. A company that has a good reputation for quality service might charge a little more up front, but you'll save in the long run by avoiding callbacks and extra charges. Look for a company that warrants its service for up to a year for major installations or repairs.

6. Be wary of price quotes that are strikingly lower or higher than competitors'. Get a minimum of three bids. Estimates for an average-size job should be within a few hundred dollars. Be suspicious of anything that is substantially lower or double the price of the rest, and watch out for hidden fees, like charges for travel expenses. A good plumber will not nickel and dime you like this, and many of us will offer free estimates.

7. Yes, it's against the rules to remove flow inhibitors from your showerheads, but some of us will do it if you ask.

8. Sure, we'll be happy to check those supply valves under your sink free of charge after we finish the work you're paying us for. Just ask. Same goes for checking your water pressure.

TOP SECRET! There's often an Allen wrench that comes with the garbage disposal. I keep it under the sink. When the thing jams, follow the directions in the manual and I won't need to come out.

9. I'm not a babysitter, a mover, or an auto mechanic. Don't ask.

10. You're calling to say your garage-door opener doesn't work ever since I fixed your faucet? Get a clue—and an electrician.

11. I see this all the time: Women want a new toilet seat and ask their husbands to make the switch. If the seat is old and has metal bolts, you probably need to cut it off with a hacksaw, not unscrew it. A wrench may slip, damaging the bowl and bloodying your knuckles.

12. Don't hang clothes on those exposed pipes in your basement. I've seen them break and flood a basement.

13. I was working in one bathroom while my client was using the whirlpool in another one. And blow-drying her hair at the same time. Her husband had told her it was fine. I told her he was trying to get rid of her.

SOURCES: Bill Stevens, owner of Berkey's Plumbing, Heating & Air Conditioning in Texas; plumbers in California, Connecticut, New Jersey, New York, Texas, and Wisconsin.

Great Advice

SIMPLE TIPS AND FIXES THAT WILL KEEP YOUR WALLET FLUSH

A burst washing machine hose is a top homeowner-insurance claim. I'd replace those flimsy rubber hoses with stainless steel ones.

No bricks in the toilet tank. They can keep your toilet from flushing correctly. No liquid drain cleaners either. They eat away at the pipes. Try a plunger or, better yet, a $30 auger.

If you're going away for any length of time, like on vacation, turn off your water, and if on any of those days the temperature drops below freezing, have someone check in on your house. I've been called to homes where the family returned from vacation and there was water flooding out from the front door.

Buy a drain strainer or hair snare if you've got a Rapunzel at home (or even a rapidly balding man). Or tell her to use a paper towel to clear the drain. (Soap can gum up the pipes, too, so use as little of that as you can.)

Small drips can waste over eight gallons of water a day, and a continuously running toilet can waste more than 200 gallons of water daily. If you ignore them, you'll pay for it when your water bill arrives.

Those "flushable" baby wipes are one of the main culprits for clogging pipes. They don't break down the way toilet paper does.

Always jiggling the toilet handle? You need to replace the flap valve. The part costs $4, and it's an easy fix. I charge $100 just to walk in the door.

WHAT YOUR HANDYMAN WON'T TELL YOU

It's easy to spend money at the hardware store. But we got home-repair experts to cough up their secrets about what you don't need to buy.

1. One way to condition tools and keep rust from invading is to rub them down with hair conditioner when you clean them.

2. You don't have to have a fancy drawer system. Keep nuts and washers on metal shower curtain rings hung from a hook in your workshop. The ring's pear shape and latching action ensure secure storage.

3. An ice cube tray is a great assistant. Use an old plastic ice cube tray to help keep small parts in the right order. If you really want to be organized, mark the sequence by putting a number on a piece of masking tape in each compartment.

4. Next time you have something that needs painting, place an aluminum pie pan under the paint can as a ready-made drip catcher. You'll save a lot of time cleaning up, and you can just toss the pan in the trash when you're done.

5. To keep small items like screws, nuts, and nails handy without taking up workbench space, drill a hole near the top of empty coffee cans so you can hang them on nails in your workshop wall. Label the cans with masking tape.

6. If you like to see everything you have at a glance, keep all your nails, screws, nuts, and bolts organized by screwing jar lids to the underside of a wooden or melamine shelf. Then put each type of hardware in its own clear jar, and screw each jar onto its lid.

7. Since they're highly resistant to corrosion, aluminum pie pans are especially well suited for storing hardware accessories in your workshop. Cut a pan in half and attach it (with staples or duct tape around the edges) open side up to a pegboard. Now get organized!

8. Hold small tools with an old leather or canvas belt. Tack it along the edge of a shelf, leaving small loops between nails. Slip tools into the loops.

9. Hinged handles like those found on metal garbage cans are great ways to hold large tools. Mount them so the handle hangs away from the wall. You can slip a hammer or wrench into the handle for safe storage.

10. Don't confine perforated hardboard to workshop and garage walls. It's also great for inside cabinet doors and on the sides of your workbench. Lightweight 1/8-inch perf board is fine for hand tools, but you'll want to use 1/4-inch perf board for heavier items. To keep perf-board hooks from coming loose, put a dab of hot glue on the end that hooks into the board.

11. Round up rolls of tape by slipping them onto a toilet paper holder mounted on a wall or workbench.

12. Tires are great places for "snakes." An old bicycle tire is just the right size to store metal snakes used to clean plumbing lines or "fish wires" used to run electrical cables inside walls. Just lay the snake or fish wire inside the tire, where it will expand to the shape of the tire and become encased within it. Then you can hang the tire conveniently on a hook.

13. Repairing small items, such as broken china, with glue would be easy if you had three hands. Since you only have two, try this: Stick the biggest part of the item in a small container of sand to hold it steady. Position the large piece so that when you set the broken piece in place, the piece will balance. Apply glue to both edges and stick on the broken piece.

Who Knew?
AMAZING USES FOR WD-40

Protect a Bird Feeder
To keep squirrels from taking over a bird feeder, spray a generous amount of WD-40 on top of the feeder. The pesky squirrels will slide right off.

Separate Stuck Glassware
What can you do when you reach for a drinking glass and get two locked together, one stuck tightly inside the other? You don't want to risk breaking one or both by trying to pull them apart. Stuck glasses will separate with ease if you squirt some WD-40 on them, wait a few seconds for it to work its way between the glasses, and then gently pull the glasses apart. Remember to wash the glasses thoroughly before you use them.

Get Off That Stuck Ring
When pulling and tugging can't get that ring off your finger, reach for the WD-40. A short burst of WD-40 will get the ring to slide right off. Remember to wash your hands after spraying them with WD-40.

Remove Chewing Gum from Hair
It's one of a parent's worst nightmares: chewing gum tangled in a child's hair. You don't have to panic or run for the scissors. Simply spray the gummed-up hair with WD-40, and the gum will comb out with ease. Make sure you are in a well-ventilated area when you spray and take care to avoid contact with the child's eyes.

Remove Tough Scuff Marks
Those tough black scuff marks on your kitchen floor won't be so tough anymore if you spray them with WD-40. In fact, you can use WD-40 to help remove tar and scuff marks on all your hard-surfaced floors. It won't harm the surface, and you won't have to scrub nearly as much. Remember to open the windows if you are cleaning a lot of marks.

Wipe Away Tea Stains

To remove tea stains from countertops, spray a little WD-40 on a sponge or damp cloth and wipe the stain away.

Clean Toilet Bowls

You don't need a bald genie or a specialized product to clean your toilet bowl. Use WD-40 instead: Spray it into the bowl for a couple of seconds and swish with a nylon toilet brush. The solvents in the WD-40 will help dissolve the gunk and lime stains.

Winter-Proof Boots and Shoes

Waterproof your winter boots and shoes by giving them a coat of WD-40. It'll act as a barrier so water can't penetrate the material. Also use WD-40 to remove ugly salt stains from boots and shoes during the winter months. Just spray WD-40 onto the stains and wipe with a clean rag. Your boots and shoes will look almost as good as new.

Prevent Snow Buildup on Windows

Does the weather forecast predict a big winter snowstorm? You can't stop the snow from falling, but you can prevent it from building up on your house's windows. Just spray WD-40 over the outside of your windows before the snow starts and the snow won't stick.

Keep Wasps from Building Nests

Don't let yellow jackets and other wasps ruin your spring and summer fun. Their favorite place to build nests is under eaves. So next spring, mist some WD-40 under all the eaves of your house. It will block the wasps from building their nests there.

Remove Doggie-Doo

Uh-oh, now you've stepped in it! Few things in life are more unpleasant than cleaning doggie-doo from the bottom of a sneaker, but the task will be a lot easier if you have a can of WD-40 handy. Spray some on the affected sole and use an old toothbrush to clean the crevices. Rinse with cold water and the sneakers will be ready to hit the pavement again. Now, don't forget to watch where you step!

WHAT YOUR GAS AND ELECTRIC COMPANY WON'T TELL YOU

These secrets will help you get a lower energy bill every single month.

1. Heat food in your toaster oven—it uses up to 50 percent less energy than a full-size oven. Your stovetop is more efficient than your conventional oven as well, so if you can start something there then transfer it to the oven to cut the cooking time, do so. And when you need to reheat leftovers, use your microwave.

2. Cut the amount of time you use your stove or cooktop by covering pots when you boil things. This brings the pot to a boil faster. If you're boiling potatoes, dice them to roughly ½-inch in size so they cook faster, start them in the cold water, and bring to boil. Once the water has come to a rolling boil, turn off the heat. Leave the pot on the burner, cover, and let sit for 15 to 20 minutes, until fork tender. Do the same for pasta, except add the pasta after the water is boiling and boil it for two minutes before turning off the heat. Let it sit, covered, for the amount of time remaining according to the directions on the box.

3. Your refrigerator and freezer run most efficiently when they're full. A near-empty fridge will run more frequently, sucking up more energy and costing you more money. The same is true for your freezer. You don't have to buy more food. Just fill more ice-cube trays for your freezer and pitchers with water, iced tea, or whatever you like to drink for your fridge. If you're a white wine drinker, keep a few unopened bottles in the fridge. Still empty? You can always load up the spaces with those blue ice packs.

4. Store refrigerated food and beverages in closed containers. If left uncovered, they release moisture and overburden the appliance's compressor.

5. Your programmable thermostat only saves money if you program it right. Many people mistakenly believe that these devices will automatically set themselves to operate in the most energy-efficient way. But they don't. You have to program them so that they stop your ducted air-conditioning coming on when it isn't really needed—at night or when you're at work or on holiday. Learn how to set your thermostat to suit your particular needs—lowering it by just 1° can reduce your bill by up to 15 percent.

6. Place lamps and TVs far away from thermostats so the heat given off doesn't cause air-conditioning systems to run longer than they need to.

7. Keep the heat out by opting for white window shades during warmer weather. Keep them closed during the day to reflect the sun's heat away from your house.

8. Weatherproofing saves. You could weatherproof your home yourself, of course, but even if you delegate the job, you can still come out ahead financially in the long run. Merely sealing leaks in windows and doors and insulating ducts could save you at least $100 a year and reduce CO_2 emissions by at least 1,000 pounds per year—and possibly much more. Adding insulation to your home could double the savings.

9. Water temperature matters. You can easily save money, and hundreds of pounds of CO_2 per year, by lowering the temperature of your water heater to 120° and washing clothes in cold or warm water instead of hot. You can save even more by replacing a water heater that's more than 10 or 15 years old.

10. Run your dishwasher, but only when it's full. Otherwise you are wasting water, energy, and money. And if it's full, it uses less than a third of the water you'd use by doing the job by hand. Next, if you have a six-hour delay button on your model, use it. Start it at 6 p.m. (you can always go back in and add more dishes after dinner). This way it will run at midnight, during off-peak energy hours.

11. Choose an Energy Star–compliant computer, which uses 70 percent less electricity than a non-designated model. Choose other appliances with the Energy Star designation, as well.

12. Don't believe the screensaver myth. All a screensaver does is prolong the life of your monitor by displaying a moving image while you are not using your computer, as any fixed image left on would eventually "burn" itself into the screen, ruining it. Screensavers do nothing whatsoever to save electricity—in fact, they burn up quite a lot. If you want to save energy without turning your computer off, check if it has a special energy-saving mode: Go to your operating system's control panel or preferences and explore the power-management options.

> 🔒 TOP SECRET! Fans do not actually cool the air in a room. They cool the people in it by creating a wind-chill effect on their skin. So there is no point leaving a fan on when you're no longer in a room. Instead, treat it like a light and turn it off when you leave the room. Otherwise, you will just be wasting electricity and running up a large bill.

13. Stand-by mode doesn't cost less than turning it on and off. Leaving a machine constantly in stand-by mode consumes a surprisingly large amount of electricity. If you want to save energy—and money—you should always turn your computer off at night or when you will be away from it for a long period of time. Remember also to switch off other computer hardware, such as scanners, printers, external hard drives, and speakers at the mains. If they are powered via a plugged-in transformer, that will remain on even when the power button on the appliance has been switched off.

Who Knew?
ANSWERS TO YOUR TOP 3 ENERGY QUESTIONS

. . . .

Q. Should I turn off the lights every time I leave the room?

A. Turn off incandescents if you're leaving the room for more than five seconds; compact fluorescent lights, if you'll be gone at least 15 minutes.

Q. I know cold-water washes are greener, but will they get my clothes clean?

A. The good news is, washing your clothes in warm or even cold water will get rid of almost any grime, except for the worst dirt or oily stains.

Q. In public restrooms, paper towel or electric hand dryer?

A. Go for the hot air. Far less energy is needed to heat and blow air at your hands than to make paper towels and haul them around. One study found that nine trees are cut down to supply an average fast-food restaurant with paper towels for a year; the tossed towels then create 1,000 pounds of landfill waste.

WHAT YOUR EXTERMINATOR WON'T TELL YOU

You don't always need to call in the experts for ants. Try these common ways to nix them first.

1. Create a "moat" around the object the ants are going for. Simply surround it with adhesive tape placed sticky side up.

2. Draw a line with chalk around home entry points. The ants will be repelled by the calcium carbonate in the chalk, which is actually made up of ground-up and compressed shells of marine animals. Scatter powdered chalk around garden plants to repel ants and slugs.

3. Some other household things ants hate are talcum powder, cream of tartar, borax, powered sulfur, and oil of cloves. You can put these items around your foundation and other points of entry to keep ants out.

> **TOP SECRET!** Stop ants from carrying off your picnic. Place each picnic table leg in a plastic container, and fill it with water. The ants won't be able to crawl past.

4. A baster is the right tool for hard-to-reach spots. If you've sprinkled a powdered ant deterrent, like boric acid, along any cracks or crevices where you've spotted the intruders, use a baster to blow small amounts of the powder into hard-to-reach corners and any deep voids you come across. **Note:** Keep in mind that boric acid can be toxic if ingested by young children or pets.

5. A flowerpot can help squelch fire ants. Place the flowerpot upside down over the anthill. Pour boiling water through the drain hole and you'll be burning down their house.

6. You don't need insecticides or ant traps to ant-proof your kitchen. Just give it the lemon treatment. First squirt some lemon juice on door thresholds and windowsills and into any holes or cracks where the ants are getting in. Then scatter small slices of lemon peel around the outdoor entrance.

7. Deter ants that are beating a path to your home by sprinkling salt across the doorframe or directly on their paths. Ants will be discouraged from crossing this barrier.

8. In a blender, make a smooth puree of a few orange peels in 1 cup of warm water. Slowly pour the solution over and into anthills in your garden, on your patio, and along the foundation of your home to send the little pests packing.

9. Cayenne pepper sprinkled in spots where the ants are looking for sugar, such as along the backs of your countertops or on your baseboards, will tell them that no sugar is ahead.

10. Keep cooking essentials, including sugar and paprika, safe from ant intruders by slipping a bay leaf inside your storage containers. If you're concerned about the sugar picking up a bay leaf flavor, tape the leaf to the inside of the canister lid.

11. An anti-ant aromatherapy trick is to tape sachets of sage, bay, stick cinnamon, or whole cloves inside cabinets. This will smell pleasant while discouraging ants.

12. Ants hate the smell of vinegar. So pour equal parts water and white vinegar into a spray bottle. Then spray it on anthills and around areas where you see the insects. Also keep the spray bottle handy for outdoor trips or to keep ants away from picnics or children's play areas.

13. If you have lots of anthills around your property, try pouring full-strength vinegar over them to hasten the bugs' departure.

Great Advice

NATURAL REPELLENTS FOR OTHER COMMON PESTS

The Pest: Slugs

The Remedy: These slow-moving insects are very attracted to beer. Fill an empty tuna or cat-food can with beer, and bury it in your garden soil up to its rim. Overnight, slugs will move into the beer and drown. Throw out the entire can in the morning and replace it with a fresh batch.

The Pest: Snails

The Remedy: Put a board or two on the garden soil, and snails will take shelter in the damp shade beneath them. Pick up the boards and scrape the creatures into the trash. Always water your garden in the morning. If the soil is dry at night, critters like slugs and snails will be less active.

The Pest: Earwigs

The Remedy: In the evening, roll up sheets of wet newspaper and lay them around the garden. At sunrise, earwigs will crawl inside the wet pages to take shelter. Collect the papers before they dry out, bugs and all. Don't throw the newspapers into your trash cans, or the earwigs will soon escape and make their way back to the garden. Either burn the papers and bugs, shake the earwigs into a toilet or sink and flush them down the drain, or tie up the papers and bugs tightly inside a plastic bag—with absolutely no openings—and put them in the garbage can.

The Pest: Aphids

The Remedy: Make your own citrus-rind spray by grating the rind of one lemon or orange and combining it with 1 pint (500 mL) boiling water. Let it steep overnight, then strain through a coffee filter to remove the bits of rind. Add the mixture to a spray bottle, and spray the aphids on the leaves of the plants. Make sure to spray underneath the leaves, too. Reapply every four to seven days as long as the problem persists.

WHAT **YOUR LOCKSMITH** WON'T TELL YOU

These secrets will keep you from getting gouged—or worse—when you lock yourself or other people out.

1. Many locksmiths in the phone book or online are scam artists. They'll quote you a great price, but when they get there, they'll say you have a special lock they can't pick, so they have to drill it open. Then they charge you $125 for a replacement lock you can buy at Home Depot for $25. You can find someone reputable at findalocksmith.com.

2. It's easy to defeat the cheapo locks from big-box stores. Most are mass-produced by reputable manufacturers but to very low standards. Look for at least a grade 2.

3. The best lock is a dead bolt that's properly installed. It should have at least a one-inch "throw," and on the "strike side," there should be a security plate with screws at least three inches long that go all the way into the door's wood frame.

4. If you have a window on or near your door, a thumb-turn dead bolt won't do much good. Burglers knock out the glass, stick a hand in, and turn. Get a double cylinder lock that needs a key on the inside.

5. Keys stamped "Do not duplicate" are duplicated all the time. Ask me about high-security locks with keys that can't be replicated at the hardware store.

6. When you buy a new house, always have your locks rekeyed. Otherwise there's probably a master key out there that can easily open your home.

7. Don't believe a car dealer who says only he can duplicate keys. In most cases, a locksmith who specializes in automotive work can make you a key—usually cheaper.

8. Divorce lock-outs are a challenge. The soon-to-be-ex-wife will call and say she's locked out, so I get her in and change the locks. Then the husband calls with the same request. I refer him to a competitor.

9. Have a housekeeper who needs a key? Ask me to key your door so that your master key works on both the dead bolt and the doorknob, but hers works just on the knob. On the day she comes, lock only the knob.

10. A lot of us do undercover work for the cops. We make keys for them and get them into places at 3 a.m. so they can set up surveillance equipment or put the bugs in place. It's part of the thrill of doing what we do.

11. I've seen my share of dead bodies. It's always a bad sign when the landlord calls to get into an apartment, and nobody's seen the tenant for ten days.

12. Try the door even if you don't have your keys. I've gone to houses and found the door unlocked. (I'm still going to charge you for the service call.)

13. Don't feel bad if you have to call me twice in a short span of time. I once had a guy lock himself out of his house three times in one day.

SOURCES: Tom Rubenoff, a hardware salesman and former locksmith in Brookline, Massachusetts; Charles Eastwood, who operates Locksmith Charley in Phoenix, Arizona; Bob DeWeese, a locksmith in Baltimore, Maryland; and Rick Bayuk, owner of Karpilow Safe & Lock in Bridgeport, Connecticut.

Great Advice

5 WAYS TO MAKE YOUR FRONT DOOR MORE SECURE

1. Add a heavy-duty dead bolt. A dead bolt is a low-cost, high-value addition to your security system. Varieties include double-cylinder dead bolts, which are keyed on both sides, and single-cylinder dead bolts, keyed on one side. Whichever type you choose, make sure it has a grade-2 security rating.

2. Add a strike box. A strike box is something you can add to your lock that toughens up your entry and deters intruders by replacing existing strike plates with a structure that includes a metal pocket, oversized plates, and a solid connection into the wall stud behind the doorjamb with three-inch screws. To accommodate this addition, you'll need to enlarge both the hole in the jamb and the cover plate recess.

3. Add a reinforcement plate. Three-sided metal reinforcement plates add an extra layer of security by encasing a door around its handset or dead bolt. To select the correct size for your door, measure its thickness, the handset or dead bolt hole diameter, and the distance between its edge and the center of the handset or dead bolt (known as the setback).

4. Rekey the lock. If you're not the first to live in your present abode, rekeying the entry locks is yet another way to enhance security. Rekeying kits matching most lock brands can be found at hardware stores and home improvement centers, and work on both entrance and dead bolt locks. They also allow up to six locks to be rekeyed for the same key.

5. Install a wide-angle peephole. You'll be able to do a larger scale screening of unexpected visitors with a wide-angle peephole viewer. This easy-to-install safety accessory is designed to fit any door up to two inches thick.

WHAT BURGLARS WON'T TELL YOU

We got convicted thieves to reveal their sneakiest secrets. Here are the top 13 things to know to avoid being a victim.

1. Of course I look familiar. I was here just last week cleaning your carpets, painting your shutters, or delivering your new refrigerator.

2. And hey, thanks for letting me use the bathroom when I was working in your yard last week. While I was in there, I unlatched the back window to make my return a little easier.

3. Sometimes I carry a clipboard. There are times when I dress like a lawn guy and carry a rake. I do my best to never, ever look like a crook.

4. The two things I hate most: Loud dogs and nosy neighbors.

5. I'll break a window to get in, even if it makes a little noise. If your neighbor hears one loud sound, he'll stop what he's doing and wait to hear it again. If he doesn't hear it again, he'll just go back to what he was doing. It's human nature.

6. Your alarm only works if it's on. I'm not complaining, but why would you pay all that money for a fancy alarm system and leave your house without setting it?

7. A good security company alarms the window over the sink. And the windows on the second floor, which often access the master bedroom—and your jewelry. It's not a bad idea to put motion detectors up there, too.

8. Don't let me see your security system. If decorative glass is part of your front entrance, don't let your alarm company install the control pad where I can see if it's set. That makes it too easy.

9. I love looking in your windows. I'm looking for signs that you're home and for flat screen TVs or gaming systems I'd like. I'll drive or walk through your neighborhood at night, before you close the blinds, just to pick my targets.

10. Lock your windows. To you, leaving that window open just a crack during the day is a way to let in a little fresh air. To me, it's an invitation.

11. I always knock first. If you answer, I'll ask for directions somewhere or offer to clean your gutters. (Don't take me up on it.)

12. Do you really think I won't look in your sock drawer? I always check dresser drawers, the bedside table, and the medicine cabinet.

13. You're right: I won't have enough time to break into that safe. . . . The one where you keep your valuables. But if it's not bolted down, I'll take it with me.

SOURCES: Convicted burglars in North Carolina, Oregon, California, and Kentucky; security consultant Chris McGoey, who runs crimedoctor.com; and Richard T. Wright, a criminology professor at the University of Missouri–St. Louis, who interviewed 105 burglars for his book *Burglars on the Job*.

Great Advice

4 WAYS TO KEEP YOUR HOME SAFE WHILE YOU'RE ON VACATION

1. Burglars really do look for newspapers piled up on the driveway. They might even leave a pizza flyer in your front door to see how long it takes you to remove it. Have a neighbor collect this stuff while you're gone, and no one will know you aren't home.

2. Avoid announcing your vacation on your Facebook page. It's easier than you think to look up your address.

3. If it snows while you're out of town, get a neighbor to create car tracks into the driveway and foot tracks into the house. Virgin drifts in the driveway are a dead giveaway that you've taken a trip to warmer climes.

4. A loud TV or radio can be a better deterrent than the best alarm system. If you're reluctant to leave your TV on while you're out of town, you can buy a $35 device that works on a timer and simulates the flickering glow of a real television. (Find it at faketv.com.)

WHAT YOUR CONTRACTOR WON'T TELL YOU

Here are some of the best ways to avoid home remodeling hassles and headaches.

1. Triple-check financing before you start. You don't want to run out of money to pay me because your lender decides to lower or eliminate your home equity line of credit. (And it can, at any time.)

2. Avoid surprise fines by asking your municipal building department about permits that homeowners might need to get for construction-related services like Dumpsters. Also make sure you're familiar with noise and nuisance ordinances so you're not hit with a costly complaint from neighbors annoyed by the 6 a.m. symphony hammered out by the crew.

3. The National Association of Home Builders has a Green Building Program. Search its website for a green builder in your area: Go to nahbgreen.org and click on Certified Green Professional.

4. Look at work I've done in the past 12 months, on a budget similar to yours. (Older projects likely had bigger budgets and more expensive materials.)

5. Check me out: Any liens? Pending lawsuits? Do I have a valid state license? Do my subcontractors?

6. Test-drive me on a smaller project before you commit.

7. Do I have insurance? Check directly with my insurance company. Those papers I waved in front of you may have expired years ago.

8. Don't overimprove if home values are falling. If a contractor is trying to bolster his pitch with potential resale value, cross-check his claims with a real estate agent or appraiser.

9. Spell everything out. Otherwise, I may not prime the walls before I paint or I may not build that closet shelf and put up that rod. Expect nothing that's not in writing.

> **TOP SECRET!** Ask if you're getting a dedicated crew. If not, your project may drag on while I juggle multiple jobs. Tie the contract to deadlines for each phase.

10. Reduce the risk of upcharges. Some contractors may charge extra for upgrades required by municipal inspectors to cover extra costs—all the more reason to review your plans in advance with your municipal building staff. You can change the plans, and the project budget, to reflect the cost of complying with the code from the start.

11. Find out who will actually be doing the work on your project by requesting a list of the subcontractors. If there's an apprentice, who will be supervising him to be sure the work is done correctly?

12. Get the details of the project schedule and how the contractor has prioritized your job compared to all his work. Ask for a job schedule broken down by phase—demolition, rough construction, plumbing, electrical, and finish work.

13. Ditto for the brand and precise quality of the materials, appliances, and fixtures you are ordering. Don't let us sub in materials of "equal or better quality" that aren't.

SOURCES: Harvard Joint Center for Housing Studies; Roger Peugeot, president of Roger the Plumber, Inc., Overland Park, Kansas; Collin Johnson, director of inspection services for the City of Glendale, Wisconsin; Bruce Case, president of Case Design/ Remodeling, Inc., based in Bethesda, Maryland.

Great Advice
HOW TO AVOID HIRING A SHADY CONTRACTOR

1. Be cautious: Don't do business with someone who comes to your door without an appointment. Be especially wary if the contractor drives a vehicle with no company name and phone number or with out-of-state license plates.

2. Do your research: Before working with a contractor, research the company. Check out its rating and complaint history with the Better Business Bureau (www.bbb.org).

3. Ask around: Ask neighbors, friends, relatives, or local consumer advocates for recommendations of reliable contractors.

4. Explore your options: Get at least three written bids for the work you want done from three different contractors before choosing one.

5. Check the contractor's background: When you're ready to hire a contractor, ask for proof that the company is properly licensed and bonded (to protect you against theft and damage), that it carries liability insurance, and that it provides workers' compensation insurance.

6. Get references: Ask the contractor for references from the company's last three jobs—and check those references!

7. Get a contract: Demand a written contract that lists the specific work to be done, costs, materials to be used, start and completion dates, and warranty information on products and installation. Read the fine print carefully before signing it.

8. Be smart about payments: Do not pay more than 33 percent of the total job cost as a deposit. Hold off on your final payment until the job is finished and you are satisfied with the completed work.

WHAT YOUR REAL ESTATE AGENT WON'T TELL YOU

What you don't know can cost you. Here's how to be smart when buying and selling.

1. My number one selling tip: Clear off countertops in the bathrooms and kitchen. Americans love that wide-open counter space.

2. Your open house helps me more than it helps you. The majority of visitors aren't buyers—they're nosy neighbors—and that gives me the opportunity to hand out my card.

3. Plug-in air fresheners are a turnoff to a lot of people. If you want your house to smell good, bake cookies.

4. Yes, staging your home by getting rid of clutter and bringing in furniture or accessories can help it sell. But music, champagne glasses next to the bed, and fake pies on the countertop? That's going overboard, and it will turn off some buyers.

5. If you get a call saying that some buyers want to see your house in 15 minutes, let them in even if it's a bit messy. Those last-minute types typically make impulsive decisions, and they might just decide to buy a house that day.

6. In a slow market, don't be offended by a lowball offer. You have a better chance of getting that person to pay than finding someone new.

7. If I'm hugely successful, you may not get the benefit of my experience. A well-known agent may pass you off to a junior agent after you sign the contract. Ask me exactly who you will be dealing with.

> 🔒 **TOP SECRET!** Houses without furniture don't look larger. Empty rooms may actually appear smaller because the buyers can't get a sense of how much furniture will fit.

8. The commission is always negotiable upfront, before you sign a contract. You can even make it part of the transaction. If you and your buyer are $4,000 apart, for example, ask the agents if they are willing to reduce their commissions by $2,000.

9. Make sure you read my listing or buyer's contract carefully before signing it. There may be an extra "administrative fee" ranging from $250 to $1,500 on top of my standard commission, intended to cover my brokerage's administrative costs. Similar to my commission, this fee is negotiable.

10. Don't skip the final walk-through. Make sure that repairs were done properly, the owner's personal items have been removed, and the items you agreed should stay are still there. I've seen stoves, washers, and dryers walk right out the door.

11. Beware of sellers' agents who overestimate your house's selling price. They're hoping you'll choose them over other agents who will price it more realistically. We call that "buying your listing," and it guarantees your house will sit on the market for a very long time.

12. If I'm new in the business, my references are likely to be relatives or friends. Always ask how they found me.

13. Even if I've had my license a few years, I may be a soccer coach moonlighting as a real estate agent, and yours may be the first home I've tried to sell in years. Ask how many transactions I completed last year, and Google my name to see if it comes up on real estate forums and websites.

SOURCES: Licensed real estate agents Nicole Tucker in Dallas and Eric Bramlett in Austin, Texas; broker Karyn Anjali Glubis in Tampa, Florida; Rob Foley, a former real estate lawyer who now owns Vermont's Flat Fee Real Estate; and a realtor in Los Angeles, California.

Great Advice

10 WAYS TO INCREASE YOUR HOME'S VALUE WITH EXTERIOR PAINT

1. Color can ratchet up the price. An effective use of color on the exterior of your home can add thousands of dollars to its value, says James Martin, who has been hired by landlords and real estate developers to increase the market value of their properties or improve occupancy rates in their buildings with eye-catching color schemes.

2. Perception of color is relative. If you put a mid-value color, such as tan, next to pure white, it will look beige. But if you put it next to dark green, it will look off-white. Keep this in mind when choosing colors. And when you are choosing a color from a fan deck at the paint store, you should mask off the colors next to it with a white sheet of paper.

3. Begin with the value. Design your color scheme first according to value. That is, decide whether you want a dark, medium, or light main color.

4. Highlight detail carefully. Create a balanced effect between the top and bottom of your home. For instance, if there is a lot of detail on the top of your home, you will need to create detail and interest on the bottom.

5. Don't be top-heavy. Put darker colors toward the bottom of the house to avoid creating an "uncomfortable, top-heavy feel," says Martin.

6. Choose colors in the right light. Pick colors outside in natural light on a cloudy day or in open shade. Bright light creates glare and can distort your perception of the color.

7. Be material-minded. Make sure the paint colors you choose complement the colors of the other materials of your home, such as the roof, brick, stone, or stucco.

8. Brighten things up. Paint window sashes and overhead surfaces, such as porch ceilings and soffits, a lighter color to reflect light and lift the spirit of your home.

9. Go warm, not cool. Use warm colors as opposed to cool. For instance, use a warm yellow-white as opposed to a cool blue-white.

10. Play up the size. Use light colors to make a small house look bigger, and dark colors to make a large house that is squeezed onto a small lot look smaller.

WHAT YOUR MOVER WON'T TELL YOU

Here's what you need to know before you make your big move—including who's legit and how long it really takes.

1. Make sure your mover is legit. If you're moving interstate, search for companies that are registered with the Federal Motor Carrier Safety Administration (FMSCA) at protectyourmove.gov. For an in-state mover, visit the American Moving & Storage Association's (AMSA) consumer website at moving.org to find screened and approved companies.

2. Beware of rogue movers. Movers should answer the telephone with the company's name, rather than a generic term like "moving company." Once you've chosen a company, stop by its office to make sure it exists and is in good condition. On moving day, make sure a company-owned and marked fleet truck—not a rental truck—arrives.

3. Movers covered by federal law must view your belongings in person before giving you an estimate if they have an office within 50 miles of your home.

4. Beware those that try to give you a phone estimate; they can later say you have more stuff than you told them about.

5. Get in-person estimates from at least three companies, and don't hire one that quotes a price much higher or lower than competitors.

6. We can charge extra fees. Consider a binding agreement, which means you'll pay what the movers estimated regardless of what your shipment ends up weighing. Caveat: The movers can still charge extra for moving into a home on a steep hill, with many steps, or in a crowded city. Ask about fees ahead of time.

7. We can charge up to 110 percent of the original estimate. But under federal law, movers cannot charge you more than that (not including fees and extras), even under a non-binding agreement. They also cannot require full payment before final delivery.

8. Movers are responsible for items that are damaged or lost if you purchase insurance with full liability. Be sure to list china, antiques, and anything with a value of more than $100 per pound on shipping documents.

9. Take jewelry, important papers, and other valuable small items with you rather than packing them.

10. Pack only one room at a time. Don't start the next room until you're finished. It'll keep you organized and allow you to tackle the move in smaller steps.

11. Don't try to move without a permanent marker. Label, label, label. Write down the contents and the destination room on every box. This may seem obvious, but it can fall by the wayside during a busy move.

12. If you move between October and May, it's considered off-peak, and you'll likely receive better service. If you must move during peak season, try to move mid-month and mid-week.

13. Believe us when we say we can move your car cheaper than you can. Moving your car across the country can cost you at least $1,000, but that's less than the roughly $1,500 in mileage and gas at current prices (plus food and lodging along the way) it'll cost you to drive.

SOURCES: Associated Press; Federal Motor Carrier Safety Administration; American Moving & Storage Association.

Great Advice

DON'T TOSS IT! HERE'S HOW YOU CAN RECYCLE HAZARDOUS STUFF

In your rush to whittle down your belongings, make sure you do the right thing with the environmentally unfriendly finds you're likely to encounter. Here are the recommended methods for recycling from the EPA, Earth911.com, and call2recycle.org.

The Hazard: CFL Bulbs

What to do: Because compact fluorescent light bulbs (CFLs) contain toxic mercury, which can be released into the environment when they break, CFLs shouldn't be disposed of with household trash or recycled with glass. Visit Earth911.com to find out whether your bulbs can be collected by or dropped off at a local waste removal agency. Several hardware and home store chains also have CFL recycling programs, including Home Depot, Lowe's, Ace Hardware, and Ikea.

The Hazard: Dry-Cell Batteries

What to do: Dry-cell batteries are what's used to power most of our cord-free toys and home appliances. Button, AAA, AA, C, D, and 9-volt are all varieties of dry-cell batteries, which fall into two categories:

Single use: Single use batteries come in several varieties, including alkaline, carbon-zinc, lithium, nickel-cadmium (NiCad), nickel metal hydride (NiMH), and button cell (lithium manganese). All contain elements or heavy metals that can become environmental hazards when they end up in dumps and waste treatment facilities. Not all states require recycling of single use batteries, but there are local battery recycling agencies in most cities and towns. Do a quick Internet search to find one near you.

Rechargeable: Rechargeable batteries last longer than their single-use predecessors, but they still contain environmental toxins. Visit call2recycle.org to find a drop-off location in your neighborhood.

The Hazard: Cell Phones

What to do: In most cases, recycling a cell phone means donating it to a worthy cause. Next time you upgrade, free up some storage space and bring that drawer full of older models to your local wireless retailer (AT&T, Verizon, T-Mobile, LG, Sony, Best Buy) or big box office supply store (Staples, Office Depot). Many charities and local government offices also accept cell phone donations.

The Hazard: Household Cleaners and Containers

What to do: Unless they're labeled nontoxic, many household cleaners contain potentially hazardous chemicals. If the label doesn't contain disposal instructions, determine whether the cleaner is water-soluble (mixes with water). If so, pour it down the drain under running water. Sponges, wipes, and mop-heads can be thrown in the trash. For products that contain harsher chemicals, such as oven cleaners and drain openers, contact the manufacturer for disposal instructions if none are provided. In many areas, household cleaner containers can be recycled curbside, but it's a good idea to check your local recycling guidelines.

WHAT **YOUR** HOUSECLEANER WON'T TELL YOU

Learn how a good relationship makes for a clean house—and other neat secrets—from the people who see (and sometimes put away) your dirty laundry.

1. Please say thank you, even if it's just on a sticky note. Or if you really like me, leave something like a $5 gift card to McDonald's. If I feel like someone appreciates me, I really go the extra mile.

2. Make sure you have all the cleaning products I will need. Sometimes I show up, and my clients have nothing for me to use. You know best what kind of cleaners you want used in your home; some people want only organic cleaners, some are picky about brands, and others have allergies.

> **TOP SECRET!** I know more than you think. I see the piles of bills marked "past due" and know you're having money problems. I find drugs and condom wrappers in kids' bedrooms. And I can tell who's unfaithful because the cheaters always start hiding dirty laundry.

3. Don't forget that I need equipment! One of my bosses kept forgetting to get me a mop so I had to wash her floors on my hands and knees with a cloth. Not only is that inconsiderate, it's harder for me to get the results you want.

4. Please do not ask me to sew on buttons . . . clean the wheels of your bike, scrub out your mailbox, or pull out the refrigerator in order to clean behind it.

5. Letting us work "by the job" sometimes means you get less for your money. It can be more cost effective to pay an hourly rate, especially if it's a maintenance cleaning.

6. It's helpful if you soak dirty pans so that I can clean them more easily when I get there.

7. I need reasonable notice if you are going to move or stop hiring me. Too many clients don't think to tell me until the week they're moving. A month's notice would be nice. You give your landlord a month's notice. Please do me the same courtesy.

8. Tiny kindnesses mean a lot. One time a client left me a gift from a trip abroad, which delighted me. Those small appreciations keep me working hard.

9. It's a huge relief when clients allow me to take my child with me to work. Sometimes I just can't find a sitter, but I still need the money.

10. Please write a list of the things you would like me to do, in addition to giving me verbal instructions, to ensure I don't forget anything.

11. Be wary if I give you my price over the phone. Reputable cleaners come to your home and give you a free estimate.

12. If your house is a disorganized mess, it makes it harder for me to clean, and if you pay me by the hour, you'll pay more. Please pick up toys, piles of papers, and clutter from surfaces so that I can actually get to them.

13. Think our insurance will cover you? Hmm, maybe not. Insurance companies expect us to be trained professionals, so if we use the wrong product on your expensive furnishings, the insurance company might deny the claim.

SOURCES: Tangela Ekhoff, a housecleaner in Tulsa, Oklahoma; Lynette Haugen, owner of True Blue Maids of Pasadena, California; Theresa Peterson, owner of Quality Cleaning "Maid to Order" in Fremont, California; Torrey Shannon, former maid service owner in Westcliffe, Colorado; and house cleaners in Louisiana, New York, Vermont, Washington, and London.

Great Advice

SQUEAKY-CLEAN TIPS YOUR HOUSEKEEPER MAY NOT EVEN KNOW

The best way to dust blinds? Close them, then wipe up and down with an old dryer sheet. It'll create an antistatic barrier that helps prevent dust from building up again.

The Mr. Clean Magic Eraser is your friend. It will cut your cleaning time in half for bathtubs, sinks, countertops, and dirty walls.

To clean glass and mirrors, use coffee filters, not paper towels. They leave no streaks or lint—and they're cheap.

Vinegar and water is a great deodorizer for a musty bathroom. Spray your shower down as you're getting out. It really absorbs the odors, and the smell of vinegar goes away in an hour.

A wet pumice stone will clean a dirty oven faster than any spray-on product. Trust us.

Vacuuming bathroom mats is a nightmare. Toss them in the wash every week or two instead.

To damp-mop wood floors, use plain water or a water-based floor cleaner like Bona. Don't use vinegar. The acid in it will pit your polyurethane finish, can void your warranty, and may reduce shine over time.

Our biggest secret weapon? A powdered product called Bar Keepers Friend. We use it on everything. Its active ingredient is rhubarb powder, which really cuts through grit and grime. It cleans glass-top stoves, counters, toilets, porcelain, and more. Your sink will never be shinier.

To clean your microwave oven, microwave a cup of water with some baking soda in it until it's boiling. This eliminates odors and makes it super easy to wipe away all that stuck-on stuff.

Clean cobwebs with a yardstick covered by a tube sock. This also works for cleaning under stoves and refrigerators.

Shine your bathroom tiles with lemon oil. It also helps prevent mold and mildew.

To eliminate that ring in your toilet, drop in a bubbling denture-cleaning tablet and leave it for at least 30 minutes or overnight. The stain will come off with just a few swishes of the brush.

WHAT PROFESSIONAL ORGANIZERS WON'T TELL YOU

It's not that hard to get and stay organized. You just have to know how to go about it— here are some tips.

1. Clients tell me the same thing: When they go to clean their closets, they tend to pull everything out and then they run out of time and they push it all back in, which makes it worse than it was to begin with. So my suggestion is to divide and conquer. On a Saturday morning do your shoes, then at other times do your slacks. People have told me that breaking it up into small projects has changed their life.

2. I always recommend grouping "like with like." It enables people to find items quickly. All tank tops together, all capri pants together in one area. Some people like to group items by sleeve length—and there are a few in the spring and summer seasons.

3. I've even seen people use color-coded hangers, but I don't recommend it—too time consuming!

4. Purses on shelves tend to get messy. For those who have wall space in their closets, a great solution would be to purchase belt racks and hang them vertically instead of horizontally. That way, the bottoms of the purses don't bunch up in the same place. This also works great for ties!

5. Look around your home for things that are going unused, that might be empty—like file drawers—and store things away in there. I have had a lot of clients who collect old suitcases and use them for storage—those don't take up much room.

6. Use clear shoeboxes for hair accessories and light-weight scarves. You can even use a clear bin for small tank tops, shorts, etc. Take a Polaroid or cut out a magazine photo and tape it so you know what's in the box. Those are fun and it will make getting to things so easy.

7. I grew up in an apartment, and we had to get creative with our winter clothing storage. One solution is to purchase plastic bags that you can suck the air out of. The clothes then take up much less space and can be placed under a bed, a couch, or on a high shelf.

🔒 TOP SECRET! When you get out your spring clothes, put the hangers in backward on the rod but then when you wear a piece of clothing, hang it up facing the front. At the end of the season you'll know what you've never worn.

8. Also, some local dry cleaners will store winter clothes for people (as long as they're dry cleaning them for you, too).

9. Get together a group of friends and host a clothing swap. Have them bring clothes they are not using and certainly don't want to discard—someone's going to want it! Have a little cocktail party, and everyone gets new clothes without spending money . . . it's a win-win situation for everyone.

10. Return anything you bought more than four months ago and never used. Many stores won't let you return for cash clothing you loved in the shop but never got around to wearing. However, they are likely to offer you store credit if you insist. So instead of letting unwanted clothes pile up in your closets, a better idea is to return them for store credit.

11. Sometimes, you can sell store credit for cash on eBay. There's a very vibrant market for store credit receipts and gift cards, which trade for very close to face value. I've seen $200 gift receipts from stores like Macy's, Tiffany, and Bloomingdale's fetch $180, so you get most of your value back without having to find a buyer for your specific item or dealing with packing and shipping it.

12. Keep winter clothes dry when you're storing them in the basement by putting pieces of chalk into a small cloth bag that you can pack with the clothes you're storing. The chalk will absorb all the moisture, keeping your clothes protected.

13. Literally clean your closet. Before you put the upcoming season's clothes back into the closet, take the opportunity of having empty shelves to replace your shelf paper, vacuum the closet floor, and make the closet fresh and clean.

SOURCES: Ann Bingley Gallops, professional organizer from The Organized Life; Beth Levin, professional organizer of Closet Queen; Stacey Agin Murray, professional organizer of Organized Artistry; Dan Nissanoff, author of *FutureShop*; Mary Pankiewicz, professional organizer and author of *You Can Be Clutter-Free & Organized*.

Great Advice

INCREDIBLY CLEVER— AND CHEAP!—WAYS TO CLEAN AND STORE CLUTTER

Tennis Rackets, Baseball Bats Keep a decorated empty wine or liquor carton—with partitions and the top cut off—in your child's room and use it for easy storage of tennis rackets, baseball bats, fishing poles, and such.

Coins Instead of emptying the coins from your pockets into a jar for later sorting, cut off a four-section piece of an egg carton and leave it on your dresser. Sort your quarters, dimes, nickels, and pennies as you pull them out of your pockets.

Junk Drawer Items If your junk drawer is an unsightly mess, insert a plastic ice cube tray for easy, low-cost organization. One "cube" can hold paper clips, the next, rubber bands, another, stamps. It's another small way to bring order to your life.

Utility Closet Clutter A hanging shoe bag is a great organizer in the utility closet. Use its pockets to store sponges, scrub brushes, and other cleaning utensils—and even some bottles of cleaning products.

WHAT YARD SALE FANATICS WON'T TELL YOU

Here's the inside scoop on what really draws buyers and how to get the best price for your stuff.

1. Get your neighbors involved. A group sale will draw more lookers than a one-family sale.

2. There's more than one pricing strategy. Decide whether you're selling things to make money or to get rid of them. Price items accordingly.

3. Ask for 25 to 33 percent of the item's original cost.

4. Be less flexible about price at the beginning of the sale and more flexible at the end.

5. We can't come to your sale if we don't know it's there. Go to yardsalequeen.com for ideas about lettering, sign placement, and free ways to advertise your sale.

6. A great way to create a sign is with a brown paper bag. Write on it using big, fat, thick lettering—definitely no wispy ballpoint pen—then fill it with rocks, and tape it shut.

7. Non-holiday weekends after local paydays are the best time to schedule a sale.

8. Put the nice stuff closer to the road. Place tools and gadgets out front, too, to draw men who might otherwise try to overrule their wives about stopping at your sale.

9. Do your own math. Say no to helpful calculations from customers, thanks just the same.

10. Your house isn't a dressing room. Don't let strangers into your house to try on clothes or use the restroom.

🔒 **TOP SECRET!** People switch tags. Seriously. As if you're not already giving a discount. Just keep your eye on who's looking at your stuff.

11. Wear a fanny pack; don't keep money in a shoebox. Keep all the money in it, along with a cell phone just in case.

12. Check the bills people give you. It's not that uncommon for people to tell you they gave you a $20 when they gave you a $10.

13. Watch out for sneaks. People will take things out of boxes, put them under their clothes, and leave the empty boxes behind.

SOURCES: J. D. Roth, writer for *Time*'s Moneyland blog; and the experts at yardsalequeen.com and blog.movebuilder.com.

Insider Expertise

HOW TO AVOID LOSING MONEY ON REPAIRS YOU DON'T NEED

Each spring and summer, professional home improvement scammers roam the United States in search of victims. They often target people who live in areas recently damaged by weather events—such as the tornado-ravaged Midwest—and older adults, offering "deals" on home repairs. So how can you avoid being fooled by one? Use these tips.

1. Leaky Roof Wrangling

Water is coming through your roof. Or is it? A con artist will say water is seeping through the shingles and you need to tear off all the old layers and build a new roof, a job that typically costs $5,000 or more.

The Reality: Most of the time, roof leaks occur because the sealing around vent pipes has failed, the metal flashing on the chimney has deteriorated, or the connections between roof sections have eroded. Replacing the sealing or flashing, simply and cheaply, will often solve the problem.

Normally, an asphalt shingle roof lasts 15 to 20 years. You need to replace the roof if you see curling or missing shingles or a large amount of granular material from the shingles collecting in gutters. Don't get talked into having the bad roof torn off, at a potential 50 percent increase in costs, unless your building code demands it. Many towns will allow a second or even third asphalt roof to be installed if the home's framing can support the extra weight. And beware a roofer who says you need an entirely new deck, the wood base beneath the shingles. A completely new deck is needed only one in 1,000 times.

2. Basement Boondoggle

If your basement is chronically wet, unscrupulous contractors might tell you they need to dig out your entire foundation and waterproof it, for anywhere from $5,000 to $15,000. More often, though, the solution is simple and costs very little.

The Reality: Many basement leaks are caused by overflow from clogged gutters, misrouted downspouts, unsloped land around the house, or even improperly aimed lawn sprinklers.

"Think of your masonry foundation as a rigid sponge," explains waterproofing expert Richard Barako. If the water volume is above normal, water will wick through the cinder blocks. So before calling in professional help, try to reduce the moisture along the foundation by cleaning gutters, rerouting downspouts, repositioning sprinklers, or packing fresh soil six inches high against the foundation and sloping it back to level within about three feet.

Damp walls may be caused by high humidity. To test, attach a piece of aluminum foil to the foundation wall; if moisture shows up on the patch in a day or two, it's just condensation. Start shopping for a dehumidifier.

If water is still seeping in, repair any cracks with hydraulic cement, available at home stores, and apply a quality water-proof paint such as Latex Base Drylok Masonry Waterproofer. As a last resort, consider hiring a professional engineer, whose impartial advice would be worth the expense. Home inspectors are less expensive, but be sure they're certified by the American Society of Home Inspectors.

3. Termite Treatments

Myths about termites abound. In a recent survey by the University of Kentucky, 60 percent of people thought termites could take a house down in six months or less. Nothing could be further from the truth, yet con artists use this fear to pressure homeowners into quickly signing on the dotted line for unnecessary or shoddy work that could cost up to $3,000.

The Reality: By arming yourself with a few facts, you'll be able to ask informed questions and avoid a scam. The most common termite in the United States is the subterranean, of which there are two main kinds: workers and swarmers (or winged) termites. The workers hollow out the wood, while swarmers mate and create new colonies. Termites live underground and burrow through soil until they find wood, or woodlike products, and water. To get into your house, they'll often build moist, earthen tunnels across foundations to your home's lower frames, a clear sign of infestation.

Wood that's been damaged by termites is hollowed out along the grain, with bits of dried mud or soil lining the feeding galleries. Be wary of exterminators showing you termites on woodpiles or fences unconnected to your house: This may be a scam. You have a problem only if there's evidence of termites inside the house or close to the foundation.

Bugs flying in the home during the spring are another sign of infestation. These may be flying ants, however. Termites have a full waist, straight antennae, and wings of equal length; ants have elbowed antennae, pinched waists, and forewings longer than hindwings.

There are more than 17,000 pest control companies in the United States, but bigger doesn't always mean better. You want a firm with good recommendations, lots of experience, and a fair price. Michael Potter, a professor of entomology at the University of Kentucky, recommends questioning the company carefully about its history and asking that it send an experienced technician. If an exterminator claims you have termites, he should show you the evidence.

Some companies charge thousands for a typical job that could be done for less than $1,000, so take notes on the exact kind of treatment and compare apples to apples when getting estimates.

4. Chimney Sweep Swindle

In a classic bait-and-switch scam, a chimney sweep calls from a "boiler room" or comes to your door telling you he's just fixed a neighbor's chimney and is offering an inspection for the low price of $39.95. Once inside the chimney, he may claim to find problems, saying you need a new liner, for instance. Suddenly that $39.95 price tag rises thousands of dollars.

The Reality: There's no question that fireplace chimneys can be hazardous. An oily, blackish substance called creosote accumulates inside the chimney and may catch fire if it's more than a quarter-inch thick. Occasionally, but not as often as chimney sweeps would have you believe, a blocked chimney can route carbon monoxide into your house.

Experts recommend an annual inspection to check for

creosote buildup and the structural soundness of the chimney. This usually costs $100 to $250 (not that ridiculous $39.95), and if cleaning is required, an additional $100 to $150. Hire only certified chimney sweeps who've been taught and tested by the Chimney Safety Institute of America. Also, watch the technician as he makes his inspection. Lately, sweeps are using video cameras fed down the flue, so ask to see the video and have the technician explain it as you watch. If he balks, he's scamming you.

Chimneys for oil and gas burners are far less a concern. "An oil-heat system that's serviced every year before winter hardly ever causes problems," says Kevin Rooney, CEO of the Oil Heat Institute of Long Island. But before you look for a professional chimney sweep, call your local fire department; some conduct inspections for free.

5. Mold Mayhem

Mold is making a comeback—not in your home, necessarily, but with con artists, especially since Hurricane Katrina. Playing up fears about disease from mold, particularly over the Internet, they try to convince you to run tests costing anywhere from $300 to $600 to identify your mold. Then they recommend a remediation company for removing the mold—a firm they're in cahoots with.

The Reality: Healthy people usually have nothing to worry about. "If you're immunosuppressed or have allergies or asthma, it can be problematic," says David B. Callahan, MD, medical epidemiologist at the Centers for Disease Control and Prevention (CDC). "Other than that, mold isn't dangerous."

The CDC doesn't even recommend testing mold, because if it's a problem to the occupants, it should be removed no matter what kind it is. And you don't need a remediation company for small areas. Just clean nonporous surfaces with soap and water, followed by a solution of one cup of bleach mixed with one gallon of water. To control future growth, eliminate excess moisture by keeping humidity levels between 40 and 60 percent. Promptly fix leaky roofs, windows, and pipes, and ventilate shower, laundry, and cooking areas.

Part Two

WHAT YOU DON'T KNOW ABOUT
YOUR FOOD

Do waiters ever do things to your food when you're not looking? And how do you know if you're actually getting decaf? Veteran staff from restaurants high and low held open the kitchen door so we could see what's in the soup of the day, the truth behind why kids love the pizza at their favorite places, and how to tell if a restaurant is really clean.

Waitpeople aren't the only ones who spilled industry secrets. Bartenders exposed what whistling and waving money at them really gets you (a nice, long wait). Baristas point out that "I'll take a..." does not mean "please." And the pizza guy? Yes, he speeds (at least once a day), and he's accidentally dropped your pizza more than once—but he's also helped you move your sofa.

Welcome to the secret world of food. Learn how you can be smarter about what goes in your mouth—and savvier about what comes out of it—to guarantee a great experience every time.

WHAT YOUR WAITER WON'T TELL YOU

Here are the top 13 things restaurants don't want you to know about what goes on when you're out of view.

1. Don't order fish on Sunday or Monday. Fish is usually delivered twice a week, so you'll get the freshest fish when you order any day between Tuesday and Friday. To be sure, you can always ask the restaurant when they get theirs.

2. I've seen some horrible things done to people's food: steaks dropped on the floor, butter dipped in the dishwater.

3. I never ask for lemon in a drink. Everybody touches them. Nobody washes them. We just peel the stickers off, cut them up, and throw them in your iced tea.

4. We put sugar in our kids' meals so kids will like them more. Seriously. We even put extra sugar in the dough for the kids' pizzas.

5. At a lot of restaurants, the special is whatever they need to sell before it goes bad. Especially watch out for the soup of the day. If it contains fish or if it's some kind of "gumbo," it's probably the stuff they're trying to get rid of.

6. Your "fresh" salad might not be. At one restaurant where I worked, the salads were made up to three days before they're served. They were sitting on a tray with a thousand other salads in the refrigerator. The waiters went back, grabbed a plate and some dressing, and handed it to the customer.

7. Sometimes, we stick a fork in it. At one bakery restaurant, they used to make this really yummy peach cobbler in a big tray. A lot of times, servers don't have time to eat. So we all kept a fork in our aprons, and as we cruised through the kitchen, we'd stick our fork in the cobbler and take a bite. We'd use the same fork each time.

> 🔒 **TOP SECRET!** I have seen servers mess with your credit card. If a server doesn't like you, he might try to embarrass you by bringing your credit card back and saying, "Do you have another card? This one didn't go through."

8. There really is no caffeine in there. In most restaurants, after 8 p.m. or so, all the coffee is decaf because no one wants to clean two different coffeepots. I'll bring out a tray with 12 coffees on it and give some to the customers who ordered regular, others to the ones who ordered decaf. But they're all decaf. Oh, and if you order specific milk, very few restaurants carry whole milk, 2 percent milk, skim milk, *and* half-and-half; it's just not practical.

9. Water has a cost. My biggest pet peeve? When I walk up to a table of six or seven people and one person decides everyone needs water. I'm making a trip to deliver seven waters, and four or five of them never get touched.

10. Use your waiter's name. When I say, "Hi, my name is JR, and I'll be taking care of you," it's great when you say, "Hi, JR. How are you doing tonight?" Then, the next time you go in, ask for that waiter. He may not remember you, but if you've requested him, he's going to give you really special service.

11. If you're worried about cleanliness, check out the bathroom. If the bathroom is gross, you can be sure the kitchen is much worse.

12. If you walk out with the slip you wrote the tip on and leave behind the blank one, the server gets nothing. It happens all the time, especially with people who've had a few bottles of wine.

13. Always examine the check. Sometimes large parties are unaware that a gratuity has been added to the bill, so they tip on top of it. Waiters "facilitate" this error. It's dishonest, it's wrong— and I did it all the time.

SOURCES: Interviews with more than two dozen servers across the country at restaurants including well-known pizza chains, casual restaurants, Mexican restaurants; Charlie Kondek, former waiter at a Denny's in Central Michigan; Kathy Kniss, who waited tables for ten years in Los Angeles; Judi Santana, a server for ten years; Charity Ohlund; Jake Blanton; Chris, a New York City waiter and the founder of bitterwaitress.com; Steve Dublanica, veteran New York waiter and author of *Waiter Rant: Thanks for the Tip— Confessions of a Cynical Waiter*; and JR, waiter at a fine-dining restaurant and author of the blog servernotslave.wordpress.com.

Great Advice
RULES ON TIPPING

Twenty percent (or close to it) is the standard amount to leave on a restaurant check. But other tipping-related matters aren't so clear-cut. Steve Dublanica, former server and author of the blog *Waiter Rant* and *Keep the Change: A Clueless Tipper's Quest to Become the Guru of the Gratuity*, weighs in on some hot-button tipping issues.

1. Should you tip on the tax? I like it when you do, but you don't have to.

2. What is the correct amount to tip on drinks? At the bar, you should leave 15 to 20 percent of the total cost of that drink, which may seem kind of ridiculous. But think of it this way: At the table, you're paying 15 to 20 percent. Why does the bartender not get that money, but the waiter—who doesn't make those drinks—does?

3. When, if ever, is it acceptable to leave a bad tip? I don't suggest stiffing servers on the tip, because you are punishing all the other people connected to that food chain. I tell people to talk to the manager and say, "I had very poor service, but I'm leaving a tip anyway."

4. Should a server be able to automatically include gratuity if it's not a large group? I don't support waiters deciding who they're going to attach a tip to. That's not their job—that's management's job—and they need to have a very well thought-out policy about it.

WHAT YOUR FAST-FOOD WORKER WON'T TELL YOU

In a rush or just craving some fries? Here's what you need (and probably don't want) to know.

1. After we cook something, we put it in a holding cabinet and set a timer. When the timer goes off, we're supposed to throw it out. But often, we just reheat the food. So for the freshest meal, come between 11 a.m. and 1 p.m. or between 6 p.m. and 8 p.m. More people are in the restaurant then, so we're cooking and serving new food constantly.

2. That plain chicken breast may have been a healthy choice out of the package, but sometimes we have to slather it with butter just to make sure it doesn't stick to the grill.

3. There's usually a way to get expensive menu items for less. If you're craving a Big Mac, for example, order a $1 McDouble with no mustard or ketchup and then add shredded lettuce and Mac sauce for a small charge. It's basically a mini Big Mac, and you can get two for less than the cost of one Big Mac.

4. Those grill marks on your burger? Not real. They were put there by the factory.

5. Avoid asking for "extra" of something, like cheese or sauce. As soon as you say "extra," we have to enter it at the register and charge you for it. Instead, just tell us you want us to "put a good amount on there" or "not to be skimpy with it," and we'll load you up.

6. Yes, our chili is made from what you think: meat from old burgers.

7. It makes me laugh when someone comes in and says she's trying to be healthy—and then orders a salad with crispy chicken. At McDonald's, some of those salads have about as many calories as a Big Mac. In fact, a small order of french fries contains four fewer grams of fat than a packet of our ranch dressing.

8. Because we're timed on how fast we get customers through the drive-through, we always prioritize those in line outside over anyone at the front counter.

9. One of my coworkers once got so mad that he spit in someone's food. He was suspended for three days; most of us would never do something like that.

10. Those gorgeous pictures of our food in our advertisements? They're airbrushed and touched up with fiberglass and paint. It probably takes two hours to make that picture; obviously, we're not going to be able to replicate that.

11. Most of us will cook something fresh for you if you ask. But if you want to make sure your french fries come right out of the fryer, order them without salt; that forces us to cook you a new batch. Then you can add your own salt.

12. Most fast-food joints clean everything, including the grills and the drink machine nozzles, with super-concentrated chemicals at the end of the day. If you're one of the first customers in the morning, you may be getting some of that chemical residue on the food or in the drink you order.

13. Please, please, get off your cell phone. I've had people pull up to the window, pay, and drive away without their food because they're talking on the phone and not paying attention. Then they're mad at me.

SOURCES: Current and former fast-food workers in Arizona, Georgia, Louisiana, New Jersey, Ohio, Texas, and Washington.

WHAT YOUR BARISTA WON'T TELL YOU

Get what you want—including a fast-moving line and good service—with these 13 things to know before you caffeinate.

1. If you're not at Starbucks, don't order like you are. If you want a Venti Caramel Frappuccino, you're in the wrong place. Order from our menu.

2. There is an art to pulling a perfect shot of espresso. The ideal shot takes 18 to 22 seconds to pull. I have to make sure that the espresso grounds are packed to just the right firmness, that the right amount of water filters through, and that the temperature is controlled. If a shot isn't perfect, I won't serve it.

3. Just because they're vegan doesn't mean our cakes are good for you. They are LOADED with white sugar.

4. Yes, I went to school for this. Starbucks sends employees to barista school for two weeks, where they study the history of coffee, the entire coffee menu, and how to turn milk into velvety foam.

5. Latte art isn't merely decorative. If a heart or a pinwheel design holds in the milk, it means that the consistency of the foam is good and the shot was pulled well. If you're at a place that does foam artwork, and you don't get a good picture, that means your drink is not well made.

6. Please believe me. If you asked for decaf, I gave you decaf. You don't need to ask me repeatedly. I am not out to get you.

7. Sometimes the owners of independent coffee/espresso carts buy cheap coffee and sell it as a respected brand. Not that any of our customers noticed.

8. Tip. I know your coffee is already over-priced, but a dollar bill in a tip jar earns you infinite goodwill.

9. You are the reason for the wait. When there's a line to the door, I hate it when customers spend the whole time talking on the phone and only think about what they want when they get to the register. They are the reason the line takes forever.

> 🔒 **TOP SECRET!** Buy whole beans. Experts and coffee connoisseurs agree that the only way to prepare a decent cup of joe is to buy beans whole and grind them immediately before brewing. Oxygen causes coffee to lose flavor rapidly, and preground coffee has far more surface area for oxygen to come in contact with.

10. A real macchiato has just a stain of milk foam and no sugar. Because Starbucks uses the names of authentic espresso beverages for sugary, milky confections that bear no resemblance to the real thing, they confuse people. I'll make someone an authentic drink and they'll say, where's the milk and syrup?

11. Be nice. No matter how tired you are, it's nice to say "please" when you're ordering your first coffee of the day. "I'll take a . . ." or "Give me a . . ." is NOT "please" in anyone's language.

12. A bigger cup doesn't mean more coffee. Starbucks' Venti (20 oz.) and Grande (16 oz.) each contain two shots of espresso. The Venti just has more milk. So if it's caffeine you're after, size doesn't matter.

13. Buy the right amount of coffee. As with most things we consume, when it comes to coffee, fresh is best. So if you're going to buy something from our shop, buy the bag, and only buy what you'll use within a week or two—within a month at max.

SOURCES: Baristas from Starbucks and independent cafés and coffee carts in Seattle, New York, Pennsylvania, and London, England.

Who Knew?
COFFEE, THE MIRACLE DRUG

When was the last time you heard a doctor use the word *miracle*? Well, wake up and smell the coffee: "It's amazing," says liver specialist Sanjiv Chopra, MD, professor of medicine at Harvard Medical School. "Coffee is truly a lifesaving miracle drug."

Though he says it's still a "scientific mystery" how a simple cup of coffee works its wonders in the body, large epidemiological studies repeatedly verify its astonishing benefits. Some recent research highlights we got from the National Coffee Association of the USA, Food.com, and the website Home and Garden Ideas say:

More than three cups a day lowers women's risk of developing the most common skin cancer by 20 percent.

More than six cups a day cuts men's risk of dying from prostate cancer by 60 percent.

Drinking at least one cup of coffee a day lowers women's risk of stroke by up to 25 percent.

Consuming at least two cups daily reduces women's chances of becoming depressed by up to 20 percent.

"Drink it black, or at most put a little skim milk in it" to minimize calories, recommends Dr. Chopra, who is also the author of *Live Better, Live Longer: The New Studies That Reveal What's Really Good—and Bad—for Your Health*. The benefits from decaf may not be as prodigious, so stick with regular if you can tolerate the buzz. Dr. Chopra drinks at least four cups a day himself, though most people should limit themselves to two. And no, he jokes, "I'm not sponsored by Starbucks."

WHAT YOUR BARTENDER WON'T TELL YOU

Here's how to get served first at a crowded bar—every time—plus more tips for making the most of your next night out.

1. Know what you want, and have your money ready. Yell, whistle, or wave money, and I'm going to make you wait. Make eye contact and smile, and I'll come over as soon as I can. Don't create a traffic jam.

2. Start a tab. If I swipe your card five times this evening, that's five times as much paperwork I have to do at 4 a.m.

3. You want a drink made strong? Then order a double—for double the price.

4. You get what you pay for. Bars that don't have regulars (in hotels, airports) have started using wireless gadgets that measure how much is poured and automatically ring up each shot. They're meant to prevent overpouring and to cut losses, but I don't like them—neither do customers.

5. I've heard it all. One guy told me I had the worst smile he'd ever seen. I found out that he thinks a girl won't remember him unless he puts her down. I guess it worked; I'm telling you this story three weeks later.

6. I have the police on speed dial. And I never hesitate to call.

7. Don't order a round of drinks after last call. Last call applies to everyone—even you.

8. If I cut you off, don't argue. If anything, you should apologize if you've made a scene.

9. Get a room. The more you make out with your date, the closer you are to being cut off.

10. I can tell if your date is going well or not. And I notice if you bring in a new date every week.

> **TOP SECRET!** We'll call you a cab. Some of us get a cut from the cab company when we call a taxi for a tipsy patron. Not that I've ever done that, of course.

11. Think tending bar isn't a real career? You're wrong. The craft of bartending is appreciated in the food industry, and some of us are even called "mixologists" now.

12. I love sharing what I know. If it's not busy, ask me about the history of drink or the latest cocktail I've invented. You'll learn something new.

13. I like a sophisticated palate. You'll win points with me if you request gin in your martini.

SOURCES: David Craver, president, National Bartenders Association; and anonymous bartenders in Boston, Kentucky, Florida, California, and Illinois.

Who Knew?

NIFTIEST THINGS TO DO WITH BEER (OTHER THAN DRINK IT)

Use as setting lotion. Put some life back into flat hair with some flat beer. Before you get into the shower, mix 3 tablespoons beer in ½ cup warm water. After you shampoo your hair, rub in the solution, let it set for a couple of minutes, then rinse it off. You may be so pleased by what you see that you'll want to keep a six-pack in the bathroom.

Soften up tough meat. Who needs powdered meat tenderizer when you have some in a can? You guessed it: Beer makes a great tenderizer for tough, inexpensive cuts of meat. Pour a can over the meat, and let it soak in for about an hour before cooking. Even better, marinate it overnight in the fridge, or put the beer in your slow cooker with the meat.

Clean wood furniture. Have you got some beer that's old or has gone flat? Use it to clean wooden furniture. Just wipe it on with a soft cloth and then off with another dry cloth.

Polish gold jewelry. Get the shine back in your solid gold rings and other jewelry by pouring a bit of beer (*not* dark ale and *not* on gemstones!) onto a soft cloth and rubbing it gently over the piece. Use a clean second cloth or towel to dry.

Remove coffee or tea stains from rugs. Rub the beer lightly into the material, and the stain should disappear. You may have to repeat the process a couple of times to remove all traces of the stain.

WHAT YOUR PIZZA DELIVERY GUY WON'T TELL YOU

Have you ever wondered what is happening behind the scenes at your favorite pizza place—and on the way to your house?

1. It's a pizza, not a lifetime commitment. My other line is ringing, so choose the toppings before you call.

2. Patience, please! It takes about 20 minutes to go from raw dough to fully baked pizza. And then I have to drive to your house.

3. Why won't we deliver to some neighborhoods? In some neighborhoods, a kid getting out of a car with a pizza in his hands is like screaming, "Rob me! I have cash!"

4. At our shop, we use our own cars to deliver pizza. Last week one of our guys smashed his car into a pole on an icy road. Now he's using a rental car.

5. I'm just a kid. Many delivery drivers are teenage boys, and most parents don't like their teenage boys driving around at night in downpours or blizzards. Yet these same people have no qualms about having other teenage kids deliver their pizza in these conditions.

6. I probably break a speeding law once a day.

7. I'm a human being. When you see me drenched and shivering in the rain, it's not nice to close the door in my face while you search for some quarters in the sofa cushions.

8. I will try to be as nice to you as possible. But if you complain that I'm late, or if you get nasty about a problem with your order, I won't be so nice.

9. There are always special customers. Like the little old lady who wants to pay her bill with a $5 check. I'll take it because none of us want to be mean to a grandmother. But if she hasn't ordered from us before, I won't take it.

TOP SECRET! Accidents happen. If I drop your pizza on the way, sometimes I'll shake the box to get the cheese to slide back on right.

10. Tips should be 10 to 15 percent of your order. If you order a lot of pizza—say, hundreds of dollars' worth, for a party or something—but give me a $1 tip, well, I'm going to have a problem with that.

11. The more gated the community, the more guarded the wallet. The best tips actually come from middle- and lower-class people who know what we go through.

12. The majority of our employees work 12 to 14 hours a day. At the end of the day, we just want to go home. So please don't call for a delivery at closing time and then complain that we can't accommodate you.

13. Some people want more than just pizza. A guy once ordered pizza from me just so he'd have some help moving his sofa up a flight of stairs. I agreed to help him. He gave me a few extra bucks. I took it.

WHAT YOUR GROCER WON'T TELL YOU

Find out where and how to get the best bargains at your supermarket—and what grocers really think about people who graze while filling their carts.

1. If you hate crowds and lines, shop at dinnertime (5 to 9 p.m.) or even later. Only 4 percent of shoppers hit the aisles between 9 p.m. and 8 a.m. Least-crowded day of the week? Wednesday.

2. That star fruit has been here a lot longer than the broccoli. Familiar produce turns over more quickly than exotic things.

3. Dig and reach for the freshest produce. Older merchandise gets pushed to the front of the bin and spread across the top to encourage customers to take it first.

4. The more products you see, the more you are likely to buy. That's why the aisles are so long and the milk is usually in the far corner. Skip the center aisles. That's where you'll find the junk food, like sodas and snack foods.

5. Like employees with a good attitude? Shop at chains that are employee-owned and suggest customer-satisfaction surveys. When employees have a stake in the profits, it shows in their attitude.

6. The "grazers" order food at the deli, eat it as they're shopping, and get rid of the wrappers before they check out. We also call that stealing.

7. We're marketing to your kids, too. That's why we put the rainbow-colored cereals and other kiddie catnip at their eye level.

8. Be wary of "specials." When people see signs with numbers "8 for $10!" "Limit: 5 per customer"—they buy 30 to 100 percent more than they otherwise might have.

9. The baby formula is locked up because thieves resell it on the black market. Ditto for the cough and cold medications, smoking-cessation products, razor blades, and batteries.

10. Bring back your recyclable cans and bottles, but please rinse them out first. Leaving soda inside is unsanitary, and we find it disgusting.

11. Attention, shoppers: Don't start your shopping just as we're closing. We just want to leave. It's been a long day.

12. Signs of a store in trouble: Stocking fewer perishable items, storing nonperishables in refrigerated cases to make them look full, and "dummying up" shelves with empty boxes. If we were offering the best prices and highest quality, wouldn't there be more people shopping here?

13. Check sizes. Manufacturers are constantly trying to repackage things to make them sound like a better deal. A new peanut butter container may look the same, but look closely and you'll see it actually has less peanut butter inside. Most customers don't watch this kind of stuff.

SOURCES: David Livingston, a supermarket industry consultant; Marion Nestle, author of *What to Eat*; Maurice Nizzardo, former supermarket executive in Connecticut; David J. Livingston, an industry consultant; Brian Wansink, author of *Mindless Eating*; and others.

Great Advice

PREPACKAGED GOODS THAT AREN'T WORTH THE CONVENIENCE

. . . .

1. "Gourmet" Frozen Vegetables

Sure, you can buy an 8-ounce packet of peas in an herbed butter sauce, but why do so when you can make your own? Just cook the peas, add a pat of butter, and sprinkle on some herbs that you already have on hand. This homemade version is almost as easy and will taste a lot fresher. The same thing goes for carrots with dill sauce and other gourmet veggies.

2. Powdered Iced Tea Mixes

It's much cheaper to make your own iced tea from actual (inexpensive) tea bags and keep a jug in the fridge. Plus, many mixes are loaded with high fructose corn syrup and other sugars, along with artificial flavors.

3. Salad Kits

Washed and bagged greens can cost three times as much as buying the same amount of a head of lettuce. Even more expensive are "salad kits," where you get some greens, a small bag of dressing, and a small bag of croutons. Skip these altogether.

4. Trail Mix

We checked unit prices of those small bags of trail mix hanging in the candy aisle not that long ago and were shocked to find that they cost about $10 a pound! Make your own for much, much less—and you can include only the things you like!

5. "Snack" or "Lunch" Packs

These "all-inclusive" food trays might seem reasonably priced (from $3.00 to $7.00), but you're actually paying for the highly designed label, wrapper, and specially molded tray. They contain only a few crackers and small pieces of cheese and lunchmeat. The actual edible ingredients are worth just pennies and are filled with salt.

6. Preformed Meat Patties

Frozen burgers—beef or otherwise—are more expensive than buying the ground meat in bulk and making patties yourself. We timed it—it takes less than 10 seconds to form a flat circle and throw it on the grill! Also, there's some evidence that preformed meat patties might have a higher chance of containing E. *coli* than regular ground meat. In fact, most of the recent beef recalls have involved premade frozen beef patties. Fresh is definitely better!

WHAT **YOUR BUTCHER** WON'T TELL YOU

Here are delicious ways to eat better for less money when beef, pork, and chicken are on the menu.

1. Don't be fooled by supermarket brand names like Butcher's Brand, Rancher's Reserve, and Blue Ribbon. The label to look for is USDA Quality Grade. Prime is the best (and most expensive), followed by choice, select, and then standard.

2. Your beef may get ground in Iowa, stuffed in a long tube of plastic, and trucked to our store, where we regrind and package it.

3. Despite all the hype, most of us think "Certified Angus Beef" is a marketing gimmick that doesn't necessarily indicate the meat is any better than other beef with the same USDA grade. Though it does look spiffy on that black tray.

4. Make sure you check the price per pound or per serving. The per-pound price of the regular-size package is often cheaper than the family pack.

5. You don't have to be so wedded to the cut of beef your recipe calls for. We can suggest cheaper options.

6. My favorite cut? The hanging tender. Also known as a hanger steak or a bistro steak, it's got great flavor at a good price.

7. Take the meat tray at the bottom of the stack or the farthest in back. Just like milk, it tends to be fresher. And check the pack date. Ideally you want packages dated that day or the day before.

8. Save $1.50 to $2 a pound on boneless pork chops. Buy a whole boneless pork loin roast and slice it into chops an inch thick.

9. Want to save a few bucks per pound on beef? Try buying a whole top sirloin and asking me to cut it into steaks. Or get a whole chuck and ask me to make you some chuck roasts, beef stew cubes, and ground meat out of it. The bigger the cut, the more money you'll save.

10. Yes, that 92/8 ground beef is lean, but if you make burgers with it, you might be disappointed. Your favorite burger joint probably uses beef that's much fattier.

11. Even if those chicken breasts say "100 percent natural," they may still be injected with sodium-laden broth, salt water, or seaweed extract. Always check the label.

12. Some of the best tasting cuts are the ugliest ones, like the flap meat on the belly part of beef.

13. Ask me to help. Even if it's already on a tray wrapped in cellophane, I can cut the fat off a roast, trim a flank steak into stir-fry strips, or grind up a chuck roast. Then I'll neatly wrap it back up for you. All for no extra charge.

> **TOP SECRET!** If you throw your meat straight into the freezer in the packaging it came in, freezer burn is a virtual certainty. Instead, take the meat off the tray, rewrap it with plastic food wrap, then put it in a freezer bag and squeeze out as much air as possible.

SOURCES: Butchers in New York City; Charlotte, North Carolina; San Francisco; Kingston, New York; and Timberville, Virginia; Lee O'Hara, author of *Beef Secrets Straight from the Butcher*; and the National Cattlemen's Beef Association.

WHAT YOUR FARMERS' MARKET WON'T TELL YOU

Find out when to look for a bargain and when a specialty item is worth the price with these top secrets straight from the farmers themselves.

1. Many of us depend on this for our survival. Almost all farmers who participate in farmers' markets run very small operations, and the profit margin is slim.

2. We don't do deals. I don't encourage "dealing" with a farmer. The prices are fair, and this is a symbiotic relationship.

3. If you want a discount, the best way to get one is through consistent patronage.

4. Your money supports your community. If you spend $100 at a farmer's market, $62 goes back into the local economy—and $99 out of $100 stays in the state. If you spend $100 at a grocery store, only $25 stays here. So, where do you want your money to go?

5. Please stop saying how expensive I am. My products would sell for much more in any specialty store and are NOT available in a supermarket.

6. I love my job because my business is not about retailing and then good-bye. It's about cultivating relationships with people who are willing to spend a little bit more for something better.

7. Standing out in the summer sun is nice, but this job isn't easy. It is tough being outdoors all day in July. I'm not just working a register; I'm loading and unloading heavy boxes every day.

8. Rain is good for crops during the growing season but bad for business. When it rains, that keeps customers inside and can easily damage my products.

9. I care about where the products are coming from. If a vendor has a retail store, I WILL NOT purchase from the vendor because I do not feel they belong in a farmers' market. Unfortunately some markets are letting in franchise/chain businesses, and that hinders the small vendor.

10. We cannot get you everything all the time. We work very hard to provide you with the freshest, best tasting food we can at a reasonable price. There are seasons when certain produce isn't available (even in California). No peaches in January!

TOP SECRET! Many produce vendors are really only retailers. Ask yours if they buy from wholesalers. If they do, shop at your supermarket instead for a better price on the exact same produce.

11. Some farmers say their produce is organic, but in order to say that, they must be certified by an organic agency and undergo an inspection. Most organic farmers are proud to display organic certification, and you can always ask to see it.

12. We are sick of these buzzwords, too: Natural, specialty, estate, artisan, local, and organic.

13. If a vendor sells citrus products or tropical products in an area of the country where those clearly don't grow, they are not farmers. They are having their produce shipped in.

SOURCES: Nancy Gammons of Four Sisters Farm and Watsonville Farmers' Market; Ersilia Moreno, owner of Olive Oil of the World; Adriana Silva, owner of Tomatero Organic Farm; cowtownfarmersmarket.com; Mark Santoro, owner of Gaia's Breath Farm.

MAKE A MEMORABLE CRUDITÉS PLATTER

Ask about these delicious veggies on your next trip to the farmers' market, and you'll be sure to create a party platter that no one will forget.

1. Fennel
The crisp anise flavor of fennel is perfect with creamy dips. Fennel also pairs exceptionally well with roasted red peppers.

2. Jicama
Crunchy jicama is a sweeter alternative to celery.

3. Endive
Bitter endive leaves are perfect for scooping up hummus, dip, and even salsa. The vegetable goes especially well with blue cheese.

4. Tiny Purple Carrots
Purple carrots will add color and the wow factor to your crudités platter. Blanch until al dente and chill. Try the red and yellow varieties for extra color.

5. Asparagus
Grilled asparagus adds an upscale finger food to your platter.

6. Fingerling Potatoes
Get the longer ones and blanch. Chill.

7. Green Beans
Blanched green beans are easy to dip. You can use fresh green beans, but frozen work just as well.

8. Radishes
Peppery radishes can be a delicious counterpoint to dips.

WHAT FOOD MANUFACTURERS WON'T TELL YOU

These eye-opening insights into how your food is made will help you to eat better.

1. When we recently examined big food companies over a five-year period, we found that 99 percent of their growth was coming from lower-calorie products. That was, quite frankly, a stunning surprise. So they're not just sitting around on their hands. They are moving in the right direction.

2. The concept of "the dose makes the poison" is very important in the realm of food, especially when it comes to natural flavors and artificial colors. All food ingredients and nutrients—even those we need to survive—have a threshold for safety. When caramel color was approved, nobody anticipated how much of it would be used in the food and beverage industry. It's in a lot of foods you don't expect: certain soups, pilaf, and hamburger, for example. So if everything you eat is from a box, a can, or a bag, then you may get too much and have reason for concern. But if you eat a variety of foods, you don't have to worry.

3. Manufacturers can hide things under natural flavoring. When I started in this business and was interviewing possible partners, I was shocked at the amount of deception. Manufacturers and copackers would ask what ingredients I was using for preservation, and then they would tell me, You know you can use X or Y—just call it natural flavoring on the package. No one will know.

4. The red color in many foods comes from crushed insects. If you see carmine or cochineal extract in an ingredients list, the product contains a little powdered bug. But aside from being an allergen for a small number of people, it's considered safe. Alternatives are petroleum-derived chemicals Red No. 40 and No. 3, which some studies have linked to such health problems as hyperactivity in children and cancer in animals. I'd rather have the insects, to be honest.

5. Some producers hide sugar by giving it different names—high-fructose corn syrup, cane crystals, dextrose, evaporated cane juice, agave nectar, and fruit juice concentrate. If a product has a lot of sugar, some companies will intentionally use two or more different types so sugar doesn't end up being number one on the ingredients list. The FDA has proposed a change that would require manufacturers to add up all these types of sugar and list them as added sugars.

6. Many "high in fiber" products are stuffed with what is essentially fake fiber. It's not as healthy as the naturally occurring fiber in whole grains and vegetables. It may even cause gas, bloating, and other stomach problems. Watch out for chicory root, maltodextrin, and polydextrose on the ingredients list.

7. FDA regulation does allow some insect parts [from harvesting, the manufacturing process, etc.] in your food. Peanut butter can have up to 30 insect parts per 100 grams. It has no effect on the healthiness, but people might want to know.

8. For many additives that go into food, our regulatory system is pretty close to nonexistent. The FDA lets food manufacturers do their own safety testing and decide independently whether ingredients are "generally recognized as safe." There are no specific mandatory guidelines about the type of testing they have to do. They don't even have to tell the FDA about new additives they're using.

9. In my experience, one thing that really surprised me is that no governing body is required to precheck nutritional labels for accuracy. When we develop a product, we use software to create the label, but we don't have to submit it to anyone. It's all self-policed. I think the only time the FDA would look at it would be if customers were complaining.

10. A lot of the foods we eat have interesting origins. For example, the bacteria responsible for sourdough bread originally came from rodent feces. Any sourdough you eat has that history, yet it's all perfectly safe and delicious.

11. Cereal is nowhere near as wholesome as companies want you to believe. The manufacturing process destroys a lot of the natural nutrition, even if the product contains whole grains. That's why virtually every cereal has a long list of added vitamins and minerals. In my family, we don't eat cereal very often, and we look for ones that have less than eight grams of sugar per serving.

12. If you're prone to diabetes, stick to regular pasta instead of whole wheat. Whole wheat pasta often has more starch than regular because of the way it's ground. Or just look for a pasta with a low glycemic index, which some brands put on the box.

13. Baked, popped, or low-fat "chips" may seem healthier. But often, they're just baked conglomerations of highly refined potato flakes, refined grains, and different kinds of powders. You may be better off eating potato chips, made with real potatoes fried in a healthful oil.

SOURCES: Katherine Tallmadge; Kantha Shelke, PhD; Melanie Warner; Rob Dunn, PHD, a biologist at NC State University and the author of *The Man Who Touched His Own Heart;* Joel Warady, chief marketing officer of Enjoy Life Foods; Michael Jacobson, PhD; Jordan Pierson, chief marketing officer of Wink Frozen Desserts; Robert J. Davis, PhD, author of *Coffee Is Good for You: From Vitamin C and Organic Foods to Low-Carb and Detox Diets, the Truth About Diet and Nutrition Claims;* Walter Willett, MD, chairman of the department of nutrition at the Harvard School of Public Health in Boston; Daniel Tapper, author of *Food Unwrapped: Lifting the Lid on How Our Food Is Really Produced;* Jason Burke; Kantha Shelke, PhD, a food scientist who specializes in ingredients at Corvus Blue, a Chicago-based research firm; Former food-industry executive Hank Cardello, director of the Obesity Solutions Initiative at the Hudson Institute (a nonprofit think tank) and author of *Stuffed.*

Who Knew?

WHAT YOU DON'T KNOW ABOUT ORGANIC FOOD

1. "Organic" doesn't mean superfood. The health benefits aren't proven (studies conflict). While organics do cut your level of pesticide exposure by one third, they can still be contaminated by synthetic agricultural chemicals in the soil or during warehousing.

2. Don't picture happy animals roaming on idyllic farms just because it's organic meat. The USDA requires that, "organic meat, poultry, eggs, and dairy products come from animals ... given no antibiotics or growth hormones." But this could just mean the animals ate organic corn instead of conventional corn. Organic meat is probably worth the expense to reduce your exposure to antibiotic-resistant bacteria.

3. "Organic" doesn't mean 100 percent organic. Unless the label says 100 percent organic, any item needs only 95 percent of its ingredients to be organic to earn the USDA organic seal. Also, some ingredients—like sausage casings and celery powder—are exempt from the USDA requirement because they are too difficult to source organically.

4. "All-natural" is meaningless. The FDA doesn't regulate products claiming they're all-natural or 100 percent natural. But foods labeled organic must adhere to strict standards, including no use of synthetic fertilizers and pesticides, antibiotics, and GMOs.

5. Pregnant women and kids: Pay attention! These groups may benefit most from organics. Studies show that fetuses and young children might be harmed by exposure to even low levels of pesticides.

6. Organic seafood labels signify nothing. "Organic" seafood is not required to meet specific standards, it has not been tested for toxicity, and it likely costs more.

7. Organic junk food is still junk food. Any cookies, candy, and chips can have excess fat, sugar, and calories. Organic ones merely lack artificial ingredients.

8. You can't rinse off pesticides. Washing conventional produce doesn't remove all its pesticides and transform it into organic. Rinsing might wash some pesticides from the food's surface but not from within the flesh. (Washing does remove food-borne-illness pathogens, so don't skip it.)

9. You can save your milk money. According to a recent article in Pediatrics, researchers found that milk from cows given hormones seems safe for kids and concluded there is no significant difference in the estrogen concentration of organic versus conventional milk. Their surprising recommendation: Drink skim milk (organic or not), because higher-fat milks contain more estrogen, which has been linked to cancer and other hormonal issues.

10. Look for produce stickers with five-digit codes that begin with a "9." That means the food is organic; and those starting with a 4 indicate the food was likely treated chemically with herbicides, pesticides, or both.

11. Organic or not, don't skip your fruits and veggies. The Environmental Working Group's "Dirty Dozen" and "Clean Fifteen" were intended to help inform consumers about the level of pesticide residues on nonorganic crops. But some people mistakenly believe that nonorganic produce should be avoided. Not so: Any plant-rich diet has proven health benefits, so crunch on!

SOURCES: USDA; organicnewsroom.com; Jenny Gensterblum, chef at Léman Manhattan Preparatory School; HappyFamily; Tara Dellolacono Thies, registered dietitian and nutritionist at Clif Bar; omorganics.org; Carrie Brownstein, seafood quality standards coordinator at Whole Foods; Brendan Brazier, formulator of Vega; Alliance for Food & Farming; Organic Valley.

Insider Expertise
HOW TO BE A GREAT RESTAURANT CUSTOMER— WHO GETS GREAT SERVICE

People in the service industry are really hustling to give you a great dining experience—and get great tips. This advice straight from the waitstaff will help you get the best service by keeping on the good side of your waiter or waitress.

It's much easier to be recognized as a regular on Mondays, Tuesdays, or Wednesdays. Once you're recognized as a regular, good things start to happen. You'll find your wineglass gets filled without being put on your bill, or the chef might bring you a sample.

If you find a waiter you like, always ask to be seated in his or her section. Tell all your friends so they'll start asking for that server, as well. You've just made that waiter look indispensable to the owner. The server will be grateful and take good care of you.

Don't snap your fingers to get our attention. Remember, we have shears that cut through bone in the kitchen.

Splitting entrées is OK, but don't ask for water, lemon, and sugar so you can make your own lemonade. What's next, grapes so you can press your own wine?

We want you to enjoy yourself while you're eating. But when it's over, you should go. Do you stay in the movie theater after the credits? No.

If you're having a problem, speak to the owner if you can. Managers may have very little power. They're less likely to comp a meal, and most aren't authorized to give away free alcohol. They'll also take it out on the server if you have problems.

If you don't like something, don't muddle your way through it like a martyr and then complain afterward. If you don't like it, don't eat it. Send it back and get something else.

People think that just because your food took a long time, it's the server's fault. Nine times out of ten, it's the kitchen. Or it's the fact that you ordered a well-done burger.

Trust your waitress. Say something like "Hey, it's our first time in. We want you to create an experience for us. Here's our budget." Your server will go crazy for you.

Don't order meals that aren't on the menu. You're forcing the chef to cook something he doesn't make on a regular basis. If he makes the same entrée 10,000 times a month, the odds are good that the dish will be a home run every time.

You'll get better food if you avoid holidays and Saturday nights. The sheer volume of customers guarantees that most kitchens will be pushed beyond their ability to produce a high-quality dish.

In many restaurants, the tips are pooled, so if you have a bad experience with the server, you're stiffing the bartender who made your drinks, the water boy who poured your water, sometimes the hostess, the food runners, and maybe the other waiters.

Kindness pays. Sometimes, if you've been especially nice to me, I'll tell the bartender, "Give me a frozen margarita, and don't put it in." That totally gyps the company, but it helps me because you'll give it back to me in tips, and the management won't know the difference.

Part Three

WHAT YOU DON'T KNOW ABOUT
YOUR HEALTH

Think you know the rules of health? Sure, staying off the sugar, piling on the produce, and getting some exercise are all smart moves. But what really gets you the best care at the ER? How can you make shots less painful for your child? And why don't docs choose department heads as their own physicians?

We worked hard to get the answers to these questions and more. With interviews with scores of health professionals—from nurses to pediatricians, podiatrists, general practitioners, eye doctors, pharmacists, dietitians, and more—we uncovered the facts professionals usually only reveal to one another.

In addition to these hassle-saving—and potentially life-saving—facts, we're boldly revealing some things that usually go unsaid, like what grosses out even your doctor or what can land you next-to naked in a hospital gown (Hint: It might have less to do with how sick you are and more to do with how much you're annoying them). Find out how to save money on personal training and eat healthy at the drive-thru. We did the work, now you get the benefits!

WHAT YOUR NURSE WON'T TELL YOU

Here are some words to the wise from the one who's often handling the needle.

1. We're not going to tell you your doctor is incompetent, but if I say, "You have the right to a second opinion," that can be code for "I don't like your doctor" or "I don't trust your doctor."

2. When a patient is terminally ill, sometimes the doctor won't order enough pain medication. If the patient is suffering, we'll sometimes give more than what the doctor said and ask him later to change the order.

3. I've had people with brains literally coming out of their head. No matter how worried I am, I'll say calmly, "Hmmm, let me give the doctor a call and have him come look at that."

4. If you're happily texting and laughing with your friends until the second you spot me walking into your room, I'm not going to believe that your pain is a 10 out of 10.

5. When you tell me how much you drink or smoke or how often you do drugs, I automatically double or triple it.

6. Your life is in our hands—literally. We question physicians' orders more often than you might think. Some of the mistakes I've headed off: a doctor who ordered the incorrect diet for a diabetic and one who tried to perform a treatment on the wrong patient.

7. If you ask me if your biopsy results have come back yet, I may say no even if they have, because the doctor is really the best person to tell you. He can answer all your questions.

8. When you ask me, "Have you ever done this before?" I'll always say yes. Even if I haven't.

9. Every nurse has had a doctor blame them in front of a patient for something that is not her fault. They're basically telling the patient, "You can't trust your nurse."

10. I once took care of a child who had been in a coma for more than a week. The odds that he would wake up were declining, but I had read that the sense of smell was the last thing to go. So I told his mom, "Put your perfume on a diaper and hold it up by his nose to see if it will trigger something." The child woke up three hours later. It was probably a coincidence, but it was one of my best moments as a nurse.

11. Some jobs are physically demanding. Some are mentally demanding. Some are emotionally demanding. Nursing is all three. If you have a problem with a nurse, ask to speak to the charge nurse (the one who oversees the shift).

12. For some reason, when I ask "Are you having pain?" a lot of patients say no, even if they are. But I've found that if I say, "Are you uncomfortable?" people are much more likely to say yes. Please tell us if you're in pain. We have all sorts of medications we can use to help you.

13. If a patient is incontinent, I'm just supposed to use a washcloth to clean them. But if you're really nice, I'll get heated wipes.

SOURCES: Mary Pat Aust, RN, clinical practice specialist at American Association of Critical-Care Nurses in Aliso Viejo, California; Kristin Baird, RN, a health-care consultant in Fort Atkinson, Wisconsin; Nancy Beck, RN, a nurse at a Missouri hospital; Linda Bell, RN, clinical practice specialist at the American Association of Critical-Care Nurses in Aliso Viejo, California; Nancy Brown, RN, a longtime nurse in Seattle, Washington; Theresa Brown, RN, an oncology nurse and the author of *Critical Care: A New Nurse Faces Death, Life, and Everything in Between;* Barbara Dehn, RN, a nurse-practitioner in Silicon Valley, California, who blogs at nursebarb.com; Karon White Gibson, RN, producer-host of *Outspoken with Karon,* a Chicago cable TV show; Theresa Tomeo, RN, a nurse at the Beth Abraham Center for Nursing and Rehabilitation in Queens, New York; Kathy Stephens Williams, RN, staff development educator for critical care at St. Anthony's Medical Center in St. Louis, Missouri; Gina, a nurse who blogs at codeblog.com; a longtime nurse who blogs at head-nurse.blogspot.com; and anonymous nurses and nurse supervisors in California, Florida, New York City, New Jersey, Pennsylvania, and Texas.

Great Advice

HOW YOU CAN HELP PREVENT MEDICAL MISTAKES

According to the medical journal *The Lancet*, medical errors might be a leading cause of death, but that doesn't mean you can't help change the numbers. Use these strategies to help keep mistakes from happening:

Trust your instincts. If you have questions about a lab result, diagnosis, or treatment, speak up. And be persistent. After you have a lab test or diagnostic image, call your doctor to make sure he received the results. Don't worry about hurting your doctor's feelings. This is about you.

Choose wisely. The doctor you pick is only the first member of a team of specialists involved in your care. She'll likely assemble the rest of the team, so finding the right doctor is doubly important. So, too, is the hospital you choose. There are no guarantees, but usually, the better the hospital, the better the team.

Read the label. Many lab mix-ups start in your doctor's office. When giving a blood or other specimen, ask the nurse, politely, to show you the identification sticker to make sure it's accurate.

Carry a medical passport. A summary of your vital health information is a must. It should list diseases, medications and doses, food and drug allergies, and phone numbers of your physician and nearest relative. Take it with you to every doctor you see—even the radiologist.

Get a second opinion. It's crucial to your health. If a diagnosis requires surgery, chemotherapy, or medications with side effects, find another specialist (call the hospital's referral service for help), and send him all your pathology and radiology lab work for review, both the images and reports.

WHAT **YOUR DOCTOR** DOESN'T TELL YOU

Don't want a grumpy, tired doctor? Stay on his good side by knowing what he's thinking.

1. We generally know more than a website does. I have patients with whom I spend enormous amounts of time, explaining things and coming up with a treatment strategy. Then I get e-mails a few days later, saying they were looking at this website that says something completely different and wacky, and they want to do that. To which I want to say (but I don't), "So why don't you get the website to take over your care?"

2. When a patient isn't listening or cooperating, I was told in school to put a patient in a gown. It casts him in a position of subservience.

3. Thank you for bringing in a sample of your (stool, urine, etc.) from home. I'll put it in my personal collection of things that really gross me out.

4. It bugs me when you leave your cell phone on. I'm running on a very tight schedule, and I want to spend as much time with patients as I possibly can. Use your time to get the information and the process you need. Please don't answer the phone.

5. I wish you would take more responsibility for your own health and stop relying on me to bail you out of your own problems.

6. Doctors often make patients wait while they listen to sales pitches from drug reps.

7. Those so-called free medication samples of the newest and most expensive drugs may not be the best or safest.

> 🔒 TOP SECRET! We don't make the money you think we do. Just how much of the $100 your doctor charges for taking 30 minutes to investigate your stomach pain goes into his pocket? After paying the bills, he gets less than half.

8. Bring a spouse, but not an entourage. I know why you're bringing your husband and three kids, all of whom are also sick, with you today. No, they are not getting free care.

9. Avoid Friday surgery. The day after surgery is when most problems happen. If the next day is Saturday, you're flying by yourself without a safety net, because the units are understaffed and ERs are overwhelmed because doctors' offices are closed.

10. If you want experience, go long. In many hospitals, the length of the white coat is related to the length of training. Medical students wear the shortest coats.

11. Often the biggest names, the department chairmen, are not the best clinicians, because they spend most of their time being administrators. They no longer primarily focus on taking care of patients.

12. If a sick patient comes to me with a really sad story and asks for a discount, I take care of him or her for no charge. And though we don't cry in front of you, we sometimes do cry about your situation at home.

13. In many ways, doctors are held to an unrealistic standard. We are never, ever allowed to make a mistake.

SOURCES: Daniel Amen, MD, psychiatrist, Newport Beach, California; cardiologist, Bangor, Maine; James Dillard, MD; ear, nose, throat, and facial plastic surgeon, Dallas/Fort Worth, Texas; ER physician, Colorado Springs, Colorado; family physician, Washington, D.C.; Vance Harris, MD, family physician, Redding, California; heart surgeon, New York, New York; internist, Philadelphia, Pennsylvania; Evan S. Levine, MD; obstetrician-gynecologist, New York City; oncologist, Santa Cruz, California; pediatrician, Baltimore, Maryland; pediatrician, Chicago, Illinois; pediatrician, Hartsdale, New York; physical medicine and rehabilitation doctor, Royal Oak, Michigan; Tamara Merritt, DO, family physician, Brewster, Washington; surgeon, Dallas/Fort Worth, Texas.

Great Advice

8 TIPS FOR DOCTOR VISITS THAT WORK

1. Study up before your visit. Research your condition, as well as any other medical conditions or concerns you may have, by gathering information from reputable websites. But don't hand your doctor a huge sheaf of printouts and expect her to respond to them during your visit. And don't try to diagnose your symptoms or self-prescribe your remedies. It's still up to your doctor to do that.

2. Make a list of questions and prioritize them. In one review of 33 office-visit studies, researchers found that people who brought checklists got more time with their doctors. Once you're in the exam room, don't be afraid to give your doctor the list—or ask for it back so you can refer to it.

3. Rehearse. When older people practiced their questions just before a doctor's appointment, according to one study, they were nearly twice as likely to speak up during the visit than people who didn't rehearse.

4. Bring a family member or friend along. Another person who knows about your health and your concerns can help you listen carefully, ask the right questions, and even help you make important decisions during an appointment.

5. Use your phone to record. Replaying an audio of your visit could assist you in better understanding instructions and information that you may have missed or not fully understood at the time.

6. Bring in your meds. Get a bag, toss in all your prescription drugs as well as herbal supplements, vitamins, and over-the-counter remedies, and bring it to your appointment. This will help your doctor understand if you're experiencing any problems with drug interactions or if you're taking any drugs you really don't need.

7. Ask what tests you need and when and where to get them.

8. Evaluate your doctor. Is she too bossy? Is he too deferential? Does your doctor interrupt you? Does he take your views as seriously as you'd like? Try discussing your concerns first, and make a good-faith effort to build a relationship of trust and respect with your physician. But if it's not working out, don't feel obligated to stay. Studies show that patients who don't trust their doctors simply don't get well as quickly, probably because they're less motivated to follow advice and treatment.

WHAT YOUR URGENT CARE CENTERS WON'T TELL YOU

Take a peek into the not-so-urgent secrets of urgent care.

1. ER or urgent care? Always head to the ER for chest pain, severe bleeding, difficulty breathing, a neurological issue such as a seizure, or a serious head trauma with loss of consciousness.

2. The next time your regular doctor says it will be months before you can get an appointment, we may be able to help. Many urgent care centers offer STD tests, school and sports physicals, adult vaccinations, Pap smears, skin allergy treatments, and more.

3. Some primary care docs don't like us because they say we skim the easy work and avoid responsibility for more complex matters. For instance, we'll sew up the laceration on an inebriated person, but we won't address bigger issues like alcoholism and high blood pressure.

4. Sorry, you won't save money if you come here when you really need to go to the ER. If we transfer you by ambulance to the hospital, you may be responsible for co-pays at both places, plus the ambulance ride, which can double your fee.

5. All urgent care centers are not created equal. Some can handle only basic ailments: sore throats, simple wounds, colds, and coughs; they don't have an X-ray machine or a lab. Others can take on diagnoses and tests.

6. We're happy to give you a sample of the latest drug for your treatment. But that tends to be the most expensive. Ask for a less pricey but equally effective option so you can refill your prescription with ease.

7. If I suggest a specific test or procedure, ask whether you really need it and what it will cost. To protect us from potential lawsuits, our clinic guidelines may require us to suggest various treatments even when they're not really needed.

8. If you're paying cash, don't be afraid to negotiate on price. We may be able to reduce your bill, but there has to be a reason. Some urgent care centers even have special cards you can purchase that guarantee you a discount at every single visit.

9. To save time, call to see if you can get on the waiting list before you come. Some centers will send you a text message 30 minutes before someone can see you.

10. Very few of our doctors start in urgent care. Many are burned-out ER or primary care doctors looking for less stress and easier hours.

11. Because we're partially judged by patient-satisfaction scores, we're under pressure to please. So if you want a steroid shot or an antibiotic for your cold, we'll probably give it to you, even if it's not necessary. The one thing we're stingy about? Narcotic pain medications, since we know drug dealers can sell them.

12. Even if there's a doctor on-site, you may never see him or her. Most urgent care centers are staffed with physician assistants and nurse practitioners; typically, a doctor is consulted for complicated cases.

13. We don't have time to sanitize our waiting room after every patient. If you're coming in at the height of flu season, stay safe by asking for a mask and using the hand sanitizer we have out.

SOURCES: Ryan Welter, MD, PhD, of Tristan Medical Primary Care Centers in Massachusetts; Richard Young, MD, of Fort Worth, Texas; Gerry Cvitanovich, of MHM Urgent Care in Louisiana; Mitchel Schwindt, MD, author of *The Patient's Guide to Urgent Care and the Emergency Room;* and Abimbola Fasusi, PA-C, physician assistant for Metro Immediate & Primary Care in Washington, DC.

WHAT YOUR ER STAFF DOESN'T TELL YOU

Take special note of these life-saving ER facts they usually don't show on TV doctor dramas.

1. We're not in it for the money. We're the only doctors who will take care of you first and ask questions about payment later, so we end up giving one third of our care for free—and lose about $100,000 of income a year. Yet we still do it. This is the best specialty in the world.

2. Say thank you. In the ER, nurses provide most of the hands-on care. So be nice.

3. Waiting is good. It means you're not going to die. The person you need to feel sorry for is the one who gets rushed into the ER and treated first.

4. We mean it. If we tell you to stay in bed, do it. Some medications make you uncoordinated, and we hate it when people fall down.

5. We don't believe you. One of our favorite lines is "You can't fix stupidity." If you complain of nausea and then eat a bag of chips, that's what we're thinking.

6. We can only do so much. Not all ERs are equally equipped to deal with children. Check with your pediatrician in advance of an emergency to see which local ER he or she recommends.

7. If you haven't had your child immunized, admit it.
That's important information for us to have.

8. Get the details. If you don't understand what you're supposed to do when you leave the ER, ask—and ask again if necessary. We don't want you to have to come back.

9. Call, don't drive. It's incredible how many people having a heart attack drive themselves to the emergency room instead of calling 911. That's just dumb. What are you going to do if you're driving and your heart stops?

10. We don't usually speed. If the patient is stable, and 97 percent are, there's no reason to drive 60 miles an hour on city streets. Have you ever tried to put an IV into someone's arm in the back of a speeding ambulance?

11. Never tell an ER nurse, "All I have is this cut on my finger. Why can't someone just look at it?" That just shows you have no idea how the ER actually works.

12. Help us out. We don't have time to read the background on every patient. So if you're having stomach pain, and you've had your appendix or gallbladder removed, tell us so we don't go on a wild-goose chase. Be honest about whatever happened. Don't be a hypochondriac, know what medications you are on, and don't answer yes to every question. It will only screw up your care.

13. Speak up, please. An ER in a rural area might not have a doctor who is certified in emergency medicine, and the likelihood of having specialists on staff is very low. If you wind up in one, ask to transfer to a hospital that has more resources.

SOURCES: Jeri Babb, RN, Des Moines, Iowa; Marianne Gausche-Hill, MD, emergency physician, Torrance, California; Dana Hawkins, RN, Tulsa, Oklahoma; Leora Horwitz, MD, assistant professor, Yale University School of Medicine, New Haven, Connecticut; Arthur Hsieh, paramedic; Ramon Johnson, MD, emergency physician, Mission Viejo, California; Denise King, RN, Riverside, California; Linda Lawrence, MD, emergency physician, San Antonio, Texas; Don Lundy, paramedic, Charleston County, South Carolina; Donna Mason, RN, ER consultant, Nashville, Tennessee; Connie Meyer, RN, paramedic, Olathe, Kansas; Allen Roberts, MD, emergency physician, Fort Worth, Texas; Dennis Rowe, paramedic, Knoxville, Tennessee; Joan Shook, MD, emergency physician, Houston, Texas; Robert Solomon, MD, emergency physician, Waynesburg, Pennsylvania; Joan Somes, RN, St. Paul, Minnesota; emergency medical technician, Middlebury, Vermont.

Who Knew?

HOW TO SAVE YOUR OWN LIFE IF YOU THINK YOU'RE HAVING A HEART ATTACK

If you're experiencing crushing chest pain with or without pain in your left arm, are short of breath, or have a sense of impending doom, you may be having a heart attack. Women are more likely to have atypical symptoms like severe fatigue, nausea, heartburn, and profuse sweating. If you are having the symptoms of a heart attack, even if you're a twenty-some-thing, vegetarian triathlete, you need to:

Use a landline to call 911. Using a landline can save your life because we can pinpoint your location instantly. If you call from a cell phone, we waste a lot of time asking where you are or searching for you.

Chew one 325 mg uncoated aspirin to get it into your blood-stream fast. This will thin your blood, often stopping a heart attack in its tracks.

While waiting, lie down so your heart doesn't have to work as hard, says Sandra Schneider, MD, a spokeswoman for the American College of Emergency Physicians.

If you think you might pass out, try forcing yourself to cough deeply. It changes the pressure in your chest and can have the same effect as the thump given in CPR, says Dr. Schneider. "Sometimes it can jolt the heart into a normal rhythm."

If someone else goes into cardiac arrest, note that the American Heart Association now recommends CPR without the mouth-to-mouth. Call 911, then push hard and fast on the person's chest until help comes.

WHAT YOUR PEDIATRICIAN WON'T TELL YOU

Find out how to make the most out of each trip to the pediatrician with these behind-the-stethoscope secrets.

1. Want to avoid the wait? Schedule your appointment for the middle of the week, and ask for the first time slot of the morning or right after lunch.

2. When you tell me you gave a decongestant to your toddler, I cringe. Studies show that cold medicines never work well for children under age six, and the risk of overdose and side effects far outweigh any benefit.

3. Want to make vaccines less painful for your child? Ask if you can breast-feed while we give your infant his shots. Or if you have an older child, see if we can use cold spray or a numbing cream to decrease the pain.

4. Do you really believe that we'd be recommending vaccines if we had any concerns about their safety? Almost all pediatricians immunize their own children.

5. If I prescribe a newer, more expensive medication, it may be because a drug rep just left my office. They constantly bring us presents and flatter us, and their only goal is getting us to prescribe the latest medication, which is usually no better than the older ones. In fact, the older ones have longer safety track records and really should be the ones we prescribe first.

6. Don't ask if I'll take a "quick look" at the sibling who doesn't have an appointment. If your mom went with you to the gynecologist, would you ever say, "Doc, would you mind putting her on the table and giving her a quick look?" Every patient deserves a full evaluation.

7. As soon as you say, "He doesn't like it when you look in his ears," you remind your child of the last time and set us up for another failure. Be matter-of-fact: "It's time for the doctor to look in your ears." Kids have also figured out that "This won't hurt" is code for "This is going to hurt," and they get all worked up. It's really best not to even use the word *hurt*. It just creates anxiety.

TOP SECRET! If you have an urgent concern and the front desk tells you there are no appointments available, ask for a nurse and explain your situation. Often she can work you in even if the schedule indicates there's no time.

8. Sometimes we have less than ten minutes per patient, so make the most of your time and ask about the most pressing problems first. If you have a lot of questions, request an extra-long appointment.

9. Even though I tell you to let your baby cry himself back to sleep once he's older, don't ask me if I always followed that advice with my own kids. I didn't.

10. Don't tell your kid the doctor will give him a shot if he doesn't behave. I won't.

11. Yes, you can talk to your pediatrician on the phone. Be persistent, be polite, and explain to the staff that you have a pressing, personal issue that you think would be best handled over the phone. We'll call back as soon as we can. This especially applies to older children, who often don't even need a visit. It may only take a call to find out that your child's fever, cold, sore throat, ear infection, and even pinkeye will most likely get better on its own.

12. Listen to your intuition. You know your child better than anyone, and that's why when you tell me something "isn't right," my ears perk up.

13. Don't delay treating your child because you want me to see the symptoms. People do this a lot: "I didn't give him Tylenol, because I wanted you to feel the fever." "I didn't use the nebulizer, because I wanted you to hear the wheezing." Trust me, I will believe you that the child had a fever or was wheezing. Delaying the treatment only makes your child suffer.

SOURCES: Pediatricians David L. Hill, MD, in Wilmington, North Carolina; Robert Lindeman, MD, in Framingham, Massachusetts; Allison Fabian, DO, in Grand Rapids, Michigan; Amanda Moran, MD, in Charlotte, North Carolina; Roy Benaroch, MD, author of *A Guide to Getting the Best Health Care for Your Child*; and a pediatrician in Virginia who preferred not to be named.

Great Advice

11 TIPS FOR A HEALTHIER AND MORE ACTIVE FAMILY

1. Go on a treasure hunt. Take your kids to a local park and set an expedition course on a map, circling various "checkpoints." Take turns navigating to each point on the map and leading the team to each destination.

2. Hold a sports party. Rather than the typical pin-the-tail-on-the-donkey birthday party, hold your child's birthday party in an active location, such as a roller-skating or ice-skating rink, laser tag center, wall-climbing gym, or indoor playground center. Or you can have your own "no particular reason" party. Kids won't think of what they're doing as exercise—but it is.

3. Wash the car together. The scrubbing is good exercise, but everyone getting wet and soapy is just plain fun for kids.

4. Plant a garden together. Digging holes, planting seeds, and pulling weeds build upper body strength. As an added bonus, research shows that children are more likely to eat the vegetables they help grow, which means your gardening forays will help your child follow a more nutritious diet.

5. Take a hike at least twice a month. Grab a backpack, plenty of water (everyone should drink eight ounces every half-hour), and a light lunch and head to a local trail for a hiking expedition. Wear hiking boots for rocky terrain or sneakers for smoother trails, and pack sunscreen and insect repellent. To make this more fun for kids, make it about something else, such as looking for a particular animal or bird, climbing to see a lake or pond, or seeing how many rocks you can scamper over without touching the ground. Kids like hiking much better when they don't realize it's about hiking!

6. Dance during commercial breaks. Make it a family rule that whenever you watch television, you have to stand up and dance around during the commercials. This goes for everyone! Whoever gets caught sitting on the couch during a commercial break must perform his or her least-liked household chore for one week.

7. Sign up for a race. Check your local paper for a list of 5K and 10K walk/run events in your area. Many of these events also raise money for charity, which can inspire your children to train for the event.

8. Walk around the world. Place a map of the country, state, or world somewhere prominently in your home. Work with your children to arrive at a walking destination. Then, based on your daily family walks, plot your progress on the map using thumbtacks. There are about 2,000 steps in a mile, so you can plot your progress by using a pedometer. To add some incentive, promise to actually take a vacation to your walking destination once you complete the number of steps to get there.

9. Act like a child. Remember duck-duck-goose, hopscotch, and red-light-green-light-one-two-three? You probably thought of these games as just that, games. But they also require movement and count as exercise. Teach them to your kids and play along. As you laugh, you'll burn extra calories. Don't forget Simon Says!

10. Place small children on the floor at least once a day—and let them crawl, move, and toddle. Children are inherently active when given the opportunity to move. Yet we often confine children and prevent the very exercise they need.

11. Design your backyard for activity. What you put in your backyard helps determine how fit your children become. If they see it, they will play. If they don't, they will watch TV. Older children enjoy climbing on ropes or ladders and playing in forts. Make sure you have a swing set, sprinkler attachment for your hose, sandbox, wagon for hauling toys and dolls, and outdoor sporting equipment for basketball, badminton, soccer, and other games.

WHAT YOUR DENTIST WON'T TELL YOU

You can't sneak as much past your dentist as you think you can. Here are 13 things they know about you—and what you need to do to see them less.

1. No pain doesn't mean "no problem." Some truly educated people think that if nothing in their mouth hurts, they're fine. High cholesterol doesn't hurt, either, but it's a big problem.

2. Bleeding is not OK. If your hands bled when you washed them, you'd run to the doctor. But in the public's mind, bleeding gums are okay. Unless you're really whaling away with your brush, if your gums bleed even a little, that's periodontal disease, period.

3. Your dentist does need to see you. The advice to see your dentist twice a year applies only if you have healthy gums. Most people don't.

4. The problem might not be what you think it is. People come to me with a mouthful of tooth decay and say, "I got my grandfather's soft teeth." I don't even know what soft teeth are.

5. The more time you spend, the less we have to. Proper oral hygiene requires ten minutes of brushing and flossing every day. The average adult spends two or three minutes total, and kids do even worse.

6. Chewing gum can be good. If you want to reduce the bad bacteria in your mouth, you should be all over xylitol, a sugar substitute found in chewing gum. It changes the chemistry of your mouth. Six or seven pieces of xylitol gum every day will help keep cavities away.

7. Mouthwash is a very short-term strategy. A mouthwash with alcohol dries out your mouth—you'll smell nice and minty for a half hour, but then the bad breath comes back worse than ever.

8. The electric toothbrush is one of the best things to ever happen to dentistry. The newer ones replicate professional cleaning—they won't reach much below the gum line, but they're far superior to regular toothbrushes. The cheap ones are okay for kids, but you'll have to pay more than $75 for a really good brush with a warranty and replacement heads.

> **🔒 TOP SECRET!** Minty mouthwash or breath mints don't fight bad breath! Most mouthwashes contain alcohol, which dries up saliva and makes your breath worse afterward. Mint candy is just a cover-up; it actually feeds the odor-causing bacteria more sugar! For a natural mouthwash, mix 1 tablespoon of baking soda with 1 cup of a 2 to 3 percent solution of hydrogen peroxide. The foam it kicks up has a powerful oxidizing effect that kills odoriferous bacteria.

9. We think X-rays do more good than harm. A lot of patients are worried that dental X-rays can cause cancer, but if you're outside for an hour, you're exposed to more radiation than you'd get from a full set of dental X-rays. What I worry about is that if I don't take an X-ray, I might miss something serious.

10. There's no way to make implants cheaper. If you're missing teeth, chances are that your insurance company won't cover implants—only one out of 22 insurance companies I deal with covers them, even though they're better than dentures in every way.

11. Sometimes, we can fix your headache. Misaligned teeth can cause migraine headaches. If we can align the teeth and fix the bite, the pain often goes away.

12. Teeth get whiter when they dry out. Some dentists promise that their office procedures will make your teeth four shades whiter. But if you leave your mouth open for an hour, you could easily be two shades whiter just from dehydration.

13. We need you to know what your insurance covers. People think we have a crystal ball that tells us everyone's insurance information. We don't. And we need to find out what's covered before we can do anything.

SOURCES: Michael Alkon, DMD, general dentist, Holmdel, New Jersey; Damian Dachowski, DMD, general dentist, Horsham, Pennsylvania; Danine Fresch Gray, DDS, general dentist, Arlington, Virginia; Jay Grossman, DDS, cosmetic dentist, Brentwood, California; Gary Herskovits, DDS, family dentist, Brooklyn, New York; Paul Hettinger, DMD, general dentist, Orlando, Florida; Jennifer Jablow, DDS, cosmetic dentist, New York, New York; Jim Janakievski, DDS, periodontist, Tacoma, Washington; Chris Kammer, DDS, cosmetic dentist, Middleton, Wisconsin; Mark Mutschler, DDS, pediatric dentist, Oregon City, Oregon; Mai-Ly Ramirez, DDS, general dentist, San Francisco, California; Ron Schefdore, DMD, general dentist, Chicago, Illinois; Bryan Tervo, DDS, expert at JustAnswer.com; Joel Slaven, DDS, general dentist, Valencia, California; Ned Windmiller, DDS, general dentist, Stillwater, Minnesota; Careen Young, DDS, prosthodontist, Beverly Hills, California.

INSTANT BAD BREATH FIGHTERS

....

Dry mouth is a haven for the bacteria that cause bad breath. So find a tap, and swish the water around in your mouth. Water will temporarily dislodge bacteria and make your breath a bit more palatable.

At the end of your power lunch or romantic dinner, munch the sprig of parsley that's left on your plate. Parsley is rich in chlorophyll, a known breath deodorizer with germ-fighting qualities.

If you can get your hands on an orange, peel and eat it. The citric acid it contains will stimulate your salivary glands and encourage the flow of breath-freshening saliva.

Cloves are rich in eugenol, a potent antibacterial. Simply pop one into your mouth and dent it with your teeth. The pungent aromatic oil may burn slightly, so keep that spicy nub moving. Continue to bite until the essence permeates your mouth, then spit it out. Don't use clove oil or powdered cloves—they're too strong and can cause burns.

Chew on fennel, dill, cardamom, or anise seeds. Anise, which tastes like black licorice, can kill the bacteria that grow on the tongue. The others can help mask the odor of halitosis.

Suck on a stick of cinnamon. Like cloves, cinnamon is effective as an antiseptic.

Vigorously scrape your tongue over your teeth. Your tongue can become coated with bacteria that ferment proteins, producing gases that smell bad. Scraping your tongue can dislodge these bacteria so you can rinse them away.

WHAT YOUR EYE DOCTOR WON'T TELL YOU

Here are 13 things about what helps and hurts your eyes (carrots included).

1. Never use tissues or toilet paper to clean your eyeglasses. Paper is made of wood, and it will scratch your lenses. I like to use my tie because it's silk and really smooth.

2. Polarized sunglasses are great at reducing glare, but they can make it difficult to see the LCD on your cell phone or navigation system. It's harder to see an ATM screen when you've got polarized sunglasses on, too.

3. Life doesn't go on as normal after I dilate your eyes. It'll be two or three hours before you can do anything that requires concentrated visual attention.

4. You wear your sunglasses only when it's sunny? That's like saying "I only smoke sometimes." Most people know that UV radiation can damage skin, but they don't realize it's also bad for eyes. Wear sunglasses big enough to block the light from above and below—they should have thick sides or wrap around.

5. Eyedrops (any kind) sting less if you keep them in the refrigerator.

6. **Some doctors pressure patients to have cataract surgery right away,** but if it creates financial problems for you, there's usually no harm in waiting. Cataracts rarely hurt you—they just make it hard to see, like looking out of a dirty window.

7. **Reading in dim light won't hurt your eyes,** but you might get a headache.

8. **Take extended-wear contacts out before bed.** Your chance of infection is 10 to 15 times greater if you sleep in them.

TOP SECRET! Carrots aren't the best food for your eyes, despite what generations of parents have told their kids. That honor goes to spinach, kale, and other dark, leafy veggies.

9. **Don't grab just any old bottle of eyedrops** out of your medicine cabinet when a new problem comes up. If you have an infection, steroid drops might make the redness look better, but the infection could get worse. I've had to remove people's eyes because of that!

10. **Pinkeye isn't always benign.** A number of patients end up with light sensitivity and even vision loss. But many physicians treat it with antibiotics that won't help if the cause is a virus. We do a rapid test for adenovirus—if that's what you have, we treat it very differently than if your pinkeye is bacterial.

11. **No, it's not OK to wait for symptoms to appear.** Some blinding eye diseases have few warning signs. A yearly exam is the only way to catch things early.

12. **If you're over 60, considering LASIK,** and at risk of developing cataracts, wait until you develop one. Then we can fix your vision as part of the cataract surgery and your insurance may pay for it.

13. **If you wear contacts,** ask for UV coating.

SOURCES: Brian Bonanni, MD, an ophthalmologist at Gotham LASIK, New York City; Stephen Cohen, OD, past president of the Arizona Optometric Association; Eric Donnenfeld, MD, editor of *Cataract and Refractive Surgery Today*; Paul Harris, OD, associate professor at the Southern College of Optometry, Memphis, Tennessee; Janice Jurkus, OD, professor of optometry at Illinois Eye Institute; Robert Noecker, MD, an ophthalmologist at Ophthalmic Consultants of Connecticut; Robert Sambursky, MD, an ophthalmologist in Sarasota, Florida; Andrea Thau, OD, associate clinical professor at the SUNY College of Optometry.

Great Advice

EASY WAYS TO IMPROVE YOUR VISION

1. Mix a cup of blueberries with a cup of yogurt for breakfast. In one study, women and men who ate the greatest amount of fruit were the least likely to develop age-related macular degeneration (ARMD), the leading cause of blindness in older people.

2. Cook with red onions, not yellow. Red onions contain far more quercetin, an antioxidant that may protect against cataracts.

3. Aim your car vents at your feet—not your eyes. Dry, air-conditioned air will suck the moisture out of eyes like a sponge. Serious dryness can lead to corneal abrasions and even blindness if left untreated.

4. Move your computer screen to just below eye level. Your eyes will close slightly when you're staring at the computer, minimizing fluid evaporation and the risk of dry eye syndrome.

5. Walk at least four times a week. Some evidence suggests that regular exercise can reduce the intraocular pressure, or IOP, in people with glaucoma. In one study, glaucoma patients who walked briskly four times per week for 40 minutes lowered their IOP enough so they could stop taking medication for their condition.

6. Turn down the heat in your house. Heat dries out the air, which, in turn, dries out your eyes. In the winter, you might also try adding some humidity with a humidifier or even bunching a lot of plants together in the room in which you spend the most time.

WHAT YOUR DERMATOLOGIST WON'T TELL YOU

If you think the dermatologist is there to just take care of your blemishes, think again.

1. I can tell which way you sleep. Sleeping on your side or stomach creates a furrow on one side of your face. For an easy way to minimize wrinkles, sleep on your back. You may snore, but you'll age better.

2. If you hit the pillow at night without washing, every single thing you came into contact with that day is on your skin. If you're usually too tired to lather up, keep a box of alcohol-free towelettes on your nightstand. Don't be surprised when you break out.

3. Anything that makes your skin feel squeaky-clean is stripping out all the moisture, and that's not a good thing. If you have dry or sensitive skin, wash with gentle or moisturizing cleanser, not soap.

4. If you're a woman who's losing her hair, apply some men's Rogaine 5 percent minoxidil formula. We recommend it off-label all the time. The women's version is only 2 percent minoxidil.

5. Many drugstore-brand antiaging creams—including those from Olay, Neutrogena, and Aveeno—have the same active ingredients and can be just as effective as products that cost four to ten times as much at department stores.

6. Please, please, throw away your magnifying mirror. It makes you want to pick and squeeze, which is the worst thing you can do.

7. Young men don't often come to see me. So if I have an appointment with a younger guy, I bet that either A) a woman dragged him in, or B) he has something going on in his private area, usually genital warts or jock itch.

8. Yes, you do have to take off your underwear for the full-body skin exam. And please don't wear makeup or nail polish. I need to see every inch of your skin. I've found skin cancer underneath toenails, between toes, in armpits, and in other places where the sun doesn't shine.

9. Drinking eight glasses of water a day is not going to hydrate your skin, which is affected by your environment. If you're in the dry heat of Phoenix, you can drink water all day long and your skin will still be dry. If you're in Hawaii, where it's humid, your skin will be plumped up no matter how much water you drink.

10. A rigorous exercise regimen will make you fitter, but it won't make you look younger. Thinner and more athletic people over age 40 have less fat under their skin and can look older than overweight people.

11. Got cracks between your toes? It's often caused by fungus. Over-the-counter creams will clear it up. Sprinkle antifungal powder into socks and shoes so they don't get reinfected.

12. Yes, that could be poison ivy down there. To prevent allergic rashes in your genital area, wash your hands when you come in from the yard—before you go to the bathroom.

13. Are razor bumps ruining your life? Shave either every day or never. Shaving every other day causes the most problems because the hairs get long enough to curl back in.

SOURCES: Kathy Fields, MD, a San Francisco dermatologist and cofounder of Rodan + Fields; Jeffrey Benabio, MD, a dermatologist at Kaiser Permanente in San Diego; Diane Madfes, MD, a dermatologist in New York City; and Jonathan Kantor, MD, a dermatologist in St. Augustine, Florida.

WHAT YOUR PODIATRIST WON'T TELL YOU

These 13 secrets can keep your feet from hurting—or stinking—for good.

1. Your feet don't have to smell. You use antiperspirant on your armpits to keep them from getting stinky, don't you? The same stuff works on your feet. Try the spray kind.

2. You can fight stink without buying anything. Make some really strong black tea, then soak your feet in it two or three times a week for 20 minutes. The tannic acid has been shown to temporarily shrink sweat ducts so they don't work as hard. Always alternate your shoes so they have a chance to dry completely, and wear socks. Otherwise, the sweat will promote the growth of bacteria that stay in your shoes.

3. Infections from nail salons keep us in business. If you want a pedicure, book the first appointment of the day, when the equipment is cleaner. Those footbaths can be especially germy. Even if technicians spray the basin between customers, many of the tubs have drains and filters that don't get cleaned. No matter what, don't shave before you go. Bacteria and fungus can enter the microscopic nicks on your ankle and give you an infection.

4. Toe separators, bunion splints, and "yoga toes" may help you feel better, but they aren't going to get rid of hammertoes and bunions. You've got to come to me for that. If you have a structural problem, a $6 device isn't going to reverse anything.

5. Some podiatrists will shorten toes or do injections so you can wear high heels more comfortably. But I don't believe in cosmetic surgery for feet. You shouldn't have surgery if you're not in pain, because you will have pain after surgery—that's a guarantee. It has to be worth it. Otherwise, you're asking for trouble.

6. Get your bunions taken care of now. If you wait until they get really bad, they'll be much harder to fix.

🔒 **TOP SECRET!** I wear flip-flops, too, but if you wear them every day, all day, you will end up in my office eventually. Those shoes are designed for the beach and pool, not for walking all over the place.

7. I've seen all sorts of things, including people who have shot their feet. You really shouldn't clean your loaded gun after you've had a couple of beers. Another dumb move: mowing the lawn in flip-flops. The first weekend of every spring, doctors see a lot of injuries.

8. Over-the-counter "custom-fit" orthotics are a bit of a gimmick. They'll help if you just need some arch support and padding, but they're nothing like the orthotics I make after creating a mold of your feet in my office. Orthotics and arch supports should be firm. If it's jellylike or soft and smushy, then that's not support—that's cushioning—and it's probably not going to help your problem.

9. A lot of you hurt your foot or ankle exercising and head straight to an orthopedic surgeon. But unless he or she is specifically trained in the foot and ankle, coming to me is a better bet.

10. Your cuticles are there for a reason. You can push them back, but don't cut.

11. I have people who tell me that I changed their life, and it turns out all I did was tell them to wear a bigger size shoe. I think, *did that really change your life?* But if they had a lot of pain, it's a big deal.

12. When you go into a shoe store, your salesperson should measure your feet. A lot of you have been wearing the same shoe size for the past 30 years because no one measures you anymore, but feet often get bigger as you age.

13. The best socks today are not 100 percent cotton. Look for materials that promise to wick moisture away.

SOURCES: Jane Andersen, a podiatrist in Chapel Hill, North Carolina; Marlene Reid, a podiatrist in Naperville, Illinois; Carly Robbins, a podiatrist in Columbus, Ohio; Jacqueline Sutera, a podiatrist in New York, New York; Cary Zinkin, a podiatrist in Deerfield Beach, Florida.

WHAT YOUR SLEEP DOCTOR WON'T TELL YOU

A good night's sleep is vital to your health and happiness. Here are 13 ways to get better sleep—and become aware of what's really robbing you of it.

1. We expect to sleep for eight solid hours, but that's actually not normal compared with global populations and our own evolutionary history. People naturally wake up two or three times a night. It's worrying about it that's the problem.

2. Digital clocks blare time at you. If you look at the time when you awaken during the night, it's likely to increase your anxiety about not being asleep. If you need a clock to wake you in the morning, just turn its face to the wall right before bed. You'll hear it just as well.

3. If you're not sleeping well, you may have acid reflux, even if you don't feel heartburn. Try elevating your head by putting blocks under the top of the bed and sleeping on your left side.

4. If you like a firmer mattress and she likes a softer one, you don't have to compromise. Get two singles, push them together, and use king sheets. You can also buy a strap that attaches the mattresses to each other. I also tell couples that each person should have a sheet and blanket. One of the biggest disrupters of sleep is the pulling and tugging of sheets and blankets. If you pull a big comforter or duvet over the top when you make the bed, you really can't tell. Couples call me after I suggest that and say, "Wow—you changed our marriage."

5. Memory foam is very temperature dependent. The foam can get a little hard in a cold bedroom. And if you're a hot sleeper, it may make you hotter.

6. My research has found that any new smell, even one associated with relaxation, like lavender, can make you more alert and vigilant. You're better off with a scent that makes you feel safe and comfortable. There really is something to cuddling up with your spouse's undershirt.

> **TOP SECRET!** Women aren't used to putting their needs ahead of others', but sleep is so necessary to health and happiness, they must. If the dog's snoring wakes you up, put him in another room. If your partner's snoring wakes you up, help him get treatment. If he refuses to cooperate, put him in another room.

7. Watching TV at night may seem relaxing, but it beams light into your eyes, which is an "alert" signal for the brain. Read a book before bed instead.

8. Give yourself an hour—the one right before bed. You need it to wind down and make the transition from the person-who-can-do-everything to the person-who-can-sleep.

9. To keep your room dark, use blackout draperies or shades—not blinds, because they never completely block out light. Install the shades as close to the glass as possible. If you don't have the depth for an interior mount, extend the fabric several inches past the width of the window.

10. A hot bath will increase your skin temperature, which eventually decreases your core body temperature, and that's helpful for sleep. Do the same thing for yourself that you'd do for a young child—make sure you take a bath a half hour or so before bedtime.

11. There's no solid explanation for it, but studies have found that wearing socks to bed helps you sleep. It may be that warming your feet and legs allows your internal body temperature to drop.

12. A lot of people take bedtime pain relievers that contain caffeine and don't even realize it. Excedrin has 65 milligrams of caffeine per tablet—if you take two, that's as much as a cup of coffee. Check the label: Caffeine is always listed as an active ingredient.

13. I'm not a fan of sleeping with two pillows if you're a back sleeper because it makes your upper back curve and strains the neck and back. If you need to sleep up high for medical reasons, get a wedge and put your pillow on it.

SOURCES: Tara Brass, MD, a psychiatrist in New York, New York; Pamela Dalton, PhD, odor-perception expert and sensory psychologist at Monell Chemical Senses Center, Philadelphia, Pennsylvania; Jan Engle, professor of pharmacy at the College of Pharmacy, University of Illinois at Chicago; Karen Erickson, a chiropractor in New York, New York; Mary Susan Esther, MD, director of the Sleep Center at South Park in Charlotte, North Carolina; Ian Gibbs, cofounder of the Shade Store in New York, New York; Colin Grey, a time-management coach in London, England; Alan Hedge, PhD, professor of ergonomics at Cornell University, Ithaca, New York; Robert Oexman, chiropractor and director of the Sleep to Live Institute in Joplin, Missouri; Patricia Raymond, MD, a gastroenterologist in Virginia Beach, Virginia; Carol Worthman, PhD, an anthropologist at Emory University in Atlanta, Georgia.

Great Advice

HOW TO STOP STRESS FROM WRECKING YOUR SLEEP

When worry drives your life, studies show you're more likely to develop chronic insomnia. Here's how to prevent that—and get a good night's sleep.

Stop those thoughts. Once you hit the sheets, worry time is over—especially about sleeping. There's a therapy trick called "thought-stopping" that works like a charm, says Mary Susan Esther, MD, director of the Sleep Center at South Park in Charlotte, North Carolina. "If you find yourself thinking about tomorrow and saying, 'It's going to be a bad day because I'm never going to sleep,' immediately think: 'STOP. Don't go there. I know I've done this before. If I don't fall asleep, I'll get out of bed, flip through a magazine, but I am NOT going to focus on this stuff!'" Sounds simple, but once you try it, you'll find it works.

Dump the 24/7 routine. Even if we manage to drop into bed in enough time to get our optimal amount of sleep, our minds are full of what-if's, why-did-we's and what's-on-the-agenda-tomorrow's. All this rumination and agitation ignites stress hormones that keep us in a state of perpetual arousal. That's why we should make a serious attempt to simplify our lives, says Cecile Andrews, PhD, author of *Slow Is Beautiful*. Draw up your to-do list, then take a big breath and start crossing things off, she says. It's a bit humbling to realize, but you really don't have to do it all.

Don't work so late. The prevailing thought is that you have to stay late to get the job done. But working right up until bedtime is bound to affect your sleep. Go home at a reasonable hour. The truth is that it's better to go get some sleep, then come back and do more work in the morning. Studies show that after a good night's sleep, your increased ability to concentrate means that you can work faster and more accurately.

Recognize yourself. How do you deal with stress? Pig out on chocolate mousse? Skip meals? Refill your wine glass a couple of times after dinner? All of these classic stress responses actually make falling asleep and staying asleep more difficult. But if you know your stress response will sabotage your sleep, plan ahead of time how you're going to handle something you just know is going to raise your stress level. If you know the big sales conference is coming up next week, for example, get into bed an hour early every night this week, which will give your body a biochemical boost of stress-proofing growth hormone to ride into the week. If you know you're going to see your ex when he drops off your daughter Saturday evening, take time out and meditate for 20 minutes before he's supposed to arrive.

Get physical. Burn off a rush of stress with a 15-minute walk. Studies show that those who regularly exercise sleep better than those who don't.

Forgive the past. Anger toward someone who has wronged you can trigger a cascade of stress hormones that can haunt you through the night. To prevent that effect, think about how you were hurt, your response, and how you feel right now. Then think about whether or not there's anything in the background of the person who hurt you that explains what he or she did. If there is, put yourself in their shoes—and see if you can't forgive them. If you can, you'll sleep like a baby.

WHAT **YOUR SURGEON** WON'T TELL YOU

Surgeons have our lives in their hands, but most of us know more about the people who cut our hair than the doctors who cut our bodies. Here, insider tips that will help you become a smarter, healthier patient.

1. To know which doctor is good, ask hospital employees. "Their word trumps an Ivy League degree, prestigious titles, and charm."

2. Always ask "Who is going to take care of me after surgery?" You want to hear "I will see you on a regular basis until you have recovered fully." Often it can be residents or physician's assistants. Sometimes it's not anybody, especially after you've been discharged from the hospital.

3. It's better to have an elective surgery early in the week. Lots of doctors go away for the weekend and won't be around to make sure you're OK. If you go in on a Friday, and then on Saturday or Sunday something icky is coming out of your incision, you're going to get someone who's covering for your surgeon.

4. Some doctors hire practice management consultants to help capture more revenue. The consultants may want the practice to sell equipment like knee braces or walkers at a markup. They may want the doctors to buy or build a surgery center to capture facility fees. They usually want orthopedic surgeons to get an in-office MRI. Every time a doctor does this, he becomes more financially conflicted. As soon as you put in an MRI machine, you order more MRIs so you won't lose money on it.

5. **Always ask about nonsurgical options and whether there's anything wrong with waiting a little while.** Surgeons are busy, and they like to operate. A professor from my residency would say, "There is nothing more dangerous than a surgeon with an open operating room and a mortgage to pay."

6. **When we get polite in the operating room,** when we start saying "please" and "thank you" and talking in a monotone, that's when nurses know things aren't going well. We use this mechanism to maintain calm. When we become unglued, everyone becomes unfocused, and that's when patients die. How you handle stress is absolutely critical.

7. **The only real way to understand what happened in the operating room** is to read the operative note dictated by the surgeon. If you have unanswered questions about your surgery, ask for the report.

8. **About 25 percent of operations are unnecessary, but administrators e-mail doctors telling them to do more.** This is not an insurance company putting pressure on doctors; this is not a government regulation. This is private hospitals pushing doctors to generate more money by doing more procedures. It goes on at America's top hospitals. The Cleveland Clinic has said this system of paying doctors is so ethically immoral that it started paying its doctors a flat salary no matter how many operations they do.

9. **That tiny thank-you card that took you 15 seconds to write?** It was very meaningful. Letters are a good reminder of how important this is and how people entrust themselves to us.

10. **Products like ScarEase, Scarguard, and Mederma do work to reduce scarring.** Start applying daily as soon as your wound has healed, and avoid sunlight or use a sunscreen with zinc oxide for at least six months after surgery.

11. The biggest mistake during recovery is not giving yourself enough of a break. Give yourself time to heal. If you don't, you can cause complications and prolong your recovery.

12. If we had any kind of serious medical condition, we'd go to a teaching hospital. You'll get doctors involved with the latest in medicine. Even for simple cases, if there's a complication that requires an assist device or a heart transplant, some hospitals may not be able to do it. At a university hospital, you also have the advantage of having a resident or physician bedside 24-7, with a surgeon on call always available.

13. If you need a medical device, ask if your doctor has a financial relationship with the vendor. If so, chances are you're going to get that type of joint or screw, even if it's more expensive or not the most appropriate.

SOURCES: Marty Makary, MD, author of *Unaccountable: What Hospitals Won't Tell You and How Transparency Can Revolutionize Health Care;* Ezriel "Ed" Kornel, MD, clinical assistant professor of neurological surgery at Cornell University; General surgeon who blogs under the name Skeptical Scalpel; James Rickert, MD; Kevin B. Jones, MD; Kathy Magliato, MD; Paul Ruggieri, MD; Marc Gillinov, MD; Andrew Ordon, MD; Tomas A. Salerno, MD.

WHAT YOUR PHARMACIST WON'T TELL YOU

Here's how to spend less at the pharmacy, get what really works for you, and avoid dangerous—and sometimes deadly—pill mix-ups.

1. Don't try to get anything past us. Prescriptions for painkillers or sleeping aids always get extra scrutiny.

2. Generics are a close match for most brand names. But I'd be careful with blood thinners and thyroid drugs, since small differences can have big effects.

3. I hate your insurance company as much as you do. Even if something's working for you, the insurance company may insist you switch to something else. I'm stuck in the middle trying to explain this to customers.

4. We can give flu shots in most states.

5. All pharmacists are not created equal. A less-qualified pharmacy technician may have actually filled your prescription. Currently, there is no national standard for their training and responsibilities.

6. We're human . . . And we make mistakes (about two million a year). Ask if we use a bar code system to help keep us from pulling the wrong drug off the shelf or giving the wrong strength of the right drug.

7. If you don't like a generic, ask if there are alternatives. I can give you a generic refill that's different from the one you started with.

8. We'll save you money if we can. A good part of a pharmacist's time is spent dealing with patients and their incomes. Part of that is suggesting generic alternatives. Or if a doctor has prescribed a newer drug with no generic alternative available, I'll call the doctor to suggest an older drug that's equally effective.

9. Look into the $4 and $10 generics. Chains like Target, Kroger, and Walmart offer them.

10. It gets busy Monday and Tuesday evenings, since many new prescriptions and refills come in after the weekend.

11. Don't put up with the silent treatment. Pharmacists are required by law in most states to counsel patients and answer their questions. If your pharmacist seems too busy to talk, take your business elsewhere.

> **TOP SECRET!** There's not some big computer database that tracks your drugs and flags interactions for pharmacists everywhere. Use one pharmacy. If you start using a new one, make sure we know what you're taking.

12. People take too many drugs. Two out of every three patients who visit a doctor leave with at least one prescription for medication, according to the Institute for Safe Medication Practices. Drugs are an easy solution, but there are other solutions.

13. Talk to me—and check my work. Every year plenty of prescriptions are taken wrong—the FDA has recorded an incident where a man overdosed after his wife mistakenly applied six prescription painkilling patches to his skin. And many people don't ask questions about how to use their medications. When you pick up your prescription, at least ask, "What is this drug? What does it do? Why am I taking it? What are the possible side effects? and How should I take it?" Not only does this help you to use the drug correctly; it's also a good way to double-check that you're getting the right drug.

SOURCES: Cindy Coffey, PharmD; Greg Collins, pharmacy supervisor, CVS/pharmacy, California; Stuart Feldman, owner, Cross River Pharmacy, New York; Dr. Daniel Zlott, oncology pharmacist, National Institutes of Health.

Great Advice

HOW TO TELL WHICH ONLINE PHARMACIES ARE LEGITIMATE

Plenty of online pharmacies are honest businesses—experts think they actually outnumber the sham ones—and they offer big advantages. You can shop the Internet for the best prices; you can buy certain drugs without embarrassment; and you can do it all from the comfort of your armchair.

But how can you be confident an online pharmacy is legitimate? One sure sign is if the site has the VIPPS (Verified Internet Pharmacy Practice Sites) seal of approval. That's a certification from the National Association of Boards of Pharmacy (NABP), and the seal must be displayed prominently on the business's website. You can also check the NABP's website for a list of pharmacies that have earned the VIPPS seal (nabp.net).

You should be suspicious of any online pharmacy that:

❋ Doesn't require you to mail in a prescription.

❋ Doesn't speak to your doctor to ensure your prescription is valid.

❋ Doesn't ask you to do more than fill in an online questionnaire.

❋ Doesn't have a toll-free number and street address listed on its website.

❋ Doesn't make pharmacists available to answer questions about the medications. Be on guard, too, if the site sells only "lifestyle" medications, like drugs for impotence, obesity, or pain.

WHAT YOUR THERAPIST WON'T TELL YOU

Ever wonder if the one being paid not to judge you, is actually judging you? Here's an inside look into the minds of the mind connoisseurs.

1. Sometimes, when we say, "That's interesting," it's really not. We say that when we get caught thinking about something else.

2. Don't take it personally if you see me outside the office and I ignore you. If I'm with someone, introducing you as my patient would violate patient confidentiality.

3. Do we talk about you at cocktail parties? Absolutely. The stranger your story, the better.

4. Mental illness can damage the brain. You can't just wait for it to go away. The longer you wait to get treatment, the worse it will get and the greater the chances that prescription drugs won't work.

5. Anyone can call him- or herself a psychotherapist or a therapist. You want a psychologist, a psychiatrist, a clinical social worker, or a marriage, family, and child counselor. You have to be licensed to use those titles.

6. It never hurts to ask for a lower fee. Some of us will actually say yes.

7. Long-term therapy makes some patients much more self-absorbed. Some start to believe that every thought and dream they have is important.

8. I might exaggerate a diagnosis to get an insurance firm to pay for more coverage. I use a diagnosis I call adjustment disorder, which means you are having trouble adjusting to your life. That can apply to almost anybody.

9. Sexual fantasies about patients? Unfortunately, it happens. When it does, it's very distracting and troubling.

10. The people who pay for their therapy themselves seem to get better faster. The patients who rely on insurance are typically not as motivated.

11. Sometimes I tell you to do the opposite of what I really want you to do. For instance, I might tell you that this week I want you to be really depressed, to think about all the reasons you are depressed each day. It works for two reasons: First, nobody likes to be told what to do. And it helps you realize that you have a choice in how you feel.

12. Please don't ask things like "Don't you agree?" If you're looking for approval, you're not going to get it. A good counselor is not there to say yes to everything.

13. No matter what you tell me, I've probably heard it before. You are not going to shock me.

SOURCES: Psychologists and psychiatrists in California, Washington, Pennsylvania, and Texas.

WHAT YOUR PERSONAL TRAINER WON'T TELL YOU

What's a waste of energy and what really works? Find out from trainers who've seen it all in the gym.

1. Do not arrive at a training session in the following states: On an empty stomach, coming off a cold/stomach bug, or on four hours' sleep. It wastes your time and mine when your body isn't fueled, hydrated, and ready to work.

2. If you concentrate on the exercise you are doing with me with the same intensity as telling me the latest gossip about your life, you would find it easier.

3. If you're on a budget, recruit a few friends for a small group session. These cost less per person.

4. We know you are eating more than you tell us.

5. It takes more than writing a check or showing up for training sessions to make you fit and healthy. It's what you do before and after you meet with your trainer, including choices with food, alcohol, workouts, and a commitment to a new lifestyle.

6. Ask you trainer what she or he does to keep educated in the field. An educated trainer will get better results and provide variety to keep you engaged and motivated in your workouts.

7. When you are late it is a waste of your money, a waste of my time, and disrespectful.

8. There is a difference between pain and burn. You need to be honest with your trainer about which you're feeling. If you push so hard that you injure yourself, we both lose.

9. Whatever the text or e-mail says, it can wait until we're done. And no, you cannot text and put forth 100 percent effort at the same time.

10. Gear matters. Don't expect to get maximum performance and results by working out in the ratty gym shoes and shorts you dug out of that old box of college dorm clothes. Invest in a good pair of sneakers. Your feet and joints will thank you and so will your trainer.

🔒 TOP SECRET! Drink a bottle of water on your way to the gym. If you're dehydrated, you can't work as hard, you don't feel as good, and your mental function is compromised. So you won't get as much out of your workout.

11. We see through your stall tactics. "I think I need to fill my water bottle." "Let me get a dry towel real quick." "Oh, I need to go to the bathroom again." Nice try. But you're paying for the session, so make every minute count.

12. Remember that a 30-minute session at max effort is better—and cheaper—than 60 minutes of dawdling and half-effort.

13. Turn off the TV when exercising on your own. Although TV may take your mind off your workout, it also causes you to lose touch with your effort level. You unconsciously slow down or use poor form as you get caught up in what's on screen.

SOURCES: Personal trainers in Vermont, Florida, California, and Louisiana.

Great Advice
SURPRISING TIPS FOR A BETTER WORKOUT

1. Avoid the mirrors. Many fitness centers line exercise rooms with mirrors, yet a study of 58 women found that those who exercised in front of a mirror felt less calm and more fatigued after 30 minutes of working out than those who exercised without staring at their reflections.

2. Set a short-term workout goal. Of course, goals motivate you to work harder, and the best exercise programs include measurable goals to achieve weeks or months down the road. Sometimes, though, when your motivation is drooping, a goal focusing on what you can complete over the next 30 minutes is what you need. So pick something achievable: Maintain a sweat for 20 minutes, give your arms a good workout, or cover 2 miles on the treadmill. A target like that gives you focus to get through.

3. Invent a competition with the person on the next treadmill. If you're on the treadmill and you're bored, glance at the display on someone else's nearby treadmill. If you're walking at 3.5 miles per hour and he or she is chugging away at 4 miles per hour, see if you can increase your speed and catch up, as if it were a race. The other person won't even know you're racing.

WHAT **YOUR DIETITIAN** WON'T TELL YOU

Here are the experts' secrets to resisting food temptation in its many guises.

1. Eat the cake. Just decide how much ahead of time. Passing on your colleague's cake looks as curmudgeonly as refusing to sing "Happy Birthday." The socially acceptable way out is to ask for a thin slice, and then eat a small number of bites you've decided on beforehand. Or just eat the cake and leave the icing.

2. Kiddie cones are not that bad. When your best pal wants to go out for ice cream and you can't shake off 1,360 calories and 89 grams of fat—the going rate for a banana split at Ben & Jerry's Scoop Shops—a 3-ounce kid-sized cone weighs in at about 220 calories at the same shop. Frozen yogurt or sorbet may have even less.

3. Beer isn't off-limits when you choose lite—or right. The most refreshing, easy-to-drink beers are the highly carbonated, lower alcohol "lite" brews. As a rule the darker the beer, the more calories, so if your yen is for craft-beer flavor, stick to the trendy new wheat and white (weiss) beers and avoid higher alcohol ales, even so-called "pale" ones.

4. You can do OK at the drive-thru. The big boys have begun to grasp that customers want some reasonable options: "395-calorie meal for $3.95" read one sign outside a fast food franchise recently. Just stay away from anything with the word "crispy"; steer clear of mayo-heavy sauces (use mustard!); and keep dressings no-fat.

5. Starbucks has low-calorie options. This chain isn't just about additions that turn a cup of coffee into an ultra-sweet high-calorie dessert. While the tempting, calorie-rich offerings are generally at eye level, look down. Starbucks now offers sensible snacks, but they're going to make you find them. As for drinks, begin any order with the word "skinny" and you can cut the calorie count by up to a third.

6. Don't skip the sauce; share. A meal in a top-flight restaurant is all about the sauces and special preparations made by a chef who is closer to an artist than a cook, and you're not going there to skip them. Instead, order less food, and be confident that the intense flavors will satisfy you.

7. Appetizers to share, broth soups, and salads are great options when you're out to eat. If you can't resist a delectable dessert item, share that, too.

8. Nibble on the move. If you are shopping and fading from hunger, avoid settling in at the food court. Instead nibble your way through a shopping marathon. Pick up a snack, such as a hot pretzel, a small bag of roasted nuts from a kiosk, or even a chicken taco, and nibble on the move. Portable meals, of course, can still seriously weigh you down; check calorie counts before you go or on your mobile phone.

9. Have the hot dog. If the only foods at the picnic are hot dogs, hamburgers, and drenched-in-mayo "salads," then go ahead and smell the burgers, but eat the hot dog. A dog on a bun with a smear of ketchup will set you back about 250 calories. That's as many as the burger has in fat alone. Load up your plate with the low-calorie burger fixin's, like lettuce, tomato and onions, to round out your meal.

10. Douse your afternoon slump or hunger pangs with water. The energy drop that hits in afternoon is likely a combination of perfectly natural factors: the result of a light lunch,

> **TOP SECRET!** Toast with a something-and-soda. When you hit the bar to raise a toast to Bob-in-Accounting's promotion, have a lower-calorie cocktail that doubles easily for a soft drink, and then alternate between the two. For example, a gin (or vodka) and tonic has only 180 calories and no one will be the wiser when you make your second round an equally bubbly and transparent zero-calorie diet Sprite, dressed up with a twist.

mild dehydration, a momentary lack of iron, or a crash off that coffee you had at the late-morning meeting. Before wandering to the cafeteria or fridge, start your recovery with a tall glass of water, which boosts your blood flow and, as a side benefit, makes you feel full.

11. Ideal snacks for clearing a cobwebby head are hummus or almonds, but if your only option is an office vending machine, look for any hint of protein—those orange crackers with peanut butter, at 200 calories, are better than a sugary cookie. Wash it down with a cup of coffee doused in iron-rich cinnamon.

12. You can eat less and still make Mamma happy. Food is love, and when Mamma tells you "mangia" and you don't, she acts like you're rejecting her, not her pot roast. The answer: Have some of everything pushed at you during the holidays or a weekend visit home, but only a spoonful. That means your plate will be more of a tasting sampler than a full meal. Remember: Just one bite of a dish, preceded by a loud "I can't resist!" will do your parents good and won't kill you.

13. Another strategy: Make yourself useful serving people and cleaning up. It gets you away from your plate, but still makes you a vital part of the meal.

SOURCES: Marion Nestle, nutrition professor at New York University; Elizabeth Somer, author of *Eat Your Way to Happiness*.

Great Advice

WEIGHT LOSS SECRETS FROM AROUND THE WORLD

Start with soup. This Japanese tradition is one of the best weight-loss strategies. That's because eating soup, particularly the broth-based vegetable kind, before your entrée fills you up so you eat less during the meal, explains Barbara Rolls, Guthrie professor of nutrition at Penn State University in University Park, and author of *The Volumetrics Eating Plan*. A two-year French study of 2,188 men and 2,849 women found that those who ate soup five to six times a week were more likely to have BMIs below 23 (considered lean), compared with infrequent- or non-eaters whose BMIs tended to be in the 27 range.

Make lunch your main meal. Although they do this through-out Europe, a good explanation for eating your big meal at midday comes from ayurveda, India's 5,000-year-old approach to wellness. "According to ayurveda, we're actually designed to eat the larger meal at lunch because our digestive 'fire,' called agni, is strongest between 10 a.m. and 2 p.m., so we digest more efficiently," explains Jennifer Workman, a Boulder, Colorado–based ayurveda special-ist, registered dietitian, and author of *Stop Your Cravings*. "I've seen people in my practice lose 5 to 10 pounds just by doing this."

Think quality, not quantity. The French snub processed "diet foods" not found in nature, opting instead for high-quality meats, fish, produce, dairy, even desserts. When food is fresh and flavorful, you can be satisfied with smaller portions. This is the opposite of the American approach, which is to fill up on bland diet foods, then gorge on sweets later. "The French set the standard for small por-tions with their haute cuisine," says David Katz, MD, author of *The Way to Eat*. "If we consider that part of eating is to induce pleasure, if you can get there with quality of choice, you get there in fewer calories."

Insider Expertise
SHOULD YOU REALLY BE EATING THAT?

. . . .

The healthy choice isn't always obvious. For optimal weight and health, here's what to pick from these popular pairs.

1. Bacon or sausage?

Answer: Bacon. A slice of bacon, cooked thoroughly, has fewer calories than a typical serving of sausage. Your best bet is a slice of lean back bacon with the rind and fat cut off, rather than fatty, streaky bacon.

2. A packed lunch or a purchased lunch?

Answer: A packed lunch. It'll be healthier; it'll probably have fewer calories; it'll be cheaper; and it'll save you lots of time that you can use for walking, reading, or socializing instead.

3. Lunch or graze?

Answer: Graze. Nibble food throughout the day, rather than having a large, formal lunch. Spreading out your calories stabilizes blood sugar and insulin levels; provides more frequent relief from stress, tension and boredom; and avoids post-meal fatigue, because you don't have a big meal. Plus, you never get really hungry and so are less likely to make the regrettable food choices that you might when you're starving. But if you are going for meals over munching, make lunch your big one.

4. Coffee or tea?

Answer: Tea. Choose black or green tea. These are jammed with heart-healthy antioxidants that provide more than just an energy-boosting punch. As well as contributing to healthier arteries, they may also help to prevent cancer.

5. Natural sugar or white sugar?

Answer: Neither. They're both sugar. Neither has any nutritional benefit or is any better than the other. Here's a case where the brown color does not imply a healthier version.

6. Strawberries or blueberries?

Answer: Blueberries. Of course, both are great for you, so try to eat lots of these two fruits. But when you compare the nutrients in an equal amount of each, blueberries have a slight edge. Blueberries are particularly rich in fiber—four times that of strawberries—and contain much more vitamin E and some unique micronutrients that are good for memory.

7. Fruit juice or fruit?

Answer: Fruit. Get the real thing. Not only are most fruit juices loaded with sugar, they've been stripped of an important element found in fruit—fiber.

8. Broccoli or cauliflower?

Answer: Broccoli. At 2.6 grams of fiber per 100 grams, broccoli has twice the fiber oomph of cauliflower.

9. Apple or orange?

Answer: Apple. The old adage is true after all. A study from the University of Nottingham found that people who ate more than five apples a week had improved lung function, less wheeziness, and fewer asthmalike symptoms. Eat them raw, try them baked, add them diced into a salad, or sauté an apple with onions as a side dish for chicken or fish.

10. Green olives or black olives?

Answer: Green olives. Green olives haven't ripened fully, so they contain roughly half the fat levels that they would have achieved had they ripened and blackened.

11. Sparkling water or club soda?

Answer: Sparkling water. There's a reason soda and sodium sound similar. Club soda is based on the use of sodium bicarbonate to "carbonate" it; thus it should come as no surprise that club soda is salt-rich. With only 3 milligrams of sodium, sparkling water beats club soda's 75 milligrams hands down.

12. Sirloin steak or rib-eye?

Answer: Sirloin. A 300 grams sirloin steak contains 325 calories and 13 grams of fat, 6 of them saturated, compared to the 423 calories and 23 grams of fat (12 of them saturated) found in the same size of rib-eye steak.

13. Soup or salad?

Answer: It depends. Some soups are far healthier than some salads and vice versa. You're better off with a salad of mixed greens and raw vegetables coupled with a light, healthy dressing over a creamy soup. You'll get more fiber and thus more filling for your calories, not to mention the healthy dose of disease-fighting antioxidants found in raw vegetables. But broth-based soups are very healthy and contain way less fat and calories than a salad covered in a creamy dressing.

14. Bottled salad dressing or homemade?

Answer: Homemade. Homemade is healthier almost every time. Not only can you use cholesterol-lowering monounsaturated fats such as olive oil, but also many bottled dressings contain extra salt and additives.

15. Café au lait or caffe latte?

Answer: Café au lait. Café au lait comprises equal parts brewed coffee and steamed milk. A caffe latte is one or two shots of espresso with steamed milk and foam filling the rest of the cup. For a tall drink made with semi-skimmed milk, the au lait has just 91 calories and 3.4 grams of fat, while the tall semi-skimmed latte, because it uses so much more milk, has 148 calories and 5.6 grams of fat. You may find that the au lait has a bolder, more coffee-rich flavor, so you win on all counts.

16. Fresh tomatoes or tomato sauce?

Answer: Tomato sauce. Tomatoes are rich in lycopene, an antioxidant believed to reduce the risk of prostate cancer and possibly several other cancers. But only by cooking it will you release the lycopene from the tomato cell walls so that your body can absorb it. What's more, lycopene is fat-soluble, meaning your body is better able to absorb and use it when you get it with a bit of fat—such as the olive oil found in most tomato sauces.

Part Four

WHAT YOU DON'T KNOW ABOUT
YOUR FAMILY

Who's watching your kids and your spouse when you aren't? Plenty of people, and they'd love to tell you a few things. From marriage counselors and nannies to mall Santas and mothers-in-law, there are a slew of behind-the-scenes insights (and some funny stories, to boot) you'll be glad to know.

What makes a wedding planner pretend to be booked? Which of your secrets are your kids telling their teacher? What do your kids really eat at camp, and should you worry about it? What do all happily married people agree on? (Looking out for each other is one thing, but part two may surprise you.) And Santa? That beard the kids are tugging on may be worth thousands! Learn the secrets to a happy family at all stages of life with these insider truths.

WHAT YOUR WEDDING PLANNER WON'T TELL YOU

What do you get for that often hefty price tag? If only you knew. Wedding planners around the country reveal the good, the bad, and the very ugly secrets about preparing for the big day.

1. I keep secrets. At one wedding I planned, the cake went missing after the bride and groom cut it. The bride soon asked where the cake was. Turns out the servers had taken it upon themselves to eat it! We cut the pieces smaller and the bride never knew. Keeping things quiet is the secret behind making the bride think the wedding was flawless.

2. I hate feeling devalued. When a potential client begins to nickel and dime me, I know they do not understand what it is I will be doing for them.

3. The biggest mistake you can make is choosing the cheapest vendors in the hopes of saving money. You truly get what you pay for.

4. Don't forget the tax and service charge. Many couples overlook the "plus plus" when planning a menu. Everything has a tax and service charge, and it really adds up—trust me!

5. Just because you planned your own destination wedding doesn't mean you can do my job better than I can. Yes, you may have found lower rates on Orbitz, but you don't have access to the contract and package perks that I'm able to offer to my brides.

6. I do manual labor and other dreadful tasks. I cannot even tell you how many times I've been on my hands and knees, sweating. I sometimes have to count the napkins and linens before they go back to the rental company. I'm talking dirty, smelly napkins, with food, lipstick, and whatever else is on them. Talk about gross!

7. Reuse flowers from ceremony to reception if at all possible. Be sure to tell your florist so your flowers aren't arranged to look good from only one side.

8. You can always elope! It's never too late to run away and have a relaxing wedding. You'll have great memories to share with your friends and family once you're home.

9. This is a full-time job, and on the big day we are steaming the bridal gown, pinning boutonnieres, making sure that the timelines are being met, making sure there are no spots on the glasses or silverware, allowing gum to be spit out in our hands before the ceremony, dealing with any situations that arise, and the list goes on!

> 🔒 **TOP SECRET!** If you've been engaged for a week and your wedding planning organizer is thicker than mine (which usually contains paperwork for the five or six weddings I'm currently planning,) then I automatically tell you that I'm booked on your date . . . and your backup date.

10. Make sure the things you spend money on can be reused. Don't have "bride" and "groom" etched on your flutes and toasting glasses. The same rule applies to serving pieces. If you must get something engraved, make it your initials, and then you have an heirloom.

11. Some things will not go perfectly. We'll do our best to fix mistakes without you knowing and bill you later at our discretion. I'll go to great lengths to make sure your wedding is perfect. Your wedding is my job, and I'll do everything I can to make it memorable, including walking miles to a florist in Jamaica to correct the $700 bouquet that arrived spray-painted purple.

12. I'll make sure everything you're offered is in the contract. If the first manager you work with offers you a complimentary toast, get it in writing. If that manager leaves for whatever reason, you won't be forced to argue about these details with his or her replacement.

13. Stay focused on the big picture. It's easy to micromanage all of the details at the expense of the big picture. As long as people marry for the right reasons, the details of wedding planning are really secondary. Don't make decisions to please or impress others.

SOURCES: Candice "Candy" Cain, Candy Cain Travel; Karen Clark, SomethingBorrowedSomethingBlue.com; Denise Georgiou-Newell, WPICC, DWC, CSP, TICO, WeDDings Jubilee Planning Services; Wayne Gurnick, AIFD, MomentsByWayne.com; Jill Higgins, Jill Higgins Photography; Lynn Jawitz, Florisanllc.com; Bryant Keller, bryantkeller.com; Gregorio Palomino, CEP, CWP; Tanya W. Porter, Weddings, Etc., LLC; Jules Rupae, Jules Rupae Events; Holly Schoenke, Simply Sweet Weddings.

Who Knew?

8 CREATIVE WAYS TO CUT WEDDING COSTS

1. Skip the custom-printed invitations. Your guests will probably never even notice the scalloped edges and silver ink that cost you an extra $2 per print. They probably also won't know if you've made your invitations yourselves. Although they are the enemy of wedding invitation designers, invitation software packages offer modern fonts and graphics, and they are easy to use.

2. Book a budding musical talent. If you have always dreamed of having a live string quartet or even a rock band at your wedding reception, but can't afford their fees, hire music students—just listen to them perform at a concert or gig before you hire them.

3. Take a class in wedding planning. Although these courses are designed for people embarking on wedding planning as a career, you'll pick up huge amounts of inside information.

4. Use local expertise. Ask around and you'll quickly discover bargain talent in your area, whether you want a wedding dress or outfit stitched, a cake baked, special ties or cravats made for the bridegroom and his party, or flowers arranged for your church and reception.

5. Consider nonfloral centerpieces. The flowers in the bride's bouquet and on your mom, dad, bridesmaids, and other relatives are the flowers that will be in your photos, so that's where you want to invest. Rather than having floral centerpieces, "Put beautiful, tall candles on the tables and surround them with glass pebbles, or float votive candles in water," says Deb McCoy, president of the American Academy of Wedding Professionals.

6. Buy booze by the head, not by the drink. Even if most of your wedding guests are nondrinkers, don't let the caterer talk you into paying by the drink. The secret about teetotalers is that many actually do imbibe when the liquor is free, and what's free for them costs you about $10 per cocktail. Plus, there will be no surprises when the bill comes.

7. Cut to the cake. Cut your cake and toss your bouquet early in the night so your photographer and videographer can leave early. Plus, after the professional photographers leave, your guests will be more likely to start snapping pictures with the inexpensive, disposable cameras on their tables.

8. Consider your credit card your secret weapon. Paying for everything related to your wedding and reception with a credit card will protect you should anything go wrong with your vendors. If the first-rate photographer you booked gets hit by a bus the day before the wedding and you put the deposit on a credit card, your money will be refunded. If you had paid with cash, your money would have gone down with the photographer. Your credit card is like a free wedding insurance policy in your wallet, so use it.

WHAT HAPPILY MARRIED PEOPLE WANT TO TELL YOU

Not everything about marriage is pretty. And the couples who make it accept and love that fact. Here's what they want you to know.

1. Only puppies want to be on top of each other—and they get tired of it, too. Sometimes, you need space.

2. Is there anyone who hasn't, at least once, remembered they left the car windows open when the rain, and sex, started at the same time?

3. A date isn't all candlelight and dinner. The true criterion for a date: anything that lets you focus on each other. That could be weeding the garden while you chat amiably, a weeklong trip to Bermuda, or ten minutes over morning coffee.

4. There's a couple who randomly asks each other, "How's your love tank?" They want to see if each other's love tank—how loved they feel—is full, half-full, or getting near empty. If it's low, it's not taken personally; it's just a signal that the other partner needs something.

5. Most people have at least one thing about their partner they really can't stand. Of course you're going to be seriously annoyed at some of a partner's habits. For example: snoring, hygiene, sloppiness, or foot-in-mouth problems. You are lucky if it's just one habit.

6. Over time there is less that you have to say—you know your partner's response! Long silences are OK.

🔒 **TOP SECRET!** Most good friendships are made, not inherited. There is usually at least one friend of your partner you hope will disappear.

7. Almost everyone has had a fantasy lover—either a real one that didn't work out or a movie star or some famous person who you dream about. There is that "What if . . ." thought that comes now and then.

8. Sometimes you just want to chuck it all. Hey, life is sometimes just hellish or boring—or both. Or you feel underappreciated and overworked. Not taking care of yourself happens sometimes, too. Everyone knows it's important to stay fit and attractive, but it's just so much work.

9. Sometimes the mojo isn't working, but you don't want to hurt your partner's feelings. It's normal sometimes to fake more sexual arousal than you're experiencing. Good partners tend to be kind about this sort of thing—angry partners telegraph that, on the whole, they'd rather be watching TV.

10. A calm, mature, trustworthy babysitter is worth her—or his—weight in gold. Even better than one babysitter: Develop a stable of two or three to boost your odds that one will be available when you need a date night.

11. Quiet sex is OK. So is afternoon sex or sex when the kids are out for the evening. But nothing beats unhurried, loud, whenever-you-want-it sex, followed by a cuddle, a nap, a shower, more lovemaking, a wonderful walk. For this luxury of uninterrupted time, you need to get away—or find a trusted friend, relative, or overnight camp so that the kids can get away.

12. There are ways to feel awake after the kids go to bed.
One couple used to take turns taking naps during the day so
they wouldn't be too exhausted to be together at night.

13. Maybe there are some long-term couples who have
never told a lie to each other about anything—yes, conscious
omissions count—but I wouldn't make a money bet on that.

SOURCES: Pepper Schwartz, PhD, professor of sociology at the University of Washington
in Seattle; Don Howard and Teresa Titus Howard, a married couple in Blue Springs,
Missouri; Susan Vogt; and anonymous couples throughout the United States.

WHAT YOUR MARRIAGE COUNSELOR WON'T TELL YOU

How can you figure out when fighting is a good thing? Find out this and much more with these 13 stable-union secrets.

1. I love couples who fight in the waiting room. At least they still care about each other. If one or both of you seems indifferent, my job is a lot harder.

2. The earlier you come in, the quicker you can get the problem solved, the less your therapy will cost.

3. When you say your feelings "just aren't there anymore," I know you're probably cheating.

4. Sometimes I'll tell a couple "no sex until the next session. Don't touch each other, period." What I'm really hoping is that they'll fail and feel a sense of unity from their mutual rebellion.

5. What do I wish I could say? "Grow up!" "Stop whining!" "Get a life!" When I feel this way, I know I need a vacation.

6. Don't try to convince me you're the good one. In most marriages, there isn't a good one.

7. Yes, you should go to bed angry. If you try to resolve everything before you hit the sack, you'll both be sleep-deprived and cranky the next day. Instead, get a good night's sleep and talk once you're rested.

8. Three signs that a couple is not going to succeed: name-calling, finger-pointing, and when one or both partners fails to accept even the tiniest bit of responsibility for the situation.

9. Sometimes two people love each other but have such different styles of living that I recommend they live together in a duplex. It sounds strange, but it works for some people.

10. I've seen couples I thought didn't stand a chance end up staying together. Often it's because they're both willing to try. But sometimes it's just that they are too dysfunctional to leave each other.

🔒 **TOP SECRET!** I'm not going to tell a couple that I have no idea why they're together. But take the hint if I say something like "You both have to make a decision about whether this is going to work long term."

11. Don't expect your spouse to be everything you need: your lover, your best friend, your massage therapist, and your confidant. You need other relationships outside your marriage to fill those roles.

12. The big thing most women don't understand: Men are not mind readers. If you don't tell him how you feel, he's not going to know. The big thing most men don't understand: If you hardly acknowledge your wife all day, she's not going to want to get intimate with you at night.

13. The person who complains about things that happened in the past is usually more of the problem than the spouse they're complaining about. And if I ask you how long you've had problems and your answer is "ten years," you're not going to change things in ten minutes or ten sessions.

SOURCES: Susan Fletcher, PhD, a psychologist in Dallas, Texas; Lawrence J. Levy, PsyD, a licensed psychologist in Boca Raton, Florida; Nancy Mramor, PhD, in Pittsburgh, Pennsylvania; Jeff Palitz, a marriage and family therapist in Chula Vista, California; Meghan L. Reitz, LCPC, NCC, in Schaumburg, Illinois; Karen Sherman, PhD, in New York, New York; Tina B. Tessina, PhD, a psychotherapist in Long Beach, California; and a marriage counselor in Pennsylvania.

Great Advice

HOW TO STRENGTHEN YOUR RELATIONSHIP

. . . .

As nice as it would be, your relationship won't just thrive on its own while you're taking care of the other business of life. Here's how to take it off autopilot and keep the excitement and partnership.

Schedule time for your marriage first. Don't relegate your relationship to scraps of leftover time. "In mapping out your schedule for the next several weeks, why not start with writing in date times for you and your mate?" suggest Claudia and David Arp, founders of Marriage Alive International and coauthors of marriage books including *10 Great Dates to Energize Your Marriage*. "Unless you're willing to make your relationship a higher priority than other relationships and activities, you won't have a growing marriage," notes Claudia Arp.

Create couples rituals. Do something regularly that bonds you, such as 10 minutes to chat before bed, always having morning coffee together, or saving Saturday for date night.

Institute a daily check-in. Marriage experts recommend couples do something that big business has employed for decades to keep workers happy, productive, and in the loop: hold regular team meetings. Luckily yours will be more fun than listening to Bob from accounting go over the last month's sales numbers. In a daily check-in, you might start by appreciating something about each other, offer some new information about your day, and end with a hope that could be small ("I hope we can go see that new movie Friday night") or lavish ("I'd love to retire at age 50 and sail the Mediterranean with you.")

Ask "Is it good for our relationship?" When you bump up against any important decision in your marriage, don't just talk about whether it's good for you and for your spouse. If you don't even want to ask the question, that's a red flag that whatever it is—from working late to "surprising" your spouse with an expensive new living room sofa to making individual plans on your usual date night—isn't going to be good for your marriage.

Cheer each other on. "One of the most important things to me is that my wife, Rebecca, is for me and I'm for her," says Lee Potts, a retired computer programmer from St. Louis, Missouri. "It sounds simplistic, but it's really important. I've been married twice before, and I don't think we had each other's best interests at heart like this. We had our own agendas." Look for the positive in your new spouse; develop a sense of humor; and give honest, specific praise.

Disconnect from the 24/7 office. Push the "off" button! When researchers tracked the technology use and moods of 1,367 women and men for two years, they found that those who sent and received the most calls and messages were also most likely to say that this "work spillover" left them tired and distracted at home. Not to mention stressed: "Your boss doesn't tend to call you with the good news," says lead researcher Noelle Chesley at the University of Wisconsin–Milwaukee. "You do hear that suddenly there's a deadline crisis." Set limits on when you'll check e-mails and when your phone will be on.

Create a code word for love. Find a secret way to express your love that only the two of you understand. It comes in handy if your spouse calls when the boss is standing beside your desk, and creates that "just us" feeling anytime you use it.

In a survey of over 10,000 married couples, 97% of happy couples listed togetherness as a top priority, while only 28% of unhappy pairs listed it. Enjoying free time together and not letting friends and family interfere in the relationship were also valued by the large majority of happy couples.

SOURCES: Pat Love, EdD., marriage and sex therapist; David Olson, PhD at the University of Minnesota, and daughter Amy Olson-Sigg.

WHAT YOUR MOTHER-IN-LAW WON'T TELL YOU

Here are some reasons why she's secretly glad you're in her life—even when it doesn't seem like it.

1. It hurts to be downsized. I spent a couple of decades being the leading lady; now I have a smaller role.

2. I know he's your husband now. But he's still my son.

3. You don't have to call me Mom. But it would be nice if you did.

4. Thank you. I don't always say it because I'm afraid you'll think I'm sucking up. But I've never seen my son happier than he is now, married and with children.

5. A little gratitude wouldn't hurt. Every year, I send you a birthday present, but you never even pick up the phone to thank me. This year, I said, "That's it. No more." Yet look at me: I'm about to send another present. I guess that's how I am.

6. I want the best for both of us. We mothers say to our children, "I want you to be happy." And we mean that. What we don't say is, "But I would like to be happy, too."

7. I know a little something. I've bought and sold 13 houses in my life. Why won't you ask for my advice?

8. When I visit you, I'm just coming to see the family. I'm not coming for a white-glove inspection.

9. I'm lucky to have you! Whenever I stay at your house, you always have my room ready, my towels, everything. You do all the right things.

10. I'm truly appreciative. I'm happy that you allow my son—your husband—to visit me on Mother's Day. It's a long trip and a big expense.

11. I have a dirty little secret. I'm afraid that if I don't get this right, you'll cut me off.

12. I've got his number. When I really want to talk to my son privately, I don't call your house. I call his cell phone.

13. I really want to make you happy. If you hate that green sweater I bought you, please, please tell me.

SOURCES: Susan Abel Lieberman, PhD, author of *The Mother-in-Law's Manual*; Jane Angelich, author of *What's a Mother (in-Law) to Do?*; and anonymous mothers-in-law in four states.

Great Advice

WHAT TO DO IF YOUR MOTHER-IN-LAW TRIPS YOUR SWITCH

Even a great mother-in-law can frustrate you now and then, which is why the coauthors of *Anger Kills*, Virginia Williams, PhD, and Redford Williams, MD, recommend these ways to cope with your ire (and avoid the defibrillator):

1. Recognize that anger is universal. We're stuck with it, and making sure it doesn't hurt you means understanding when to express it—and when to let it go. It's having only one way to react—always or never—that can make anger a problem.

2. Ask yourself if whatever made you angry is important. Is what you're thinking and feeling appropriate to the objective facts of the situation? Can you modify this situation? Is it worth taking action?

3. Talk yourself down: a) yell "Stop!" to yourself (silently) when you start replaying an offense; b) distract yourself (surf travel sites for dream vacations); c) breathe in, clench your fist, breathe out, release fist. Repeat.

More than 60 percent of mothers-in-law see their son's wife as either a daughter, a friend, or the right woman for their son. Just 10 percent see her as the enemy, according to a survey of 1,868 mothers-in-laws and 2,000 daughters-in-laws, conducted jointly by ThirdAge.com and GalTime.com.

WHAT **YOUR PARENTS** WON'T TELL YOU

Do you still feel like you're seven around your parents even though you're the boss in your own house? Well, here's how to forge a rewarding, adult relationship with your mom and dad.

1. We're adults, too. If your parents still treat you like a kid despite the fact that you have kids of your own, you may have to help them let you "grow up." The key is thinking of them as adults, not parents, and acting like an adult when you're around them. A simple way to do this is to ask yourself a question before each interaction with them: "How would I act in this situation if Mom or Dad was a friend or an acquaintance?" Then behave accordingly.

2. We like to talk about the world with you. Model your conversations with Mom and Dad on those you have with friends. Don't limit conversations strictly to family memories, or gossip about family members, or your personal life. There's a whole wide world out there—why not explore it with Mom and Dad as you would with a friend? Current events, sports, work, local neighborhood issues, or national politics (if you can manage such a conversation and still be on speaking terms the next day) are all fair game.

3. Keep your sense of humor. When you're dealing with your parents, laughter can be a lifesaver—both to help you handle the stress of dealing with sometimes crotchety individuals and to help you bond together. Tell a few jokes you know they'll enjoy, share some comics from the paper, or e-mail with them. If you can laugh together, you're doing OK.

4. Sometimes you have to speak up. We're not always going to like it. If you love your mom and dad but they drive you batty, your resentment can eat away at your relationship. So don't seethe silently. Communicate, with gentleness and respect. For instance, if your mom keeps calling you at work, tell her that your boss is starting to notice and, while you love talking to her during the day, it's beginning to affect your job performance. Arrange a call you can both count on at a mutually convenient time.

> **TOP SECRET!** Grant us some independence, too. Sometimes it's the grown-up kid who doesn't want to cut the nurturing relationship off. If you are past 25 and still find it necessary to talk to Mom every night, then you may be the problem, not your folks. They deserve freedom, too.

5. Why ask our advice unless you really want it? Sometimes asking for a parent's advice is really a way of asking for Mom's or Dad's approval. If that's the case, remember that you're an adult now, perfectly capable of choosing a living room carpet or a car on your own. If your parents are bent on offering you advice whether asked or not, smile, nod, and take it in (who knows—it may actually be helpful!). Focus on the fact that they have your best interest at heart. Then make your own choice.

6. Don't ask us to help straighten out your latest personal or financial crisis. While you may depend on their emotional support, relying too much upon their resources, rather than your own, can lead to mutual resentment. So get used to solving your problems, big or small, on your own. You'll be amazed how good doing it all by yourself can make you feel—and what a positive effect it can have on your relationship with your parents.

7. Create opportunities for exploring and uncovering memories. If your parents are older, look through old scrapbooks with them, asking them for stories about the people in the photos. We help our parents discover the meaning in their lives by encouraging them to talk about their accomplishments, the high points in their lives, and the joys and sorrows they have experienced.

8. We wouldn't mind creating a video, audio recording, or scrapbook with you. The finished product will not only be a testament to a renewed closeness between you, but also provide a wonderful legacy.

9. Expressing your appreciation is always welcome. Yes, Mom may be a buttinsky, but she always makes your favorite Christmas cookies. Dad is a bit of a stuffed shirt, but just the other day, he came to your rescue when your car died at the mall. The point is, your parents still do things for you that deserve your notice—and gratitude.

10. Rediscover and share mutual interests. When you were a kid, did you and your dad share a passion for a particular football team? Did you and your mother spend time each summer canning tomatoes? Make these happy memories the foundation for new, shared activities.

11. Be honest about who you are and what you want. Maybe there are things about your growing up that your parents regret. But as long as you don't regret it, they have to adjust. Be clear about who you want to be, and help your parents accept you on your terms.

12. Look for common activities. Baking, shopping, hiking, skiing, carpentry, etc. At any age, sharing a common task or activity is a great way to build closeness.

13. We know your hot buttons. Do not allow parents to channel guilt at you. If your parents are the type to complain about you never calling, never visiting, forgetting an uncle's birthday, not sending enough pictures, or whatever irks them that day, don't take the bait and feel guilty—unless you honestly regret the oversight. In which case, apologize immediately and seek a way to make amends. Otherwise, let it roll off your back. You have no obligation to play parent-child guilt games. You are a mature, independent adult, and act on your own volition.

SOURCES: Tom Swanson, PhD, director of support services education at VistaCare, a hospice care provider in Scottsdale, Arizona; Tina B. Tessina, PhD., a licensed psychotherapist in Long Beach, California, and author of *It Ends With You: Grow Up and Out of Dysfunction* and *The 10 Smartest Decisions a Woman Can Make Before 40.*

WHAT YOUR NANNY WON'T TELL YOU

Here are top things even *The Nanny Diaries* didn't bring to light.

1. Treat your nanny with respect and as an equal, and you will have a loyal friend for life. Most of us become lifelong friends of the babies we helped raise, as well as their parents.

2. When you're hiring a nanny, don't just rely on references; go with your gut. If you really like—or don't like—a candidate when you first meet her, trust that instinct.

3. Don't come home drunk or on drugs, wake up your children to play with them, and then wake me up to put them back to bed.

4. Don't treat me like a maid. Respect that I'm here to do an important job—watch your children—so don't expect me to start doing your errands and cleaning non-kid messes.

5. Nannies from other cultures need orientation. Tell me which foods are fancy gourmet foods to be used sparingly and which are everyday foods. I kept eating up the best caviar and spitting it out in the trash, thinking it had gone bad.

6. Ask tons of questions when you're interviewing. How would she deal with a child who won't stop crying? Has she ever been fired from a job? Seeing how she reacts under tough questions will give you answers you need to know and an idea of how she responds to pressure.

7. Don't misrepresent yourself to an agency. If you don't have an extra room for the nanny, say so. Don't claim to have a bedroom and bathroom for her, and then ask her to sleep with your child.

8. Pay us well. Value your child a little more and cut corners elsewhere.

9. I am not paid enough to be a substitute parent for your child all the time. If you do not have the time or patience to raise a child, don't have one.

10. I have my own family. Many of us have kids in other countries. We'd like to see them, but we need vacation time.

11. If you want to save a little money, try hiring a nanny in training. They are eager to please and probably have a lot of background babysitting.

12. If your child bites me, don't reward her. One parent actually said, "Oh honey, are you hungry?" to her child while ignoring my bleeding face.

13. Start off with a trial basis. That way if you don't get along, or anything isn't to your liking, your not locked into an agreement.

SOURCES: Nannies or former nannies in Boston, New York, Seattle, Pennsylvania, and Los Angeles. (Including playwright Lisa Ramirez—whose off-Broadway play, *Exit Cuckoo*, deals with nannying—and an English nanny who worked for a Hollywood couple).

WHAT YOUR KID'S TEACHER WON'T TELL YOU

What really happens behind the classroom door? Find out the truth and how you might be helping—or not!

1. We know if you've been "helping." We can tell the difference between parents helping their children with homework and doing it for them (especially when they're clueless in class the next day). Please stop doing everything for your children and allow them to make mistakes. How else will they learn? Kids are not motivated to succeed if they feel their parents will bail them out every time.

2. The truth is simple: Your kid will lie to get out of trouble.

3. Please, no more mugs, frames, or stuffed animals. A gift card to Starbucks or Staples would be more than enough. A thank-you note: even better.

4. We know what your kids really want, and it's not what you think. Parents give their kids the pricey gadgets and labels, but what kids really crave is for you to talk to them. They want to know you're interested in their lives.

5. We're sick of standardized testing and having to "teach to the test."

6. We don't arrive at school 10 minutes before your child does. And we don't leave the minute they get back on the bus. Many of us put in extra hours before and after school.

7. Encourage your child to keep reading. That's key to success in the classroom at any age.

8. My first year of teaching, a fifth-grader actually threw a chair at me. I saw him recently, and he told me he just graduated from college. *That's* what makes it all worthwhile.

> 🔒 **TOP SECRET!** Kids dish on your secrets all the time—money, religion, politics, even Dad's vasectomy.

9. Teaching is a calling. There's not a teacher alive who will say she went into this for the money. Guys who dribble a ball for a couple of hours a game can make up to $20 million a year. We educate future leaders and make about $54,000 a year. And while having the summer off is great, many of us have to take on extra jobs—teaching summer school, tutoring—to make ends meet.

10. We get jaded, too. Teaching is not as joyful as it once was for many of us. Disrespectful students and belligerent parents take a toll on us.

11. We spend money out of our own pockets. Teachers often buy things our students need, such as school supplies and even shoes.

12. Please help us by turning off Internet access on your child's phone during school hours.

13. You do your job, I'll do mine. I have parents who are CEOs come in and tell me how to run my classroom. I would never think to go to their offices and tell them how to do their jobs.

SOURCES: American Federation of Teachers; interviews with elementary and middle-school teachers in California, Connecticut, Georgia, Iowa, Minnesota, New York, and Texas.

Great Advice
BEAT BACK-TO-SCHOOL STRESS

. . . .

The challenge with school stress is that kids don't always know how to talk about it—so you don't always know what's up. Here are expert tips from *USA Today* and the website *Shine* that are sure to help both of you out.

1. Listen. Try to casually find out what's going on with them. Even if they aren't talking, watch for nonverbal cues and trust your instincts if your kid just doesn't seem himself or herself. Begin the conversation by offhandedly asking about school while you're driving home, at the supermarket, or doing a chore around the house together. Don't pressure them, and refrain from pressing for answers.

2. Talk about homework. If they're new to homework, discuss the work with them before they sit down to work. Talk about what is due when and help them plan how to get the work done. Don't focus on grades, but rather focus on completion and understanding the concepts of the assignment. Learning to manage their workload efficiently will help them succeed not only in school, but also in the workforce.

3. Establish a routine. Set a breakfast and morning routine that works for everyone. Try to make mornings calm and be enthusiastic about what's planned for the day. Lead by example by happily sharing the plans that you have for your day.

4. Unschedule kids. Extracurricular activities are great, but it's just as important that kids take time to relax and have some unscheduled time at home or outdoors. Keep one weekday after school as a "free day," and stick to that schedule for the school year. It's easier to be relaxed and prepared for the rest of the week when your child has had proper downtime.

WHAT YOUR KID'S CAMP COUNSELOR WON'T TELL YOU

You might not want to know how much fun your kids are having without you!

1. They're not as homesick as you think they are. For the first week, the cries of the homesick are almost unbearable. After that: "Mom? Who's Mom?"

2. Your kid is a lot less shy and a lot more competent than you think.

3. Your son may go without showering for weeks and will shun clothing.

4. We don't always know where your kids are. As long as he or she is eventually found, we're not going to tell you about all the times we had to call a search-and-rescue for your child.

5. Some of us are hungover every morning and rigidly enforce afternoon naptime not because the kids need the rest but because our heads hurt.

6. Even if it's not a coed camp, your teen is going to learn more about the opposite sex (accurate or not) than you want them to know.

7. If they want to eat peanut butter and jelly for weeks in a row, there's really nothing we can do about it.

8. We confiscate the "illegal" candy you send and eat it ourselves. For your kid's own good, of course.

9. Your kids will be plunged into icy water, submitted to exotic "tortures," and scared witless countless times—just because we think it's funny. . . . Oh, and they'll love it.

10. Camp builds self-esteem. The typical camper return rate is about 60 percent, according to the American Camp Association (ACA), and 92 percent of campers surveyed say the people at camp "helped me feel good about myself."

> 🔒 TOP SECRET! **Don't think labeling their stuff means things will make it home. Everything's going to get hopelessly mixed up.**

11. Your child is going to speak in incomprehensible camp slang for weeks after coming home. And they'll pine for people named Lunchmeat, Fuzzy, and Ratboy.

12. We actually do this because we love your kids—and we'll probably do it again next year. According to the ACA, the average return rate for staff is 40 to 60 percent. Camp is even more fun as a counselor than it is as a camper.

13. Learning to make wallets may seem silly, but the real value is the self-confidence kids get when they make something they can actually use.

Great Advice

GIVE YOUR KIDS A GREAT CAMP EXPERIENCE—WITHOUT BREAKING THE BANK

1. Make a rough list. With a sense of your kids' interests—do they want a general camp or one for sports, arts, academics, or other interests—search for accredited local camps through the American Camp Association (find.acacamps.org) and pick some affordable options. Then call camp directors and ask how they operate, how long they've been around, and whether they offer financial aid. Even better, take the kids to visit, if you can.

2. Ask about discounts. While some camps offer financial aid, many more have discounts for early registration, multiple and returning registrations, as well as for getting others to sign up. But as with many potential money-savers, you won't know unless you ask. Also find out if there are extra fees or expenses (like uniforms, equipment, or field trips), and how refunds work.

3. Get creative. If everything but the price sounds perfect, and discounts aren't working out, consider a shorter stay—maybe four weeks instead of all summer.

4. Mine your affiliations. If traditional summer camp is out of your budget, being affiliated with certain groups might mean more affordable alternatives. If your kids are members of a scout troop or council, Boy or Girl Scout camps may be only $150 to $400 a week. Some camps allow non-scouts to participate. Don't overlook church, school, or community camps. And if your kids are on a school or community team, there may be summer training or team-building opportunities.

WHAT YOUR MALL SANTA WON'T TELL YOU

It turns out that Santa has a few requests of his own when it comes to managing this holiday tradition.

1. Some of us get bonuses for making our daily photo quota. So please forgive me if I try to move things along.

2. Never force your screaming kid onto my lap. Just bring him close and give me a few minutes.

3. Want to have more than just a few seconds with me? Skip the mall. Let's meet at your kid's preschool or a photo studio that invites Santa in for special portraits.

4. Between October and December, most of us work about 40 ten-hour days and listen to 30,000 children.

5. You're ruining the fun. I've noticed a lot of you have started telling your kids the truth about me a lot younger than you used to. Sometimes you spoil things before your child even asks the question, just because you're worried he'll hear it from someone else. Please stop.

6. I'm not an orthodontist, either. Don't ask me to tell your child why she needs to stop sucking her thumb.

7. As a matter of fact, I did go to school for this. Topics of study: how to hold children, manage sticky conversations, and care for my hair and beard.

8. I don't have total recall. Don't come back after a few minutes and ask what your kid requested. Stand close enough to listen.

9. It's hard not to sweat in our heavy wool suits. To make sure we smell nice, some of us sprinkle baby powder in our beards; others use evergreen-scented colognes and sprays. And we're always sucking on breath mints.

10. Please take your barely potty-trained two-year-old to the restroom before you get in line. Soil my suit, and it's coal for you, buster.

11. Those of us with real beards think we're superior. But the best of the rest of us pay as much as $3,000 to wig makers to make us authentic-looking whiskers.

12. I see you vigorously nodding your head, but even so, I will never, ever promise anything to a child.

13. I've been kicked in the shins, hit in the groin, scratched, bitten, and peed on. But there's a reason I keep doing this year after year: This is the best work I've ever found.

SOURCES: Santas in California, Iowa, Illinois, and Rhode Island, including "Santa Tim" Connaghan, a traveling Santa instructor.

Great Advice

TEACH YOUR KIDS THE TRUE VALUE OF "STUFF"

1. Show them money going in, not just out. If your kids only see you with drawing those $20 bills from the ATM, they're going to think machines hand out money. Make sure they also see you depositing funds.

2. Teach them to set goals and save for them. Label a jar with a set amount of money to be used for something specific. Start small—say, $5 to buy some ice cream and sprinkles. Keep this money separate when you go to the store, so your child can buy the ice cream himself with the cash.

3. Differentiate between wanting and needing. You *need* shoes, but you *want* the trendiest brand. Apply this rule to anything you buy and to any of their requests for "stuff."

4. Make choices, not sacrifices. Instead of saying, "We can't afford that," "That's too expensive," or just saying no, substitute a comment that expresses an intentional choice. Examples: "I want to stay home and visit state parks this year so we can save for a special vacation next year." Instead of feeling that "no" means sacrifice, scarcity, or embarrassment, children learn that life is about making choices.

5. Show them you're planning for the future. In addition to using a change jar to save for special treats, let your kids hear you talk about saving for a new roof, paying off the car, saving for their education, and paying bills on time.

6. Give to others. Along with that jar for ice cream, label another jar for charity. Make sure your children put a fixed percentage of their earnings and allowance in it. Make sure they see you giving to others.

WHAT YOUR VET WON'T TELL YOU

Insider tips and cautionary tales, which can save time, trouble, and trauma—for everyone in the family.

1. People always ask, "How do you handle pit bulls and rottweilers and big German shepherds?" The truth is, the dogs that scare me most are the little Chihuahuas. They're much more likely to bite.

2. New staff or training students sometimes practice injections or catheter placements on your pet. If you'd rather not allow your pet to be used this way, make sure you say something beforehand.

3. Behavior issues are the No. 1 cause of pet re-homing, euthanasia, and death. Yet, because it's not medical, most of us don't learn much about that in veterinary school.

4. Your vet may not have gotten into vet school! Vets who can't get into traditional U.S. veterinary programs due to bad grades and poor test scores often go to for-profit schools in the Caribbean, where, basically, if you can pay the tuition, you get in.

5. No regulation says vets have to check certain lists before they euthanize an animal, and lots of vets still do convenience euthanasia for owners who prefer the easy way out. We see a lot of euthanasia in November and December, for example, just because people are getting ready for the holidays. I refuse to do it.

6. I hate to break it to you, but your $2,000 designer dog is a mutt. Puppy stores and breeders have created these cute names like morkipoos and puggles, and now people are paying $2,000 for a dog they couldn't give away at the pound ten years ago. Whoever started the trend is a marketing genius.

7. Even though you see vitamins on the shelves in pet stores, healthy pets don't need them. The pet food companies have spent billions of dollars to make sure their food is properly balanced with every vitamin and mineral a pet needs.

🔒 TOP SECRET! To give a cat a pill, buy pill pockets (available from vets), which many cats love. If that fails, wrap your cat in a towel and sit on the floor with them between your legs. Calmly wrap your dominant hand around the head so your fingers are under the cheekbone. Tip the head back; the lower jaw should slacken. Use your middle finger to ease the jaw down, and place the pill near the back of the tongue. Release the head and stroke the cat's throat to encourage it to swallow. Watch in case the cat spits the pill out.

8. After their kitten vaccinations, indoor cats don't really need to be vaccinated. They're not going to get rabies sitting inside the house. Vaccines have the potential to create a lot of harm for cats, including possible tumors at the vaccine site.

9. If your animal is really sick, it's better to bring him in during the morning. A vet I once worked with would do a huge workup when a sick animal came in early. But if the animal came in late in the day, the vet would actually encourage the owner to euthanize. But I would add that this is not common.

10. The vets who work for most corporate-owned vet hospitals are paid monthly bonus checks based on how much money they bring in from clients. So if it seems like you are paying more at one of those hospitals, you likely are.

11. When you're looking for a new vet, always check out the staff. A lot of times they'll be listed online. Look for technicians who are certified or licensed (they'll have RVT, LVT or CVT after their names).

12. You can go to an online pharmacy and get the same exact drugs you would get from your vet for 10 to 20 percent off. But check first to make sure it's certified as a Verified

Internet Pharmacy Practice Site (VIPPS certified). Some vets will also match online prices—you just have to know to ask.

13. Just because a food is premium priced doesn't mean it's good stuff. That's especially true with many foods that come in those little gourmet pouches or cans. You pay $3 a package, and it's basically just junk food with little nutritional value. Do some research, and have your vet read the ingredients list with you.

SOURCES: Mark Howes, DVM, owner and medical director of Berglund Animal Hospital in Evanston, Illinois; Patty Khuly, VMD; MeiMei Welker, DVM, outreach vet at DoveLewis Emergency Animal Hospital in Portland, Oregon; Jessica Stout-Harris; Jill Elliot, DVM, owner of Holistic Vet in New York and New Jersey; Dennis Leon, DVM; Oscar Chavez, DVM; Anonymous vets in California and South Carolina.

Great Advice

DOGGIE TRAINING DOS AND DON'TS

....

Cesar Millan, the Dog Whisperer, is a canine shrink with an uncanny ability to turn even the most aggressive pooch around. Millan reveals how to bring out the Lassie in your Brutus:

Wake up and walk. Most dogs are wired to be active. When they're not, pent-up energy leads to whining and chewing. It's a must to take your dog on a 45-minute walk or run before work. If you can, hire a dog walker for midday. "A dog that's tired doesn't bite, dig holes, or bark."

Touch, but never hit. Don't be afraid to use touch to tell a dog he's broken the rules: Millan pulls at the tuft of the neck and gives a gentle nudge—not to hurt the dog, but to surprise and correct.

Be the boss. "Everybody wants to be a dog's best friend, but dogs don't follow friends; they follow a leader," says Millan.

Establish leadership from the get-go: head and shoulders up. "Remember the popular people in high school? They walk in the room and people move—act like that." Walk ahead going out the door; only let him bound ahead if you give the OK. And be firm. Dogs need consistent structure and routine.

Go to the pros. If your dog bites or is overly aggressive, seek help from a dog trainer.

Insider Expertise
LIFE'S 25 TOUGHEST QUESTIONS ANSWERED!

....

Reader's Digest's "Ask Laskas" columnist, Jeanne Marie Laskas, answers what you've been wondering about your friends, family, and more.

1. Can love really last a lifetime?

Absolutely—but only if you chuck the fairy tale of living happily ever after. A team of scientists found that romantic love involves chemical changes in the brain that last 12 to 18 months. After that, you and your partner are on your own. Relationships require maintenance. Pay a visit to a nursing home if you want to see proof of lasting love. Recently I spoke to a man whose wife of 60 years was suffering from advanced Alzheimer's disease. He came to sit with her every day and hold her hand. "She's been my best friend since high school," he told me. "We made a promise to stick together." Now, that's a love story.

2. Why do married folks begin to look like one another?

Watch any two people who like each other talking, and you'll see a lot of mirroring. One smiles, and so does the other. One nods or raises her eyebrows, and so does the other. Faces are like melodies with a natural urge to stay in sync. Multiply those movements by several decades of marriage, all those years of simultaneous sagging and drooping, and it's no wonder!

3. Can a marriage survive betrayal?

Yes. It takes time and work, but experts are pretty unanimous on this one. In her book *The Monogamy Myth*, Peggy Vaughan estimates that 60 percent of husbands and 40 percent of wives will have an affair at some point in their marriages. That's no advertisement for straying—but the news is good for couples hoping to recover from devastating breaches of trust. The offended partner needs to make the choice to forgive—and learn to live with a memory that can't simply be erased. Infidelity is never forgotten, but it can gradually fade into the murky background of a strong, mature marriage.

4. Why does summer zoom by and winter drag on forever?

Because context defines experience. As Albert Einstein once said: "When you are courting a nice girl, an hour seems like a second. When you sit on a red-hot cinder, a second seems like an hour."

5. Do animals really have a sixth sense?

Or seventh or eighth! A box jellyfish has 24 eyes, an earthworm's entire body is covered with taste receptors, a cockroach can detect movement 2,000 times the diameter of a hydrogen atom, and your dog's sense of smell is up to 100,000 times greater than yours (some dogs have been known to smell human cancers). It's safe to say that animals experience a much different world than we do.

6. Why does the line you're in always move the slowest?

Because you're late for your kid's band practice, and you curse your luck and envy those speeding by. Conversely, when you're in the fast line, unfettered by stress, you don't even notice the poor schlubs in the slow lane. Good luck rarely commands one's attention like bad luck.

7. By what age should you know what you want to do with your life?

Any moment now. This used to be a question the young asked. The Bureau of Labor Statistics reports that younger baby boomers abandoned the American ideal of picking a job and sticking with it. Between the ages of 18 and 36, these boomers held an average of 9.6 jobs. That's a lot of exploration. The wisdom of elders in all cultures seems to be this: There's nothing to do with a life but live it. As Gandhi pointed out, "Almost anything you do will be insignificant, but it is very important that you do it."

8. Where do traffic jams come from?

Scientists are hard at work on this one, studying computer models of the physics of gridlock and inventing all new traffic-light algorithms. Some of them postulate that the rhythms of automobile traffic are influenced by the same cyclical forces that cause waves in the ocean. For the average commuter, though, it may be helpful to think of it this way: congestion. There are just too many darn people trying to do the same thing at once. (Flush every toilet in a single office building simultaneously, and see what happens.) All of this is a way of saying: Buy a newspaper, load up some favorite tunes on your MP3 player, and take the bus.

9. When is your future behind you?

When you stop chasing dreams. So don't stop!

10. Do you have to love your job?

No. Love your children, your spouse, and your country. Love your parents, your neighbor, and your dog. Loving is too important an emotion to attach to the way you make a living. But it's OK to strive for satisfaction. According to a recent Harris Poll, across America 59 percent of workers say they are extremely, somewhat, or slightly satisfied with their jobs, but a depressing 33 percent feel as if they've reached a career dead end. If you're among the latter and thinking about a new job, consider the fact that employees in small firms said they felt more engaged in their work than did their corporate counterparts.

11. Can a man and a woman ever just be friends?

For a short time perhaps. Making the friendship last requires that you find each other at least vaguely repulsive. Good luck!

12. When do you take away Grandpa's car keys?

Twenty-two states currently require frequent testing for senior drivers. The American Medical Association and the AARP, however, say safe driving has more to do with functional ability than age. True, seniors are more at risk for reduced vision, hearing loss, and impairments associated with arthritis—but all of these conditions depend on the individual. So when it seems to you that Pop is becoming a danger to himself and a danger to others, tell him straight. Point out that his reactions have slowed or his judgment is losing its edge. Suggest he not drive anymore. Be firm, but at the same time, don't treat him like a child. Allow him his dignity. Offer him a ride.

13. Do siblings who fight really end up liking one another?

I surveyed my older sisters, both of whom have vivid memories of how I tripped, pummeled, and whacked them with various large plastic dolls (hey, they started it—they teased me!), and both confirmed my suspicion that nowadays they like me just fine. I sure like them. All the experts will tell you that fighting among siblings is normal. The key is how parents handle it. Rule number one: Don't take sides. Never get into a discussion of who started what or what is more fair. Stop fights with a time-out for all offenders. My mother would send us to separate rooms. So we invented string phones and a pulley system to transport necessary treats and toys. And whatever we were fighting about was forgotten.

14. How do you know when to end a friendship?

As soon as you get that sneaking suspicion that it never really began.

15. Why do we turn into our parents when we swore we wouldn't?

Because really, when all is said and done, we admire them.

16. Can a half-empty person become a half-full person?

A current theory is that people have an "emotional set point." Some folks are just made happier than others. Pessimists will see this as bad news, believing it really doesn't matter what you do—they are never going to be any happier. But there is hope—as any optimist will see! Happiness has more to do with how you construe the events in your life than the actual events themselves.

17. When do kids become adults?

Biologically, it's happening earlier; emotionally, it seems to be happening later. Nowadays puberty occurs in females between ages 8 and 14, between 9 and 15 in males. A generation ago, when you turned 18, you were out the door and on your own. Now we see kids in the Boomerang Generation coming home to Mom and Dad after college, hoping for a hand with bills, laundry, meals, and other responsibilities of adulthood. It's cute for a while, less adorable the older the kid gets.

18. Can a mother be friends with her teenage daughter?

No. Most teens aren't ready for anything close to a mature friendship. According to current research, the brain continues to develop into a person's twenties. Mothers often want to befriend their daughters; fathers, their sons. But this is not in anyone's best interest. Teenagers need to form identities distinct from their parents. That means: lots of privacy, even some secrets. It's usually easier for a teenage girl to befriend the friend of her mother, and it's usually best for the mother to leave it at that.

19. Does money really buy happiness?

No. Because happiness isn't for sale. Many people get tripped up by this one, amassing wealth only to find themselves cycling into a bottomless pit of insatiable yearning. Turns out, joy and misery are not that far apart when it comes to very big wads of cash. Consider the case of a Kentucky couple who won $34 million in 2000. Thrilled to be released from the demands of their boring old jobs, they frittered their fortune away on fancy cars, mansions, all the usual stuff—losing everything that mattered in the process. They divorced, he died of an alcohol-related illness, and she died alone in her new house just five years after cashing the winning ticket. When it comes to happiness, only people you love, and who love you, can bring it. If you have enough dough to buy yourself a luxurious yacht, but no real friends to sail with, you're sunk.

20. Can spenders and savers stay married?

Sure—and they won't run out of things to talk about either. Disagreements over money are a leading cause of divorce, so experts advise lots of work around this issue if, financially speaking, you've found yourself married to your opposite. Tip: Always talk in terms of "ours" instead of "mine" or "yours," and work your strengths. The saver should be allowed to draft the budget; the spender gets to be in charge of vacations, celebrations, and ordering extra toppings on the pizza.

21. Is money the root of all evil?

No. Greed is. Elvis nailed this one when he said, "Sharing money is what gives it its value."

22. What do you do if you see a parent berating a child?

Cringe. Take a deep breath. If you truly believe you can help the situation, approach as someone showing sympathy—not as an accuser or member of the parent police. Empathize with the overstressed parent. Suggest that he take a deep breath. Tell him it worked for you.

23. Why is it so hard to say you're wrong?

Because it often involves saying, "I'm sorry," which is even harder. Throughout history people have found it easier to stop speaking to one another, punch, slander, shoot, and bomb rather than apologize. Tip: Next time just say, "Whoops," and see what happens.

24. When should you reveal a secret you said you wouldn't?

It's a matter of damage control. Is the person who asked you to keep the secret in danger of hurting himself or others? If so, intervene. Otherwise, mum's the word.

25. Does the toast really always fall buttered-side down?

Scientists in the Ask Laskas Kitchen conducted a study for which they first toasted an entire loaf of bread, one slice at a time. They buttered each slice, and dropped it from a variety of heights ranging from tabletop to ceiling. Among their findings: A dropped piece of toast never lands on its edge; stomping your foot and yelling "Darn!" does not change a thing; and the floor in the Ask Laskas Kitchen is not nearly as clean as we'd like. Well, life's like that. Never as neat as you'd like it to be. But keep buttering your toast. And savor every slice you've been given.

Part Five

WHAT YOU DON'T KNOW ABOUT
YOUR LOCAL BUSINESSES

Our lives depend on local services—or at least our quality of life can! They fill our day-to-day needs for everything from keeping us on the go, to cleaning our clothes, to helping us look our best. We see these neighborhood merchants every day, but what do they see?

Some businesses aren't really hiding things from you, but knowing what happens on the other side of the cash register—including what really sells and what they're trying to push on you—can help you get exactly what you need . . . maybe even with a discount. Whether you're getting a transmission overhaul or a bouquet of flowers, here's what every consumer should keep in mind.

WHAT YOUR CAR DEALER WON'T TELL YOU

Here are some tips that will put you in the driver's seat for new-car negotiations.

1. That car we advertised at the unbelievable price? It's a stripped-down model with a manual transmission and crank windows. Ever wonder about those ads that promise a minimum $3,000 trade-in value for your clunker? Those dealerships also pad the sales price to make up for the difference.

2. The best time to buy is at the end of the month, and it's best to negotiate the trade-in separately. Negotiate up from the invoice price (what we paid for the car, easy to find on the Web), not down from the sticker price.

3. Please do the math. You can't get a $40,000 Tahoe for $250 a month for 72 months! Even at zero percent, $40,000 divided by 72 months is $555 before tax, title, and license fees.

4. Despite the stories you've heard about sleazy car dealers, plenty of us are honest folks frustrated by the guys who give the rest of us a bad name.

5. Kelley Blue Book, Edmunds, and NADA (National Automobile Dealers Association) all offer guides for car values. We're the experts who do this every day and can evaluate what a 2008 Honda Accord EX is really worth in our market.

6. Don't expect retail for your trade-in and wholesale for our car. We have to recondition your trade, advertise it, warranty it, and pay interest on the amount we have in the car, then sell it for less than we want after it sits on the lot for months.

7. To get a great price with minimal haggling, call and ask for the Internet manager or fleet manager.

8. Go in armed and educated. Study the pricing of the car you like and have your financing lined up. If you walk in with nothing, you're not a customer—you're a victim.

9. Never pay the VIN-etch fee. It's a $250 optional add-on that's almost pure profit for us. And if you want us to tint your windows, apply rustproofing, or paint a pinstripe on your truck, I'll probably charge you two or three times the cost of doing it elsewhere.

10. Forget the overall cost of the car. Let's talk about what you want to pay each month. Then I can build in profit generators such as extended warranties and credit insurance, and you won't even notice. Watch out for this!

11. Once you've agreed on a price, you think you're done—but we're just getting started. I'll promise you just about anything to get you to sign on the dotted line. But if I don't put it in writing, I may not remember the next day.

> 🔒 **TOP SECRET!** Once I'm sitting behind the desk, you'll feel like I'm in control and may be willing to pay a little more. (We learn this during training.)

12. Banks almost never require you to buy a particular warranty or a particular add-on to get the loan. If the finance officer tells you otherwise, ask to speak to someone at the bank.

13. If your auto credit score is under 600, expect to get an interest rate higher than 16 percent and to put 20 percent down. If your score is under 550, we may put a tracking device in your car that will shut it off if you don't make a payment.

SOURCES: Car dealers in Florida, Ohio, North Carolina, and New York; Sarah Lee Marks, a Las Vegas–based personal car buyer who sold cars for almost a decade; and Jeff Ostroff, president and CEO of carbuyingtips.com.

Who Knew?

8 EASY WAYS TO EXTEND THE LIFE OF YOUR CAR

1. Do not race your car's engine during start-up. This is a quick way to add years of wear to your engine, especially if it's cold outside.

2. Accelerate slowly when you begin your drive. The most wear to the engine and drive train occurs in the first 10 to 20 minutes of operation.

3. Warming the engine by letting it idle in the driveway is not a smart idea. The engine doesn't operate at its peak temperature, resulting in incomplete fuel combustion, soot deposits on cylinder walls, oil contamination, and ultimately damaged components.

4. Put less strain on your engine and automatic transmission by shifting to neutral at red lights. Otherwise, the engine is still working to push the car even while it's stopped.

5. When turning your steering wheel, don't hold it in an extreme right or left position for more than a few seconds. Doing so can damage the power-steering pump.

6. Don't fill up if you see the tanker. If you happen to see a gasoline tanker filling the tanks at your local gas station, come back another day or go to a different station. As the station's underground tanks are being filled, the turbulence can stir up sediment. Sediment in your gas can clog fuel filters and fuel injectors, causing poor performance and possibly necessitating repairs.

WHAT **YOUR GAS STATION** DOESN'T WANT YOU TO KNOW

You can make fill-ups less frequent with these simple strategies.

1. Gas price increases usually take effect in late morning. Retailers also tend to raise prices on weekends, especially holiday weekends, so midweek is better.

2. Always park so that you can pull forward rather than waste gas backing up. This can improve your mileage by 25 percent (some experts say this number might even be underestimated)!

3. The speed limit also limits pump visits. The U.S. Department of Energy says that by following the speed limit and swearing off aggressive driving, drivers can improve mileage by anywhere from 12 to 55 percent. Edmunds.com found that using cruise control improved mileage by an additional 7 percent.

4. Modern cars don't become fully efficient until the engine is warmed up, so if you plan on running a series of errands, drive to the farthest location first and then work your way back—a series of short stop-and-start trips will never allow your car to reach maximum efficiency.

5. Rapid acceleration and hard braking, completely avoidable actions, just throw gas away. Instead of braking hard at a red light, coast from a distance. Come to stops slowly and gradually (if there is no one behind you, coast to the red light if you can).

6. Lace up your sneakers and get some exercise doing errands while you save gas. A bicycle can help you rack up car-free miles even faster. Or nix trips to the store altogether and do your errands online, including banking, buying stamps, and paying bills.

7. Banking your trips means fewer gas station stops. Need to pick up a prescription, mail a package, and go to the bank? Instead of spreading these tasks out over a few trips, do them all at once. Park in a central spot and walk from place to place.

8. Extra driving time means wasted gas, so figure out where you're going before you leave. Use the GPS feature on your phone or a website like MapQuest.com to get exact directions. Try to avoid making left-hand turns where you will spend more time idling your car.

> 🔒 **TOP SECRET!** Cutting out idling leads to mileage improvements of up to 19 percent. If you're going to be at a standstill for 10 or more seconds, it's better to cut the engine.

9. Check the air in your tires. The less air, the more difficult to drive.

10. A clean engine means fuel will be more efficient, so change your oil every 3,000 miles.

11. Car pools are a great way to save on time and gas. Instead of picking up your kids from school every day, ask a neighbor with kids in the same school to help. You can each take turns picking up the tykes.

12. Drive the small car. Do you own an SUV and a fuel-efficient sedan? Take the smaller car on any long trips you can.

13. For every 30 pounds of extra weight your car carries, miles per gallon decreases by anywhere from one-tenth to one-hundredth of a percent. That may not seem like much, but mile after mile it adds up.

Great Advice
MAKE CAR TIRES LAST LONGER

Keep the caps on. You step out into driveway ready to start your morning commute only to discover a flat tire. How in the heck did that happen overnight? If the tire valve is missing its cap, the culprit might be a leaky valve. Those little caps keep out dirt and moisture that can cause leaks, so be sure to keep caps on all your tire valves. Another tip: When you replace tires, remind the tire shop that you expect new valves with the tires.

Maintain proper inflation. Under-inflated tires are a tire salesman's best friend. They create excessive heat and stress that can lead to tire failure. If you want to get every last mile out of your tires, get yourself a tire pressure gauge and use it at least once a month (more in hot weather) to keep your tires inflated to the recommendation in the vehicle's owner's manual. Check tires when they are cold (driven for less than one mile) for an accurate reading.

Beware the wet thumb. If you top off your tires at a service station, check to see if there's moisture coming from the air pump. Simply depress the pin inside the inflator valve with your thumbnail. If your thumb gets wet, advise the station manager that his tanks need to be drained and go to a different station. Moisture, trapped inside a tire, can cause pressure variations and corrode rims.

Check for uneven wear. Check tires for uneven wear. If you've maintained tire inflation properly, uneven wear may indicate the need for a wheel realignment. It can also mean improperly operating brakes or shocks, a bent wheel, internal tire damage, or worn bushings.

Check tread for safety. Most states require tires to be replaced when they have worn down to 1/16 inch (1.5 mm) of remaining tire depth. Tires sold in North America are required to have "wear bars" molded into them to make it easy to see when tire replacement is legally required. However, if you'll be driving in the rain, you should change your tires when there is ⅛ inch (3 mm) of tread left. Otherwise, water may not escape from under your tires fast enough and you risk hydroplaning—a dangerous situation in which your car loses traction and literally floats on the water. Stick an American quarter between the treads in several places. If part of Washington's head is always covered, you have enough tread to drive in the rain. If you drive in snow, you'll need at least 3⁄16 inch (5 mm) of tread to get adequate traction. Stick an American penny between the treads. If the top of the Lincoln Memorial is always covered, you're ready for winter driving.

Rotate your tires. Rotating your tires helps to distribute tire wear evenly and ensures that you'll get the maximum road life out of them. The first rotation is especially important. Your owner's manual should specify both rotation period and pattern. If not, rotate your tires every 6,000 to 7,500 miles (9,700 to 12,000 km)— your tire dealer should know the correct pattern of tire rotation.

When temperatures affect tire inflation: When outside temperatures drop or soar, tires tend to lose pressure. A drop of 10°F (6°C), in fact, will decrease a tire's air pressure by 1 or 2 pounds. Tires can lose even more air in hot weather. Under-inflated tires can result in accelerated wear and poor driving performance. If you live in a place where temperatures vary a lot, check your tire pressure often and add air as needed.

WHAT YOUR CAR MECHANIC WON'T TELL YOU

Real mechanics have revealed the top 13 ways to avoid an auto-repair scam.

1. Watch out for scare tactics. Admonitions like "I wouldn't drive this another mile" should be viewed with suspicion.

2. Check their credentials. Look for ASE (National Institute for Automotive Service Excellence) or AAA (America Automobile Association) certification, as well as a state license. Reputable shops are proud to display them.

3. Ask, ask, ask. Get recommendations and find out years in business, warranties offered, licenses, and the type of equipment used. Look for a clean garage. A floor cluttered with empty oil cans, worn tires, and dirty rags is a red flag.

4. Never sign a blank authorization form. Always get a signed work order with a specific estimate for each job and warranties that apply.

5. It's nuts to take a car with engine problems to a shop without a good engine analyzer and scan tool. Any mechanic who says "I don't need fancy equipment" should be avoided.

6. When you go for a second opinion, don't tell the mechanic what the first diagnosis and price were.

7. Coolant flushes and power steering flushes are very common gimmicks at quick lubes. Check your owner's manual; many cars have fluid that is designed to go 100,000 miles.

And cleaning fuel injectors is a waste of time and money. There are additives on the market that do a great job. Transmission flushes are another one of the biggest scams going. Manufacturers don't recommend them, and your car almost never needs one.

> 🔒 **TOP SECRET!** Don't bring your car in on Friday afternoon. The mechanics might rush the job to get out for the weekend.

8. Always ask for OE (original equipment) brake pads or at least equivalent material. A $49.95 brake job will usually get you the worst friction material you can buy—it's the difference between stopping short and causing a pileup on the way to work.

9. The market is being flooded with cheap parts from China. Request a name-brand replacement and ask to see its box. Then get your old parts back. This way you'll know they've been changed, and you can tell if they were worn out.

10. Beware of a mechanic who shows you a transmission pan with metal particles in it and recommends a major job. The shavings are usually a sign of normal wear.

11. Know what your state's tread specifications are before buying new tires. Then have the mechanic measure the old tread with a gauge. Ask about your new tire's "build date." If you're getting an unusually good deal, you might be receiving three-year-old treads, especially risky for snow tires.

12. Lifetime mufflers? What would ever make you think a muffler will last a lifetime? Yes, they'll give you free replacements, but they'll hit you over the head for expensive pipe repairs.

13. Consult your dealer before you have work done on a catalytic converter or emissions parts. Some of these items carry a very long warranty, and free replacement is often required by law.

SOURCES: Domenic DiSiena, manager, Bedford (New York) Shell; Gary Montesi, owner, Montesi Volkswagen, North Haven, Connecticut; Bob Sikorsky, automotive writer, Tucson, Arizona; anonymous mechanics in Minnesota and New York.

Who Knew?
4 TIPS TO KEEP YOUR CAR BATTERY RUNNING

1. Aspirin. If your car's battery has given up the ghost and there's no one around to give you a jump, you may be able to get your vehicle started by dropping two aspirin tablets into the battery itself. The aspirin's acetylsalicylic acid will combine with the battery's sulfuric acid to produce one last charge. Just be sure to drive to your nearest service station.

2. Baking Soda. Eliminate the corrosive buildup on your car's battery terminals. Scrub them clean using an old toothbrush and a mixture of 3 tablespoons of baking soda and 1 tablespoon of warm water. Wipe them off with a wet towel and dry with another towel. Once the terminals have completely dried, apply a bit of petroleum jelly around each terminal to deter future corrosive buildup.

3. Epsom Salt. Is your car battery starting to sound as if it won't turn over? Give your battery a little more life with this potion. Dissolve about an ounce of Epsom salt in warm water and add it to each battery cell.

4. Soda. Yes, it's true, the acidic properties of soda pop will help to eliminate corrosion from your car battery. Nearly all carbonated soft drinks contain carbonic acid, which helps to remove stains and dissolve rust deposits. Pour some soda over the battery terminals and let it sit. Remove the sticky residue with a wet sponge.

WHAT YOUR CAR DETAILER WON'T TELL YOU

Keep your car looking brand-new—
inside and out—with these secrets.

1. Paint does more than make your vehicle look great. It's also the first line of defense against rusted body panels. The best way to protect the paint is to park the car in a garage. If that is not possible, park in the shade or purchase a car cover. The sun's ultraviolet rays break down paint and cause it to fade.

2. Touch-up paint won't adhere well to rust. So be sure to keep some matching touch-up paint on hand so you can touch up any minor nicks, often found around door edges and keyholes.

3. A cracked taillight or turn signal cover can be much more serious than it seems. If left alone, your light compartment could fill with water and cause some real damage. A good short-term fix is to tape over the crack. Use the red or orange tape that's available at auto parts stores and that's made for this.

4. Take your car to a windshield repair shop when the windshield has a rock chip, crack, or ding. For far less cost than replacing the windshield, they can fix chips and cracks, even quite long ones. The repairs not only keep the chips and cracks from spreading and restore structural integrity, but they also improve clarity.

5. Cracked washer/de-icer fluid tanks are fairly common once a car is of a certain age. Until you can buy a new tank or find one at the junkyard, insert a plastic freezer bag into the tank and fill it with the washer fluid.

6. Protect your car's roof from scratches with an old blanket before tying lumber, bicycles, or luggage to your roof rack.

7. The beginning of the end for the finish on many cars and trucks is a poorly stowed load. It's the same for wagon and hatchback interiors. Invest in the appropriate racks for bicycles, cargo, and luggage. To keep tall objects from sliding around in a pickup truck bed, use a shower curtain rod (or two) as a brace. Just push the cargo against the front wall of the truck bed and install the rod behind it. Twist to secure. Cargo nets will also help keep objects from banging around and damaging a truck bed.

8. Wheel-well splashguards are often flimsy, but they're important. They help keep water and winter's salty slush from splashing up into the engine compartment, where it can damage sensitive electrical components. Unfortunately, these guards tear off easily, so check for damage when you wash your car. Resecure with the appropriate fasteners or replace as needed.

9. The fastest corrosion occurs when the temperature repeatedly rises above and then falls below freezing. Washing is more important in the winter than any other time of the year. All that sand, slush, and ice mixed with road salt is exactly what makes your car rust—especially the undercarriage.

10. New self-adhering urethane films have been developed to protect the most vulnerable painted areas on your car from stone chips and other minor abrasions. You can wash and wax these surfaces, just as you would the rest of the paint job.

11. Too much pressure will scratch the clear plastic lenses on your dashboard. Use a soft damp cloth to lightly wipe the dust off. Too many scratches can make it difficult to read your gauges under certain lighting conditions.

12. Wipe a rubber protectant (such as Armor All) or silicone on door and window weather stripping to keep it in good condition. Don't use an oil-based product, such as WD-40, because the oil will damage the rubber. Bad weather stripping should be fixed immediately.

13. All manner of food bits and liquids can accumulate under a baby seat, where they can permanently stain the upholstery. Place a sheet of heavy plastic and an absorbent towel under the seat to prevent damage, and resecure the seat according to the manufacturer's directions.

Who Knew?
WEIRD THINGS THAT WORK TO KEEP YOUR CAR CLEAN

Cooking spray removes brake dust. You know that fine black stuff that collects on the wheels of your car and is so hard to clean off? That's brake dust—it's produced every time you apply your brakes and the pads wear against the brake disks or cylinders. Next time you're shining your wheels, give them a light coating of cooking spray. The brake dust will wipe right off.

Mayonnaise takes road tar or pine sap off your car with ease. Slather some mayonnaise over the affected area, let it sit for several minutes, and wipe it away with a clean, soft rag.

Socks make a perfect hand mitt for buffing the wax on your car.

Vinegar removes bumper stickers. Saturate the top and sides of the sticker with undiluted distilled vinegar and wait 10 to 15 minutes for the vinegar to soak through. Then use an expired credit card to scrape it off. Use more vinegar to get rid of any remaining gluey residue.

Vinegar also keeps frost from forming. Wipe or spray the outsides of the windows with a solution of 3 parts white vinegar to 1 part water. Each coating may last up to several weeks.

Dryer sheets are great for picking up pet hair that's stuck to your upholstery. Take a used fabric softener sheet and swipe it across the fabric. Even tenacious hair will get sucked right off the material, and the sheet will even leave behind a clean scent.

WHAT YOUR DRY CLEANER WON'T TELL YOU

These tips will let you take your clothes—but not your wallet—to the cleaners.

1. Lots of "dry" cleaning isn't. As much as 24 percent of garments are cleaned in water. Perspiration doesn't come out otherwise.

2. It's not your gender, it's your clothes. Women's clothes—silk, special trims, buttons, slacks without a crease—can take more work and cost more, too.

3. Yes, we use perchloroethylene (perc). It's a probable carcinogen, but it's the best thing we have right now. If you can smell it on your clothes, they weren't cleaned correctly.

4. Don't get too excited about so-called "organic" cleaning. Among the most common perc replacements is the petroleum-based solvent DF-2000, made by ExxonMobil. Because it's hydrocarbon-based, to a chemist—and almost no one else—it's considered an "organic" compound. The EPA cites risk of neurological damage and skin and eye irritation in workers using it, and since it doesn't clean as well as perc on its own, dry cleaners often end up adding pretreatment chemicals.

5. People never remember to pick up their comforters. That's why this place sometimes looks like a Bed Bath & Beyond.

6. You blame us for damage, we blame your clothes.
Instead of court or the Better Business Bureau, we'll suggest the
International Textile Analysis Laboratory, run by our trade asso-
ciation. It's independent (honest!), and both sides get a report.

7. Certifications aren't everything. The Drycleaning and
Laundry Institute (DLI) offers certifications for dry cleaners who
pass an official examination, including Certified Professional Dry
Cleaner (CPD), Certified Professional Wetcleaner (CPW), and Certified Environmental Dry Cleaner (CED). Those who meet even
more stringent requirements may also attain DLI's "Award of
Excellence." While some kind of certification is better than none,
it's not the ultimate arbiter of skill or knowledge.

8. Your lost clothes are probably in someone else's closet.
We'd really prefer not to write you a check. And if we say we
have to get in touch with our insurance company, we could be
stalling, hoping the clothes will turn up.

9. Many of us will reuse your intact hangers. (Thanks.)

10. We're not raking it in. The machinery is expensive. The
people who press your silk shirt get up to $20 an hour. It's a skill.

11. Things happen. We've heard stories
about dry cleaners who borrow a customer's
dress for a weekend.

> 🔒 **TOP SECRET!** If a dry
> cleaner claims "all work done
> onsite," they're either lying or
> incompetent. Only ten to fifteen
> percent of dry cleaners have
> the equipment and expertise
> necessary to handle everything
> that comes in for cleaning.

**12. Clean your leather before you need
it.** Better to bring it in during the spring or
summer. Leather cleaning specialists do
about half their business in three months in
the fall so jobs brought in then will typically
not get the same attention or may take longer
to return.

13. Quality knows quality. The best clothing store in town
can recommend the best dry cleaner in town.

SOURCES: Steve Boorstein, a former dry cleaner who dispenses clothing care advice
on his website, www.clothingdoctor.com; and Chuck Horst, president of Margaret's
Cleaners in La Jolla, California.

Who Knew?

TREAT HOUSEHOLD STAINS WITH ONE KITCHEN INGREDIENT: VINEGAR

To eliminate a fresh grease spot on a suede jacket or skirt, gently brush it with a soft toothbrush dipped in white vinegar. Let the spot air-dry, then brush with a suede brush. Repeat if necessary. You can also generally tone up suede items by lightly wiping them with a sponge dipped in vinegar.

Lift out many water-soluble stains—including beer, orange and other fruit juices, black coffee or tea, and vomit—from your cotton-blend clothing by patting the spot with a cloth or towel moistened with undiluted white vinegar just before placing it in the wash. For large stains, you may want to soak the garment overnight in a solution of 3 parts vinegar to 1 part cold water before washing.

Older, set-in stains will often come out in the wash after being pretreated with a solution of 3 tablespoons of white vinegar and 2 tablespoons of liquid detergent in 1 quart (1 liter) of warm water. Rub the solution into the stain, then blot it dry before washing.

Cola, hair dye, ketchup, and wine stains on washable cotton blends should be treated as soon as possible (that is, within 24 hours). Sponge the area with undiluted vinegar and launder immediately afterward. For severe stains, add 1 to 2 cups of vinegar to the wash cycle, as well.

Remove a rust stain from your cotton work clothes by moistening the spot with some full-strength vinegar and then rubbing in a bit of salt. If it's warm outdoors, let it dry in the sunlight (otherwise a sunny window will do), then toss it in the wash.

Remove deodorant stains from your washable shirts and blouses by gently rubbing the spot with undiluted vinegar before laundering.

Get crayon marks off kids' clothes by rubbing them with a recycled toothbrush soaked in undiluted vinegar before washing them.

WHAT YOUR HAIRSTYLIST WON'T TELL YOU

After reading these secrets, you'll know exactly what to say, do, and tip in the salon to get a style you love.

1. I work hard to make you happy, and I want you to like what I do. After you leave my salon, I worry about what you think. (I work on people, not on cars on an assembly line.) And if you feel like calling to tell me how happy you are with my work, you will make me smile.

2. You represent me. So it's in my best interest for you to look good.

3. I'm a beautician, not a magician. I can give you Gisele Bündchen's haircut, but I can't give you her face.

4. Come at least five minutes early. If you're running late, please call ahead. Show me some basic respect. This is a business, not fun and games.

5. Don't ask me to squeeze you in. If I'm already booked, I'd be taking time and effort away from other clients. You wouldn't like being treated that way.

6. My work takes time. When a client says she's in a rush, I tell her she needs to schedule her time better. Keep in mind that trim is not "just a trim." It requires my expertise, skill, knowledge, and time. Would you say to your dentist, "It's just a tooth," or to your doctor, "It's just a leg"?

7. If you cancel at the very last minute, that's lost money to me. I can't fill that appointment with little or no notice.

8. We see women at their worst. Their hair is wet; they have foils on their hair; they have no makeup on. There's nothing for them to hide behind. So they tell us everything.

> 🔒 **TOP SECRET!** Kids' haircuts aren't child's play. Why do you think a child's haircut should cost less than yours? Kids don't sit still. Kids kick. It's an intense experience.

9. Layers are the magic remedy. Some women think that if they keep their hair all one length the way it was in high school, everyone will think they're still in high school. But you're not. As you get older, you need to soften the lines around your face.

10. Bodies and hair change as hormones change. If your hair is dry, brittle, or if it's not holding your color or style the way it used to, see a doctor. If your hair isn't overprocessed, you could be pregnant (surprise!) or menopausal (yes, I can tell).

11. A dollar bill doesn't buy anything anymore. For stylists, tips should be 15 to 20 percent of the total cost of your bill. They are a significant portion of my pay. If you stiff me, I'll remember. Salon owners who style hair do appreciate tips and want them. And that single bill you stuff into the shampoo person's hands isn't doing her any favors. Tip at least $5—more if your hair is long.

12. Take a picture. Some clients will say, "Cut my hair just like you did last time." That always baffles me. The average time between appointments is six to eight weeks. I have hundreds of clients. How am I supposed to remember exactly how I did your hair the last time? If you want a carbon copy of a cut and style you loved, take a picture and show me.

13. Spend a little money on the right products. Your hair wants to be healthy. Just help it a little. Let it do its thing.

SOURCES: Hairstylists Dawn Trudden in Wellington, Florida; Ericka Sandstrom in Aurora, Illinois; Megan Moore in Salt Lake City, Utah, who blogs at thebeautysnoop.com; and Jenny Strebe in Scottsdale, Arizona, who blogs at theconfessionsofahairstylist.com.

6 WAYS TO GET GORGEOUS HAIR WITHOUT PRICEY PRODUCTS

. . . .

As much as we might all wish for it, there is one basic truth about hair care: the wash-and-go cut, simple-and-easy hairdo is essentially a myth. To keep your hair looking good, you have to spend a little time on it. The good news is that you don't have to spend a lot of money.

1. Wash, rinse, repeat—not! Washing your hair twice in one session is an old marketing trick designed to make you use up your shampoo twice as fast. Double-shampooing strips all the natural oils out of your hair as effectively as paint thinner. Hair should never be "squeaky clean" because that's the same as "super-dry." In fact, one of our top experts, a partner and senior stylist at an up-scale New York salon, recommends using shampoo on your hair not twice in one wash, but only every second wash.

2. Use baking soda. Your hair will look shinier and bouncier if you remove all traces of styling products and conditioner every six weeks or so. You don't need a clarifying shampoo. Just mix 1 table-spoon of baking soda with 2 tablespoons of white vinegar, work it into your hair, then rinse thoroughly.

3. Timing is everything. Don't use any clarifying product if you have just colored your hair, because it can remove some of the color. But it's a great idea to use a clarifying shampoo just before you color your hair. Removing all traces of buildup allows the hair to take the color much better, so the color will last longer.

4. Sleep like a princess for Rapunzel-like locks. Your hair-style rumples less if you sleep on a satin pillowcase.

Cotton pillow covers (yes, even those 400 thread-count sheets) roughen the cuticle more; satin allows the hair to slip smoothly over the surface as you roll and turn in your sleep.

5. Baby those tresses. Don't pay premium prices for high-end shampoos that are specially formulated for colored or permed hair. An inexpensive bottle of baby shampoo will treat your hair just as gently and will also allow the color or perm to last much longer.

6. Give it a natural shine. To bring out your highlights, use an astringent rinse while washing your hair. For lighter-colored hair, combine ¼ cup of lemon juice with 1 cup of warm water and pour it over your hair. To bring out the highlights in darker hair, mix ¼ cup of white vinegar with 1 cup of warm water.

WHAT YOUR MAKEUP COUNTER WON'T TELL YOU

Find out what you're doing wrong, what you're doing right, and how to avoid danger and dollar signs in your makeup routine.

1. The main difference between designer cosmetics and their drugstore counterparts? Fancy packaging. In fact, some manufacturers make both high-end and drugstore products—using similar formulas!

2. One of the governmental agencies responsible for the cosmetics industry is the FDA, but it doesn't review cosmetics before they go on the market, it can't recall a product if there's a problem, and it has banned only about a dozen toxic chemicals from beauty products, compared with the more than 1,300 that are banned in the European Union.

3. Your foundation has SPF? That's great—but you still need sunscreen. Experts say most people don't use enough makeup to fully protect their skin, and they end up missing important areas such as their ears, neck, and the back of their hands.

4. Want to look younger? Choose anti-aging moisturizers and serums with vitamin A derivatives such as retinol and retinaldehyde. The next most effective ingredient: L-ascorbic acid.

5. For the appearance of fuller lips, dab a bit of petroleum jelly or shiny lip gloss on the middle of your lower lip.

6. Sure, those spray sunscreens make application a cinch, but think about this: You may be inhaling toxic chemicals into your lungs and bloodstream. Be sure to spray an aerosol into your hands first and then apply.

7. Nearly one in five cosmetic products contains traces of formaldehyde, a known human carcinogen. You can avoid it altogether by skipping products that list DMDM hydantoin, imidazolidinyl urea, diazolidinyl urea, sodium hydroxymethyl-glycinate, or bronopol as an ingredient.

8. Go gold for a more youthful look. A little bit of gold in your foundation will neutralize redness and counteract the gray pallor that accompanies aging on all skin tones.

9. If your mascara is drying up and you're in a pinch, a couple of drops of saline solution can make it last a few more days.

10. Never wash your face with just plain soap. Made from animal fat and salt compounds, it strips your skin of its natural oils and proteins. Use a non-soap cleanser instead.

11. There is a magic potion that will stop 90 percent of your skin's aging, but, according to a Marist Institute for Public Opinion poll, only one in ten Americans uses it: sunscreen.

12. To accentuate your eyes, choose a shadow color that complements your eye color. If you have blue or green eyes, wear a shade that has brown, copper, bronze, plum, or terra-cotta tones. Enhance brown eyes with blues, purples, and greens.

13. To make your look last all night, always prep your eyelids with primer or concealer, and then set it with powder before you apply liquid or pencil liner and eye shadow.

SOURCES: Makeup artists Cristina Bartolucci at DuWop Cosmetics, Alejandro Falcon at Osmosis Skincare, and Rebecca Perkins at Rouge New York; dermatologists David Bank, MD, author of *Beautiful Skin: Every Woman's Guide to Looking Her Best at Any Age*, and Fayne L. Frey, MD, founder of fryface.com; Nneka Leiba, deputy director of research at the Environmental Working Group; and Andrea Q. Robinson, author of *Toss the Gloss: Beauty Tips, Tricks & Truths for Women 50+.*

8 MAKEUP TIPS TO MAKE YOU LOOK LESS TIRED

Pulled an all-nighter? Haven't gotten your recommended eight hours since you were a little tyke? Here are some tips to wipe the sleepiness off your face.

1. Start with a clean slate. This is especially important if you went to bed without washing your face last night and remnants of yesterday's makeup are sticking around. A gentle cleanser is ideal, Follow up with your regular daily moisturizer.

2. Smooth on tinted moisturizer. It will blend in nicely and even your skin tone, leaving skin looking sun kissed. In summer, a little illumination is a nice touch.

3. Target under-eye circles. One of the key areas to focus on when you're tired is your under-eye bags. To prep the skin, use an eye cream to battle puffiness. Next you will want to hide the appearance of dark circles. Take a concealer two shades lighter than your skin tone and apply this in a triangular shape under your eyes.

4. Set your concealer. To prevent creasing and to keep your concealer in place all day, set this area with a loose setting powder. To set, apply a generous amount of powder with a brush or damp beauty blender and let it "bake" in for a few minutes. Once the powder has started to sink into the skin, take a brush and dust the remaining powder off.

5. Add color to eyes. Swipe a goldy-pink or champagne color on lids. Focusing this brightening shade on the inner corner makes the eye appear wider and more awake. Finish the eyes by lining the waterline with a nude liner, curling your lashes, and applying a volumizing mascara. Lastly, fill in your brows with whatever product works best for you.

6. Dip into bronzer. Dust on a bronzer that has—you guessed it—a subtle shimmer to it. Apply to areas that the sun naturally touches your face: apples of cheeks, tip of nose, and along your hairline. Use a light hand. Bronzer should kiss your face—not look like a mask, which will backfire and make you appear dull and tired.

7. Add color to cheeks. Making your skin glow with a shimmery blush and highlight is key to faking well-rested, fresh skin. Dust a shimmery blush onto the apples of cheeks to add some color back into your face. Add highlighting powder to the tops of cheekbones, down the nose, across the cupid's bow, and on the chin to enhance your skin's appearance.

8. Bring focus to lips. Coat lips in a natural looking lip gloss/stain to add a nice, but subtle, pop of color without looking overdone The finished look gives the illusion of a well-awake, fresh face!

SOURCES: Emma Kapotes, photo editor/designer and makeup artist; Rich Campbell, director of education at Dermaflash.

WHAT YOUR GYM WON'T TELL YOU

Ever wonder just how germy gyms are? Or how they convince you to buy those pricey training packages? Here are inside tips to get the most out of your membership.

1. We count on you not to show up. About 50 percent of people who start an exercise program quit within six months. If more members started coming regularly, it would be chaos in here. Start slow. People who quit typically push themselves too hard at first and get discouraged.

2. It's often cheaper to pay per visit. Economists at the University of California, Berkeley, found that the average gym user who enrolls in a monthly or annual membership pays 70 percent more—about $300 more a year—than those who pay per visit.

3. Many of you use the treadmills totally wrong. Holding on for balance is OK, but some people support almost all their body weight on their arms. That's unsafe—and it prevents you from burning as many calories.

4. What's hot right now? Functional fitness, or doing exercises that help you in everyday life, which is important for older adults hoping to prevent injury. That means fewer exercises like leg extensions, and more multi-joint, full-body exercises (like squats) that strengthen you for real-life activities.

5. Don't drop your kid off at our daycare and leave the

premises. It's just rude—and it's against our rules. If you want to get your nails done or go shopping, hire a babysitter.

6. Enjoy the free personal-training session when you join. But if your trainer shows you complex exercises, it might be per management orders. The goal: to make exercise seem complicated so you buy training sessions.

7. Patience, people! TV shows may give you the idea that you can lose 25 pounds and transform your body in a few weeks, but that's not reality. Stick with us for three months, and you will see a noticeable difference in your physique.

8. Beware the smoothie station. Some smoothies pack as many as 500 calories, which may negate the workout you just did. Plus, we sell those products at a big markup. You can save money—and calories—by making them at home.

9. Want us to offer a class at a different time? We need about 12 people to come regularly to make it work. Get a group of coworkers or friends who are interested, and request it together.

10. Members can be unbelievably territorial. Once, I was teaching a spin class when two people came in late and saw other members on their reserved bikes. They started yelling and pulling the people off. It was like a scene out of a movie.

11. See those bottles of disinfectant spray and paper towels? They're not there for decoration. Please wipe down your sweaty machine after you use it.

12. Don't automatically pay the initiation fee. Most of the time, it's completely negotiable.

13. What I look for in a gym: a friendly front-desk staff, which tells me it's well managed, and a high-quality rug inside the front door, which means they take cleanliness seriously.

SOURCES: Tom Holland, MS, CSCS, former gym owner and author of *Beat the Gym;* Tiffany Richards, former employee at a fitness chain; Charlie Sims, owner of a CrossFit gym in Louisville, Kentucky; Jim Thornton, MA, ATC, CES, president of the National Athletic Trainers' Association; and economist Stefano DellaVigna, who studied gym users for three years.

WHAT YOUR COMPUTER TECH WON'T TELL YOU

Rebooting really works! Here are some other secrets that will help you be your own IT person—sometimes.

1. Turn it off, turn it back on. Nine times out of ten, rebooting your computer—and any equipment that connects to it—will solve the problem.

2. Check the cables. People are always shocked that a cable came loose. Of course, everything that needs power is plugged into an outlet, right?

3. Google will not solve everything. Google is an amazingly helpful tool where you can find most answers to your tech questions by searching yourself . . . BUT I know which solutions are true and which are not. I can do a Google search for something and weed out all the illegitimate answers.

4. Sometimes it's easier to accomplish certain things using home-based technology than the big corporate office technology. For example. Gmail vs. Microsoft Exchange. Gmail is simple and easy to use, while Exchange is super complicated.

5. Use "strong" passwords. Combine letters and numbers—but not your birth date—to create a "base" password, and add a unique suffix for each site you use. If your base password is your spouse's initials and your anniversary date (say, SP061789), your Amazon password might be "SP061789AM."

6. Make sure you have current antivirus and anti-spyware protection, and set it to update at least once a day and run a full-system scan at least once a week. Also make sure your OS system is update often as well.

7. There's no free lunch. Downloading free music, movies, and games from file-sharing sites can open holes in your system for others to exploit.

8. Remember: Public Wi-Fi is public. If you don't have to check your e-mail or bank account while sipping a latte at the mall, don't do it. While you're on a public network, a nearby hacker can capture your passwords.

9. Give it a rest. Turn off your computer when you aren't using it into "sleep mode," which uses very little energy. If you do leave your computer on, reboot it at least once a week to clear out your memory.

> 🔒 **TOP SECRET!** When searching Google, to remove out of date answers, click "Tools" along the top and you can search by the past hour, day, week, month, or year. The default is "anytime" and you can get results from 5–10 years ago, which may not be relevant to your search.

10. I can't make a four-year-old computer fast. Computers naturally slow down with age. Hard drives wear out and slow down. I'll try to fix it, but sometimes new is just better.

11. Keep it clean. On a PC, run Disk Cleanup and Disk Defragmenter at least once a month. After about four years, your computer is elderly. If you're shelling out for a blazing-fast Internet connection, pony up for a new model.

12. Got neighbors? If you do, protect your home wireless network with a password. If a person knows what he's doing, getting into a computer on a non-encrypted network is easy.

13. You backed up your data, right? External hard drives with lots of memory now sell for under $100, and automated programs like Cobian Backup or Apple's Time Machine make regular backups a no-brainer.

SOURCES: Derek Meister, Geek Squad; Aaron Schildkraut of myhometech.net; anonymous posters on TechRepublic.com; techcomedy.com; Matthew Florence and William McGhee of HCL America at Trusted Media Brands, Inc.

WHAT YOUR BABY STORE WON'T TELL YOU

You really don't have to have all those products we want to sell you. Here's what you can live without.

1. You don't need a Diaper Genie. The idea of keeping a dirty diaper, compacted or not, in a kid's room for an extended period of time isn't terribly appealing. Just throw all the dirty diapers into the trash and take it out daily. The really stinky ones go straight to the outside garbage.

2. The Wee Block may be a better concept than a reality. The sales pitch: "Just cover baby before diapering, and let the soft, absorbent dome catch your little guy's geysers." The reality: accidents still happen, and it's just another thing to constantly wash.

3. Use a pot of boiling water or the dishwasher instead of a counter-space-consuming bottle sanitizer.

4. And you can scrap the bottle warmer, too. If you're willing to wait a few extra minutes (the bottle warmer is supposed to be faster), that same pot of boiling water can be used to warm your baby's milk.

5. Hold baby wipes in your hands for a few seconds and you've done the job of a Wipe Warmer for free—and you've saved electricity, too.

6. Baby powder smells great, but doesn't seem to serve a big purpose. Plus, powders containing talc can be dangerous if inhaled.

7. Long-sleeved shirts are great stand-ins for mittens. If your baby scratches himself, mittens are tempting. The trouble: Sometimes they barely stay on for more than 30 seconds. The better alternative: Long-sleeved shirts like the ones your baby wears in the hospital. The sleeves fold over your baby's hands.

> 🔒 TOP SECRET! Receiving blankets can be cumbersome. They're too big to be used as burp cloths and too small to swaddle the baby. If you have blankets and changing pads, these may just end up in the dresser drawer.

8. Nix the baby food processor. If you already have a food processor, you really don't need another one just for your baby.

9. A video baby monitor is not really a must. The picture quality of these isn't great, and all you really need to do is hear your baby.

10. Your child may be Einstein—but a DVD series won't help. It's no surprise that watching Baby Einstein DVDs won't turn your child into a genius. She won't become a connoisseur of classical music or fine art either. Disney admitted as much when the company offered refunds on the videos and DVDs. Instead, try reading, singing, talking, and playing with your baby.

11. Shopping cart covers are just another thing to carry around. As germ-laden as shopping carts are, there's no evidence that a cover will protect your kid from getting sick. If you're worried about germs, like most of us are, wash your baby's hands often and use a baby wipe to clean your cart.

12. Unless you are an incredibly organized person, you probably won't have any use for a diaper caddy.

13. A good diaper bag is worth it. This will be your home-away-from home station for everything you need from bottles to wipes to medicine to toys. Oh, and diapers!

SOURCE: Dina El Nabli from ReadersDigest.com

Great Advice

5 SMART USES FOR BABY WIPE CONTAINERS

1. Organize your stuff. Fill washed and dried containers with everything from sewing supplies, recipe cards, coupons, and craft and office supplies to small tools, photos, receipts, and bills. Label the contents with a marker on masking tape, and you're set!

2. Make a first-aid kit. Gather up your own choice of essentials, such as bandages, sterile gauze rolls and pads, adhesive tape, scissors, and triple-antibiotic ointment, and use a rectangular baby wipes container to hold it all. Before you add your supplies, give the container a good washing—and rub the inside with alcohol on a cotton ball after it dries.

3. Use as a decorative yarn or twine dispenser. A clean cylindrical wipes container makes a perfect dispenser for a roll of yarn or twine. Simply remove the container's cover, insert the roll, and thread it through the slot in the lid, then reattach the cover. Paint or paper over the container to give it a more decorative look.

4. Store your plastic shopping bags. Do you save plastic shopping bags for lining small wastebaskets (or perhaps for pooper-scooper duty)? If so, bring order to the puffed-up chaos they create by storing the bags in cleaned, rectangular wipes containers. Each container can hold 40 to 50 bags—once you squeeze the air out of them.

5. Hold workshop towels or rags. A used baby wipes container can be a welcome addition in the workshop for storing rags and paper towels—and to keep a steady supply on hand as needed. You can easily keep a full roll of detached paper towels or six or seven good-sized rags in each container.

WHAT YOUR SHOE SALESMAN WON'T TELL YOU

These secrets make shoe shopping—and wearing—far less painful for everyone.

1. I may be kneeling at your feet, but I'm not your servant. Lose the 'tude, dude.

2. No one cares how big your feet are. Don't ask for a size 7 if you're a 9 (though we all appreciate a little foot powder, if it's not too much trouble).

3. There's more to measuring than you think. Shoes should be as wide as your feet and longer than your feet. It's not just the distance from the heel to the end of the big toe that matters. It's also the distance from the heel to the ball of the foot.

4. Please don't try on two different sizes and slip one shoe from each size into the box you're buying without telling me. A lot of people have feet that are a half or whole size different. Let me know if you're one of them up front.

5. Don't try on sample shoes if they're not your size. People smash their feet into shoes that are three sizes too small, and then I have sample shoes that have been stretched.

6. Please don't keep me waiting for ten minutes while you talk on your cell phone. What if I did that to you?

7. If we don't have exactly what you want, it may not exist. And I can't cobble it together in the back room while you wait either.

8. Leather shoes will stretch, so keep that in mind when you're buying them. If they're a little too tight you can probably break them in, but if they're really tight, they're not the right shoes for you, no matter what we say when we're pitching them to you.

🔒 **TOP SECRET!** Take our word for it if we tell you that a shoe isn't a good fit. Customers have been known to try on a shoe that's too small, and then they can't get it off.

9. There's a name for the metal gauge that measures the width and length of your feet. It's called a Brannock Device. Tell your kids it should stay flat on the floor and not go hurtling through the air toward my head. Many thanks.

10. Don't be a serial shoe returner. Once or twice, okay. But ten or twenty times a year? I don't think so.

11. I've spent thirty minutes with you, and then you tell me you need to get your wife's approval? News flash: She doesn't need yours. Next time, bring her along.

12. You get what you pay for. A $20 shoe isn't going to feel— or last—like a $120 shoe.

13. Do you really want to borrow one of the store's footies to try on shoes? The ones in that box? The ones that everyone in town has used? The ones that haven't been washed since I started working here? (I didn't think so.)

SOURCES: Shoe salespeople in New York, Texas, Pennsylvania, and Georgia.

Great Advice

12 SNEAKY TRICKS SHOPPERS SHOULDN'T FALL FOR

There are a lot of scams out there, but there are also a lot of ways to save money at your local shops and service stores. Spotting—and avoiding—these tactics will help you find real values and stave off buyer's remorse.

1. Don't fall for prices ending in 9, 99, or 95. These so-called charm prices make us think they reflect good deals, author William Poundstone tells Sonya Sobieski of *Psychology Today*. We also tend to round them down, reading a price like $5.99 as $5, a phenomenon known as the left-digit effect. Poundstone—the author of *Priceless: The Myth of Fair Value (and How to Take Advantage of It)*—also notes that markdowns don't often include these magic numbers. That's because when the discount is easy to calculate, we think it's a better bargain. Thus "Originally $20, now $15" works better than "Originally $20, now $13.97." You'll be more tempted to go with the former, even though the latter saves you more.

2. Steer clear of 99-cent stores. Not only are they loaded with charm-priced items, obviously, but they have a profit margin twice that of Walmart, Poundstone reveals. One exception: if you live alone or have a small family, reports shopsmartmag.org. These stores often sell pint-size packages of food, allowing those who consume less to avoid waste.

3. You can expect to pay a premium if you're a lazy shopper. From Dairy Queen to Starbucks, many food retailers have begun selling mini-size treats at prices that hardly make them a good value, notes *USA Today*. They know that many people would rather be seen as virtuous—eating fewer calories than a normal portion contains—than thrifty and that they're willing to spend more if they don't have to actually dole out those portions themselves.

4. Note the missing dollar signs. According to a Cornell University study quoted at cbsmoneywatch.com, diners spent much less when menus used the word dollars or the dollar sign than when only numerals were used to indicate price.

5. Know you're being tracked. If you use a store loyalty card, your buying habits are being recorded and often used to lure you to buy more. According to the *New York Times*, retailers these days are successfully tricking consumers into spending more by determining their spending "sweet spot," based on previous purchases. So three 12-packs of Pepsi are marked at $12.99 at Stop & Shop because the grocer knows you'll buy at that price, even if you don't need it.

6. Understand how certain phrases are used by retailers. "For a limited time only" creates a sense of urgency, Yale marketing professor Ravi Dhar tells mainstreet.com. And retail analyst Amy Noblin theorizes in *USA Today* that the come-on "Buy one, get one 50 percent off" incites more people to buy than if the sign reads simply "25 percent off everything."

7. See per-customer limits for what they are: a ploy. As Vicki Morwitz of New York University's Stern School of Business explains to cbsmoneywatch.com, "[People] think, 'Oh, this is scarce, I should buy this,' when it's probably not."

8. Beware new packaging. Check the ounces on that newly packaged bottle of your shampoo, and you may find you're paying the same for less, says Poundstone. One way manufacturers hide this? A big dimple in the bottom of the container.

9. Watch out for bogus "bargains." If a retailer displays a cut-rate model that's clearly inferior to the one he wants you to buy, he's trying to influence you, says Poundstone.

10. Look at what's displayed with what. Research has turned up some very specific data on product adjacency that retailers use to get you to buy more, writes Martin Lindstrom in his book, *Brandwashed: Tricks Companies Use to Manipulate Our Minds and Persuade Us to Buy*. If you see prepaid calling cards set up next to the coconuts, assume it's for a reason. One grocery chain found that buyers of the former tended to buy the latter (because people who cook with coconuts tend to be from Asia or the Caribbean).

11. Don't try on clothes you don't need. A shopper who stops to chat with a store employee and tries something on is twice as likely to buy as a shopper who does neither, Paco Underhill, author of *Why We Buy: The Science of Shopping*, tells time.com.

12. If you're a guy, shop alone. According to a *Journal of Marketing Research* study reported by money.com, a full 56 percent of men shell out more if they hit the mall with a friend as compared with women, 4 percent of whom actually racked up bigger receipts when going solo. That's because when men shop, they like to show off their knowledge and status via their purchases.

WHAT YOUR FLORIST WON'T TELL YOU

Want to know the secret ways to get the freshest, cheapest blooms—and make them last? Here they are!

1. Sure, you can order flowers at 3 a.m. from 1-800-Flowers, FTD, or Teleflora. But they'll charge you an extra $15 and then just call us.

2. If you want more flowers for your money, find a florist in your recipient's town and call him directly. But it's harder than you think: Some florists in the yellow pages and at the top of your Google search are national businesses masquerading as local ones. They even buy local phone numbers. So make sure you look for a physical address in town.

3. Most flower shops restock on Monday mornings, so that's the time to place an order. Fridays and Saturdays are good days to ask what's on special.

4. Ask for a discount. We give one to senior citizens, professional groups, and customers we like.

5. Those stay-fresh packets really work. Our smartest customers ask for a bunch of them. Most of us will gladly give you extras. Out of preservative? Try this: one part 7UP, three parts water, and two or three drops of bleach. Do not use copper pennies.

6. Put away those scissors, which can crush the stem. Instead, use a sharp, non-serrated knife to cut a quarter of an inch off the bottom of stems, at an angle. While you're at it, cut off those leaves below the water line. They breed bacteria.

7. Change the water at least every other day.

8. Don't forget to wash the vase with soap when you change the water. Otherwise, the bacteria clinging to the sides will contaminate your new water.

9. How fresh is your rose? Look closely at the bottom of the blossom and see how many outside petals have been removed. The more ripped petals you see, the older it is.

10. How about thinking outside the box? Lots of women would love a vase filled with red tulips still in the bulb for Valentine's Day.

11. That cheap glass vase that came with your bouquet? Most of us will gladly recycle it if you return it.

12. Looking for a way to jazz up your red roses? Try pairing them with purple statice or heather. Or ask us: "What can you put in that that will really make her roses stand out?"

13. Believe it or not, weddings are not that profitable for most of us. This is primarily due to labor costs. But we're banking on your future business. Once we do a wedding for you and do it right, you're a customer for life.

SOURCES: Russ Schmitt of Schmitt's Florist in Louisville, Kentucky; Sharon McGukin, author of *Flowers of the Heart: A Bride's Guide to Choosing Flowers for Her Wedding*; Larry Novak of Novak's Flower Shoppe in Maple Heights, Ohio; Tina Stoecker of Designs of The Times in West Melbourne, Florida; Bob Wollam of Wollam Gardens, a commercial cut-flower farm in Northern Virginia plus florists in Atlanta, Cleveland, Louisville, and Florida.

Who Knew?

GET THE BIGGEST IMPACT FROM JUST A FEW BLOOMS

When you know how to choose flowers wisely and strategically place them—thanks to these tips from interior and floral designer Rebecca Cole—you don't need a whole florist's shop full of them.

Place bud vases in high traffic home areas—with even just a few flowers. Any decorative glass from the kitchen will do.

The kitchen table might be the best place for flowers, because it's where people gather.

For a contemporary look, group several vases together holding just one or two stems. If you're using your own container, be creative! Use champagne glasses, china pieces, or other items that fit the décor of the room.

Old water pitchers, antique teapots, classic urns, or even tattered clay pots make fascinating containers for a casually placed flower arrangement.

For an easy, elegant table decoration, set a series of crystal vases on a fabric runner. Place fresh flowers in each of the vases and surround them with greenery.

Float two or three blooms, such as open roses or gerbera daisies, in a favorite crystal bowl.

WHAT YOUR JEWELER WON'T TELL YOU

Use these rock-solid tips to figure out if a gemstone deal is too good to be true.

1. Think you got a great deal on that beautiful ruby? It may not be real. A number of jewelers nationwide have been caught selling "composite rubies," which are as much as 40 to 50 percent glass, for almost the price of the real thing.

2. A sure sign of poor craftsmanship: rough edges on the back of the piece. If it's not finished underneath, they've probably cut corners somewhere else.

3. If your favorite color is blue, I'm going to try to sell you the most expensive stone in that color, probably a sapphire. But many other stones—including spinel, tanzanite, and tourmaline—also come in blue. You just have to know to ask.

4. Seek out jewelers who are credentialed by the American Gem Society (americangemsociety.org), which holds them to a high standard of knowledge and a code of ethics.

5. When you tell me, "I never take it off," I can't help but think, *That's disgusting.* To leave it on when you clean the house, lotion up your hands . . . yuck. You should take it off.

6. Please don't lick or spit on your finger to get your ring off and then hand it to me.

7. If you're buying a diamond on a budget, don't get stuck on the clarity grade. You can come down several clarity grades and in most cases will see absolutely no difference with the naked eye, especially once it's set in a piece of jewelry.

8. Here's a word to watch for on that diamond's certification report: laser. If your diamond has a high clarity grade, but under "Comments" it says "laser path" or "laser," that means a laser beam was used to get rid of a flaw, and it should cost 15 to 40 percent less than an untreated diamond of the same grade.

> **TOP SECRET!** For some extra shine on your diamonds (as long as they're not fracture filled), spray a little Windex on them, then wipe it off. That's actually what a lot of jewelers use, even the ones who sell expensive cleaner.

9. If your jeweler tells you that none of his emeralds are treated in any way, he's probably either ill informed or dishonest. Almost all emeralds today are treated.

10. Clean your gems in warm water with a mild liquid detergent and a toothbrush.

11. Extended warranties from jewelry stores typically aren't worth the money. If you have a rider on your homeowner's insurance for your ring and it's lost, damaged, or stolen, or if a stone falls out, your policy will usually cover it.

12. The "60 or 70 percent off" sales you sometimes see? Not possible. There just isn't enough margin in what we sell that you can discount like that and run a business and pay your bills.

13. We like to say, "If you don't know your jewels, know your jeweler." It really does come down to trust.

SOURCES: John Henne, president of Henne Jewelers in Pittsburgh, Pennsylvania; Clayton Bromberg, president and CEO of Underwood Jewlers in Jacksonville, Florida; Antoinette Matlins, author of *Jewelry & Gems: The Buying Guide;* and gemologist Renee Newman, author of *Gem & Jewelry Pocket Guide.*

Who Knew?
CREATIVE WAYS TO
STORE YOUR JEWELRY

Avoid tangles and morning "where-is-it?" hassles with these solutions.

Egg cartons and ice-cube trays. The compartments of egg cartons and ice-cube trays are just the right size for keeping jewelry separated, organized, and visible. They are especially good for keeping pairs of earrings together; just line them up side by side in a drawer.

Padded coat hangers. Put necklaces and bracelets around the neck of the hanger, then use the padding to hold pierced earrings and pin-on brooches. You could color-code hangers to hold jewelry to go with a range of outfits.

A coat rack. Draping necklaces and bracelets from the hooks on a coat rack mounted on the wall next to your dressing table is a smart idea. For one thing, your baubles are there when you need them; for another, they can add a nice decorative touch to an expanse of bare wall.

Plastic pill organizers. Clean plastic pill bottles or organizers are a great solution for traveling. The compartments are small, see-through, and perfect for holding earrings, rings, brooches, and bracelets separately. No tangling and no rooting through everything to find what you want.

WHAT YOUR FUNERAL DIRECTOR WON'T TELL YOU

Here are more than a few money-saving secrets funeral directors aren't taking to the grave.

1. Go ahead and plan your funeral, but think twice before paying in advance. You risk losing everything if the funeral home goes out of business. Instead, keep your money in a pay-on-death account at your bank.

2. If you or your spouse is an honorably discharged veteran, burial is free at a Veterans Affairs National Cemetery. This includes the grave, vault, opening and closing, marker, and setting fee.

3. You can buy caskets that are just as nice as the ones in my showroom for thousands of dollars less online from Walmart, Costco, or straight from a manufacturer.

4. On a budget or concerned about the environment? Consider a rental casket.

5. Running a funeral home without a refrigerated holding room is like running a restaurant without a walk-in cooler. But many funeral homes don't offer one because they want you to pay for the more costly option: embalming. Most bodies can be presented very nicely without it if you have the viewing within a few days of death.

6. Some hard-sell phrases to be wary of: "Given your position in the community . . . ," "I'm sure you want what's best for your mother," and "Your mother had excellent taste. When she made arrangements for Aunt Nellie, this is what she chose."

7. "Protective" caskets with a rubber gasket? They don't stop decomposition. In fact, the moisture and gases they trap inside have caused caskets to explode.

> 🔒 TOP SECRET! If I try to sell you a package that I say will save you money, ask for the individual price list anyway. Our packages often include services you don't want or need.

8. If there's no low-cost casket in the display room, ask to see one anyway. Some funeral homes hide them in the basement or the boiler room.

9. Ask the crematory to return the ashes in a plain metal or plastic container—not a stamped temporary container. That's just a sleazy tactic to get you to purchase a more expensive urn.

10. Sure, you can store ashes in an urn or scatter them somewhere special, but nowadays you can also have them crushed into a real diamond, integrated into an underwater coral reef, or blasted into space.

11. Shop around. Prices at funeral homes vary wildly, with direct cremation costing $500 at one funeral home and $3,000 down the street. (Federal law requires that prices be provided over the phone.)

12. Yes, technically I am an undertaker or a mortician. But doesn't funeral director have a nicer ring to it?

13. Never trust a funeral director who says, "This is the last thing you can do for your loved one." Always bring another person with you, ideally someone who's not as emotionally attached to the deceased.

SOURCES: Funeral directors in Illinois, New Jersey, Tennessee, and Washington; funerals.org; and Joshua Slocum, executive director of the Funeral Consumers Alliance and coauthor of *Final Rights: Reclaiming the American Way of Death*.

Insider Expertise

THE GUERRILLA GUIDE TO GETTING GOOD CUSTOMER SERVICE

· ·

As costs balloon and paychecks shrink, customers are chasing value while merchants are chasing profits. Naturally there are some nasty collisions. But good service is, in the end, good business—and it's something both sides want.

Usually this means you need to weave your way through the automated labyrinth and talk to a real, live person. These strategies can get you there, but before you call, you need to ask yourself two questions: *Do I have a valid complaint? Am I expecting a reasonable solution?* If the answer to both questions is yes, you can use the tactics here to get satisfaction for almost any transaction.

Before you Begin

1. All valid complaints start the same way. You expect one outcome but get another. It's just like algebra class: x dollars = y service. If you're getting $\frac{1}{2}y$, then you should have to pay only $\frac{1}{2}x$. Or perhaps they can throw in z, where z is something you feel equals $\frac{1}{2}y$. It's a simple matter of balancing the equation.

2. Just how much time should you spend on the problem? Calculate your income as an hourly wage. If your time is worth $30 an hour, don't spend all day chasing down a $25 refund. Life is short. Hold times are long.

3. You may have to give customer service more than one shot. Concisely and calmly explain your problem. If the first rep is stuck on no, call back and get a different one.

How to Reach a Real Person

1. Push zero repeatedly, say "operator" or "agent," or simply stay on the line until the end of the options.

2. Gethuman.com lists hundreds of companies and the phone shortcuts to quickly reach someone.

3. Try the back door. Call sales, investor relations, or the main corporate headquarters line.

4. Select the Spanish-only option. You'll likely get a bilingual operator faster than an English-only agent.

5. Call from a friend's phone instead of the one registered to your account. In some companies, potential new customers leapfrog to the top of the queue.

6. Call the company's international customer-service number collect. Its incentive for keeping you on hold will drop dramatically.

Tried-and-True Tips for When You Need to Escalate Your Tactics

1. Dictate the Options

How to Do It: Begin the call by saying, "I have a situation that you are going to fix for me today." Clearly state in a sentence or two exactly what you want them to do for you. Have your options figured out. It may help to write them on an index card and keep it in front of you.

Why It Works: You set the tone and expectations from the outset. You'll skip the "if" of helping you and get right to the "how." You'll save time, and not just for yourself. Many call centers work on commission and incentives. It's a high-stress environment. The faster the rep completes his calls, the bigger his bonuses.

In the past, it wasn't unheard of for AOL reps to hang up on customers if they tried to cancel their accounts. One insider revealed he took stress medications until he got acclimated to the job and its pressures. He became one of AOL's top guys when it came to convincing people not to cancel their accounts. His reward? Thousands of dollars a month in bonuses and an annual all-expenses-paid trip to Mexico. Not surprisingly, an AOL spokesperson says, "It is not our policy for representatives to achieve time targets by hanging up on customers. Such behavior could result in termination."

2. Threaten to Cancel

How to Do It: Tell the company that unless it solves your problem, you're taking your business to a competitor. It's helpful to cite the other company's enticing promotional offers. A deal-sealing phrase? "Give me a reason to stick around."

Why It Works: One study shows that if a business hangs on to an extra 5 percent of its customers, profits increase an average of 44 percent. In contrast, the cost of replacing you is five times the cost of making you happy. Some companies even have a special division—the "retention department"—with specialists trained to convince you not to leave, even if they must dangle credits and freebies in front of you.

3. Call the Executive Suite

How to Do It: It's a little-known secret, but many large companies like Bank of America, US Airways, Verizon, and Best Buy have a firewall of high-ranking customer-service personnel surrounding the executive offices. To reach them, find the number for corporate headquarters and the name of a top-ranking executive. The CEO works nicely. Call the main operator and ask in your most professional voice to be transferred to his or her office. Once there, quickly pitch your case to the assistant, who will likely hand you over to an elite squadron equipped with customer-service superpowers.

Why It Works: The job of the executive customer-service team is to solve all problems in their path. They like to make customers happy. They also like to keep you from bothering busy executives, complaining to regulatory agencies, and blabbing to the local news.

4. Launch an E-Mail Carpet Bomb

How to Do It: Figure out the company's e-mail address

format. It's usually something like firstname.lastname@ companyname.com. You can find sample e-mail addresses in company press releases and SEC filings (sec.gov). Next, find the names of a number of top executives, plug them into the formula, and blast your complaint letter to as many as you want. For a list of potential targets, check out the company at google.com/finance and look under Management. The About Us or Investor Relations sections of a company website are also good places to find a high-level executive roster.

Why It Works: A top executive understands he won't have a company if there are no customers. Perhaps he read the study in the *Journal of Marketing* that found the stock of companies scoring high on the American Customer Satisfaction Index outperforms the general market. Plus, he's a bigwig. If you can convince him your cause is just and he tells his people to fix your problem, it will get done.

5. Become a Town Crier

How to Do It: As a last resort, try typing up a one-page flyer telling your true tale of customer disservice. Make copies and take them with you to the store. Inform the manager that unless he gives you what you deserve, you will stand outside the store and distribute flyers to anyone and everyone who walks by.

Why It Works: Now that it has your money, a store can afford to lose your business. But what about the business of the next ten customers?

Warning

These techniques are recommended only for sane people who can speak in reasonable tones and treat strangers like humans. Threatening an individual may result in a visit from the police. Causing a company to lose money may result in a lawsuit. The right to free speech does not exist on private property and may have to be exercised just beyond the owner's property line, which usually extends from the edge of the store to where the sidewalk meets the asphalt.

And know this: One year, Sprint fired 1,000 "professional" customers (that's right—customers). Some had called customer service dozens of times over six months, begging for credits. "These were the customers who had nothing better to do but call us every single day demanding credit," one insider revealed. "And they were getting it because customer care was exhausted from arguing with them. At the end of the year, we were literally paying these customers to use our service." You want to stand up for your rights, but there is a limit. When you break it all down, these professional customers were probably spending more in "time dollars" than they got back in credits.

Part Six

WHAT YOU DON'T KNOW ABOUT
THE MEDIA

Starting to get suspicious about the seemingly perfect "reality" of reality TV? Questioning your social media presence both personally and professionally? The media itself is a whirlwind of overall distortion, making you believe whatever they want you to. And guess what, it kind of works. We are all guilty of falling into its trap. We want to save money but get caught up in deal-hunting and buy more coupons than we could ever hope to redeem; we crave the foods the chefs make on TV so we buy specific brands and spruce up our kitchen; we post all our positivity on social media in hopes of proving to other people that we are living our lives to the fullest.

Well, in this section, we open up and tear apart the façade of the media and explore what they don't want us to know. And maybe, just maybe, we can learn something valuable about the role modern media plays in our lives.

WHAT YOUR TV WEATHERMAN WON'T TELL YOU

It's not all sunshine and rainbows.

1. In many cases, the meteorologist is the highest-paid person on the broadcast because weather is one of the top reasons people watch local news. That's probably why the stations with the best weather people usually have the best ratings.

2. Looks do matter when it comes to TV weather. I've been told to trim my eyebrows and wear more makeup. (Yes, men and women both wear makeup on TV—lots of it!)

3. Bad weather is good for ratings. Really good. When there's a big storm coming, some TV stations will get three or four times as many people watching as normal. Our news directors love it.

4. The hurricane season forecasts that come out every year predicting the year's storm activity are almost always wrong. Even I was surprised when I realized how inaccurate they are.

5. Once you're under a severe weather "warning," assume it's going to happen. Unlike a "watch," a National Weather Service warning means the dangerous weather likely already exists, and you should take action immediately.

6. There's no legal definition of a meteorologist, so anybody can call him- or herself one and get away with it. Try to get your weather from someone certified by the American Meteorological Society—it just takes a quick Google search.

7. We're not very good at predicting summer showers and thunderstorms, because they're so small. It can be sunny all day a mile away from you, but you get rain.

8. The dew point—not the relative humidity—is the best measure of how humid it feels outside. When it's raining, for example, you can have 100 percent humidity, but it may not feel sticky. Yet anytime the dew point is over 65 degrees, it will feel humid. And if it's at 75, that means it's very wet out there.

9. Summer forecasting is a breeze compared with winter reporting. The toughest question: Is it going to snow? Unlike warm weather predictions, if I'm off by one degree in the winter, it can mean the difference between rain, snow, and sleet.

10. Partly sunny is actually more gray than partly cloudy. Here's the scale from least to most sunny: cloudy, mostly cloudy or partly sunny, partly cloudy or mostly sunny, and then sunny or clear.

11. Don't take a shower during a thunderstorm. You can get struck by lightning due to metal plumbing, which conducts electricity.

12. Our long-range forecasts aren't very accurate. We're quite good at one to three days out and decent at five to seven days out.

13. Watch out for phrases like "Shocking forecasts to come" before commercial breaks, as we use the hype to get your attention.

SOURCES: Joe Murgo, chief meteorologist for WTAJ-TV in Altoona, Pennsylvania; Chuck Gaidica, a meteorologist in Detroit, Michigan; David Bernard, chief meteorologist at CBS Miami; Chris Maier, a meteorologist at the National Weather Service; AJ Jain, an energy meteorologist who blogs about the weather industry at freshaj.com; and weathermen in Michigan and Los Angeles.

Who Knew?

WHY ARE TV ADS SO LOUD?

....

We all have been knocked off the couch by a blaring commercial that came on right after a tender TV moment. How do advertisers always manage to break those sound barriers?

Advertisers like it noisy. Commercials crank every sound level to maximum volume in a bid to get your attention. "In commercials, everything is equally loud—the voices, the music, the sound effects," says Brian Cooley, editor-at-large at the technology review site cnet.com.

"The peak levels of commercials don't exceed the peak levels of programming," admits Spencer Critchley, a communications consultant in California. "But the experience is similar to having a spotlight shining in your eyes all the time versus a flashbulb go off every now and then." In other words, an entire commercial can be broadcast at the same level as an extra-loud (but fleeting) explosion on 24.

And contrast counts. If you're watching a tender moment unfold on a soap opera just before a raucous ad for a monster-truck rally, the spot will be startling—making an already loud commercial seem even louder.

To combat the problem, you can purchase a TV sound regulator for about $50. Unfortunately, many aren't compatible with HDTV or TiVo, but higher-tech relief is on the way. In Japan, some televisions now come with built-in technology that automatically balances sound levels, and the technology should appear stateside soon. For now, though, you'll have to strike a deal: Whoever wields the remote must also monitor the mute button.

WHAT LINKEDIN WANTS TO TELL YOU

In today's tech-savvy world, your LinkedIn profile needs to be sharp, crisp, and impressive to both potential employers and colleagues. Avoid the profile pitfalls that could easily sink your job prospects.

1. Don't skip the profile pic. Your photo is your virtual handshake, so upload a photo that aligns with your role as a professional but also makes you seem approachable. Professionals who include a profile photo receive up to 21 times more profile views. And remember to keep it professional. Unless you're a veterinarian, a photo with your cat is probably not the best choice.

2. Don't skimp on work history. Your LinkedIn profile will be viewed up to 29 times more often if you list more than one prior position, and visual aids can really help. Illustrate your unique professional story and achievements by adding visuals like pictures, compelling videos, and innovative presentations to your experience section.

3. Don't hide your skills. When writing about your past jobs, passion projects, volunteer gigs, and schooling, consider every experience in terms of the skills you gained, not just your position title. Be sure to highlight these skills on your profile. Having at least five relevant skills will help people connect you with opportunities.

4. Don't forget to brand yourself. To land that dream job in today's world, you've got to sell yourself, especially in your digital profile. That means having a customized public profile URL. When you created your LinkedIn profile, it probably had some ugly combination of letters, numbers, and backslashes that had no value for your personal branding. If you still have this, go in right now and update it to reflect your name.

5. Don't neglect keywords in your summary. Adding a summary of 40 words or more makes your LinkedIn profile more likely to turn up in a future employer's search. A good tip is to ensure your summary includes keywords and skills featured in desirable job descriptions for your field.

6. Don't ignore your profile. A strong, regularly updated LinkedIn profile can be your ticket to a variety of professional opportunities, from jobs and mentors to new business and volunteering. And if you don't already have a summary section, add one today to really sell yourself to potential connections. Also, check your grammar. Ask friends, family members, or former co-workers to proofread your writing to catch any careless errors.

7. Don't forget to add location. More than 30 percent of recruiters conduct advanced searches based on location, so the more details you have about where you live, the more likely it is that you'll be found and connected to your next opportunity.

8. Don't post anything political or controversial. This may seem obvious, but experts have seen many LinkedIn users take a political position on their page. LinkedIn is not the place to voice your political opinions or share personal pictures and/or videos.

9. LinkedIn is also not a dating site. Stay professional. So if you're looking for love, head to eHarmony or match.com.

10. Don't forget where and when you met someone. Once you've grown your LinkedIn network, it can be a bit daunting to remember every single person you've connected with via the site. Luckily, LinkedIn can help you recall the people in your network. In the Relationship section, in addition to telling you the date when you connected, LinkedIn allows you to write notes about your contact, including how you met, or to set reminders to "check in" at various intervals. These notes and reminders are only visible to you so the contact won't be able to see them.

11. Don't hesitate to ask for recommendations. If you don't have any recommendations, yet, don't be shy about asking colleagues for them. LinkedIn makes it easy, providing an "Ask to be recommended" link, where you can specify what you want to be recommended for, who you want to recommend you, and even write a personal message. Pick specific people. Don't just randomly ask all your contacts if they can recommend you.

> **TOP SECRET!** If you are sending an invitation to connect because you are interested in an opportunity, customize the invite with a short and to-the-point message.

12. Don't upload your whole resume. There are too many untrustworthy people and staffing firms out there that will download your resume, add it to their databases and even submit to their clients without your permission. Use your LinkedIn profile as a detailed overview that will generate enough interest to spark direct communication. Only then, after building rapport and learning more about the person, the opportunity, and the company, should you pass along your detailed credentials.

13. Remember to occasionally download your connections. After you've gone to all the trouble of building a large professional network, you don't want to risk losing everyone's contact info—they may know about an excellent opportunity for you; or you may know of a career opportunity for them. Or, they may work at company you're considering applying to and you'd like to contact them to learn more about their employer. To do this, click on Connections, then Settings (the gear icon), and on the next page, under Advanced Settings, you'll see a link to export your LinkedIn connections as a .CSV file.

SOURCES: Catherine Fisher, a San Francisco-based LinkedIn career expert; Larry Kim, a business contributor to Inc.com; Amanda Neiser, a Long Island-based recruiter and founder of Plum Placements, Inc.

WHAT FACEBOOK WON'T TELL YOU

What happens with your personal information, and who sees your private posts? Improve your experience with these tips from Facebook experts.

1. Want to know how much Facebook knows about you? Go to Account Settings in the Home menu and click "Download a copy of your Facebook data."

2. You may not want to share your updates and other personal information with the whole world, but we've kept the default setting as Public. It's better for us if you share more, and we're assuming that most of you aren't going to bother changing your privacy settings.

3. You may not see every post from your friends, and only a fraction of your friends may see yours. Facebook wants users to see posts that will keep them on longer, so it moves up the posts that are the most liked and commented on.

4. If you are signed in to Facebook, we track you while you surf the Internet. Anytime you visit a page that has a Facebook Like or Share button, we log that information.

5. If your posts are set to be Public, burglars can see your status updates and figure out when you're not in town. Insurance companies may also use posted information to raise a premium or deny a claim.

6. Posting big news like your engagement, the birth of a baby, or your acceptance to grad school? Facebook will know. We target those by using something called natural language processing, and then we make sure they stick around in your friends' news feeds until they log on.

7. It may work to your benefit for us to know a lot about you. For instance, if you Like the Gap Facebook page because you shop there, you'll appreciate it when a coupon pops up.

8. Not seeing enough posts from friends you care about—and too many from those you don't? Set your news feed to sort by Most Recent, rather than Top News. Then add your favorite people to your Close Friends list and unsubscribe from any friends whose updates you're not interesting in receiving.

9. We make money by selling ad space to companies that want to reach you. They give us demographics—the desired location, career, education level—and we put their ads on the pages of those who meet the criteria.

10. If you really want to make sure your friends see your important news you can pay a fee, around $7 to $10 a post, to move your update to the top of their news feeds.

11. Lots of users hate Timeline, but it's not going away anytime soon. It's a more effective way for people to share, it's visually appealing, and brands love it because it gives them a better platform to market their business.

12. You can limit your posts to Facebook friends who live in your city, those who went to your college, or those you work with. You can even choose to allow everyone to view a post except your boss. Click the arrow in the lower right-hand corner of the status update box, and you'll see all the options.

13. Never leave your computer while you're logged on to Facebook, especially if your coworkers have a sense of humor.

SOURCES: David Jacobs, consumer protection counsel at the Electronic Privacy Information Center in Washington, D.C.; Brittany Darwell, lead writer for insidefacebook.com; Justin Lafferty, coeditor at allfacebook.com; Cameron Camp, cyber security expert at ESET in San Diego; and a former Facebook employee.

Who Knew?

7 THINGS THAT COULD HAPPEN WHEN YOU QUIT SOCIAL MEDIA

Social media is glorious fun and a colossal time-suck, not to mention pretty darn addictive. Here's what happens when you pull the plug, even for a short hiatus.

1. You'll get more work done, and you'll do it faster.
When you don't have to worry about your devices buzzing left and right, you could find your productivity levels shooting through the roof. "The thing about social media is that it constantly interrupts us," says Joanne Cantor, PhD, professor emerita of communication at the University of Wisconsin-Madison and author of the book Conquer CyberOverload. "When we stop ourselves to check social media again and again, it really becomes another form of multitasking, and multitasking makes whatever you do take longer."

2. You'll get your creative juices flowing. If you find yourself stuck in a creative block, it might have something to do with your social media habits. Dr. Cantor says the key to an imaginative mind is taking breaks every now and then while you work with something other than social media, like taking a walk or daydreaming. "Having that social media in the background and calling to you and asking you things interferes with your creativity."

3. You might feel anxious at first. While the effects of quitting social media are generally positive in the long run, your immediate reaction may be one of stress and anxiety. These feelings are caused by a neurobiological withdrawal from the sense of being constantly connected. "If you're using social media addictively, which some people are, you have elevated levels of dopamine, so when you stop doing that, there is some withdrawal," says David Greenfield, PhD, assistant clinical professor of psychiatry at the University of Connecticut School of Medicine and founder of the Center for Internet and Technology Addiction. Luckily, these feelings usually do not persist beyond the first few days.

4. You'll feel less stressed. Because social media has become so easy to access anywhere and at any time, we often feel compelled to pay attention 24/7 to what is taking place on our newsfeeds and timelines. According to Greenfield, this impulse to be constantly aware of what's going on online leads to an increase in cortisol, the stress hormone. This heightened stress can bring along a whole slew of unfavorable effects on the brain, such as a reduced memory and an increased chance of depression. Staying away from social media makes you less prone to such a high level of cortisol, leaving you calmer and more focused.

5. You'll feel more self-assured. When we post on social media, we tend to share only the happy, exciting parts of our lives that we want others to see. This may seem harmless, but when we see only people at their best, it's easy to feel like we're falling behind by comparison. This tendency to negatively compare ourselves to those who we believe are superior is what psychologists call upward social comparison. "Let's say you're struggling to have a baby," says Mai-Ly Nguyen Steers, PhD, a postdoctoral fellow and lecturer at the University of Houston. "Normally, people wouldn't come up to you and say, 'Well, look at how amazing my baby is!' Whereas it kind of feels like that on social media."

6. You'll get more sleep. You take a quick minute to check one notification on Facebook before bed, when suddenly you realize you've been browsing, liking, and commenting long past your bedtime. Sound familiar? Dr. Greenfield says this has become a common habit for many people at night, often spending one to two hours scrolling through social media in bed. "Think about it: If you're doing that every day, that's 15 hours a week you spend just doing social media."

7. You'll strengthen your face-to-face relationships.
Sure, social media can be an excellent way to stay in touch with old friends or family from out of town, but cutting ties with the Internet can work wonders for your tangible friendships. Face-to-face interpersonal relationships are generally much stronger than those conducted solely online, and taking a breather from your social media accounts forces you to focus on these real-world interactions.

WHAT REALITY TV SHOW PRODUCERS WON'T TELL YOU

Want to know how to get on a reality TV show, and what to expect if you make it? Get ready to be disillusioned.

1. Reality TV is actually not, well... real. True, there's no script, but we have writers who craft plot lines, twisting and tweaking footage to create conflict and shape a story. Oh, and we redo things all the time. On *The Biggest Loser,* the contestants have to walk up to the scale about five times so the producer can capture all the angles on camera.

2. We're always trying to get as much talent as possible while spending as little money as possible. Ninety-nine percent of the people on reality TV get their expenses covered and maybe a daily stipend of $20 or $30, but that's it.

3. Yes, we often take different clips and edit them together to sound like one conversation, sometimes drastically changing the meaning. We can even create complete sentences from scratch. It's so common, we have a name for it: frankenbiting. If you see someone talking and then the camera cuts away to a shot of something else but you still hear their voice, that's likely frankenbiting.

4. In most competition shows, a clause in the contract says the producer—not the judges—has the final say in who's eliminated. The judges usually make the picks, but producers do step in occasionally and say, "This person is really good for the show; I don't want him kicked off just yet."

5. Compelled to redo your bathroom in a day after watching a DIYer do it on a reality show? Not so fast. Maybe we made it look like it took only 24 hours, but we actually had a professional crew working on it for two weeks. And the budget we gave was completely unrealistic.

6. Here's a tip for applying to be on a reality show: Talk about your weakness—whether you're terrified of snakes or you can't stand lawyers and salesmen. The producers love that stuff.

7. Anytime you have an "all-stars" version of a show, the players are almost always on the phone with each other beforehand making deals. But most of the stars are so shady, they break their alliances before the game even starts, so it's still interesting.

8. The big shows do an extensive background check on all prospective stars. We call friends and family members, conduct drug and STD tests, make you sit through endless interviews, and do psychological and physical examinations.

9. Not all reality shows are the same, and some are heavily staged. On *House Hunters*, some of the houses toured on camera were reportedly friends' homes that weren't even on the market. And for day-in-the-life shows about different occupations, many producers fake scenarios (like a tree falling on a logger) to add drama.

10. I once had a woman cast as a villain who turned out to be the nicest lady ever. As producer, I sat her down and said, "Listen, you were cast in this role. If you want to make good TV, if you want the series to come back and make more money next year, then you need to play along. If you don't, you're going to be cut out entirely." It worked.

11. The on-camera interviews are especially produced. You can nudge a cast member to think a certain way or tell them something that will change their tune.

12. The quickest way to judge the budget of a show? Location. If they're shooting outside in parks and on the street, they pretty much have no budget. To save money, I've shot things at my own house before.

13. You're seeing only a sliver of the action on that 42-minute episode you just watched. *The Biggest Loser,* for example, has 11 cameras running eight hours a day. That's 88 hours of footage a day, seven days a week. So we end up with 616 hours of video for just one week's episode, which allows us to create the story line we want.

SOURCES: Pascual Romero, a former reality-TV producer; Rob Cesternino, a two-time *Survivor* contestant who runs robhasawebsite.com; a reality-show assistant director; and a reality show producer.

WHAT TV CHEFS WON'T TELL YOU

We went behind the scenes to hear from your favorite chefs on TV to learn their dirtiest kitchen secrets. Goodness, greatness, great balls of fire!

1. Many TV chefs don't write or develop their own recipes. Some don't have time. Other are more focused on being on TV than on cooking, so they would rather pay someone else. And a few just don't know how.

2. No, that's not my real house or kitchen. In most cases, I'm cooking on a set in New York City or Los Angeles that gets packed up when we're done filming the season.

3. When a chef forgets to say something important, we have to do what's called a voice-over. That's when you're watching and all of a sudden, you don't see the chef's face. Instead, you see a close-up of the bowl or their hands and you hear them saying, "Now add a quarter teaspoon of cinnamon."

4. Obviously, we're not all going to sit around twiddling our thumbs waiting for a roast or a lasagna to cook. So there are people in a second kitchen behind the scenes cooking a bunch of versions of the same recipe so it will be ready to go at different stages. That's called a swap-out.

5. Sometimes, the dishes we taste are stone cold because of a swap-out. So we may be saying, "Mmm," but really it tastes awful. We just smile and stomach it.

6. Sure, we burn things. When that happens, we just make sure to pick it up with the charred side away from the camera, and we never flip it over.

7. Sorry, but we are not going to tell you how bad a recipe is for you. While more chefs are acknowledging that we have a responsibility to people's health, you're never going to see calorie counts when we're making chocolate cake.

8. This job is harder than it looks. Besides just cooking, you have to describe your method step-by-step, talk about different ingredients, and make eye contact with the camera.

> 🔒 TOP SECRET! Here's how to enhance just about any dish: Add some acidity. Whether from citrus fruits or vinegar, acidity wakes uo the palate and makes food pop.

9. Before I host a cooking segment, I go through every step of the recipe with the art director, prop stylist, and food stylist. They ensure I have every tool I need, they *mise en place*—or prepare and measure out—every ingredient, and they make the finished dish look gorgeous.

10. Please don't follow my recipes to the letter. A recipe should be a loose map to guide you, but since no two ingredients are exactly the same, you should be constantly tasting the dish and adapting as you go along.

11. Most chefs, especially big names, are not involved at all in deciding what they're cooking if they're invited to do a short on a morning show. They often don't even know what they're making until they get there.

12. We make mistakes, lots of them. Towels catch on fire. Food gets dropped on the floor. We get cut and burned. One chef actually had the words "All Clad" branded onto her wrist for weeks after touching a pan that was coming out of the oven.

13. The truth is, I have no clue what brand of ketchup I'm using. That's because we have a graphic artist whose job is to "Greek" brand name products by creating fake names and labels.

Great Advice

WHAT YOU REALLY NEED TO KNOW ABOUT YOUR KNIVES

Cutting board materials matter. Using a proper cutting board and hand washing your knives are absolutes; you're either doing it or you're not. Wood, bamboo, and plastic are better for your knives than composite boards; harder boards like glass, metal, stone, and ceramic will quickly destroy knives.

A sharp knife actually causes fewer cuts. The reason you cut yourself less with a sharp knife is because it takes less force to cut through anything. Sharp knives aren't scary—blunt ones that need loads of force and are liable to go anywhere are. Use the right tool for the job and use it the right way.

Proper cutting technique is easy to learn. Tuck your fingers under and use the knuckles as a guide for the knife. Watch your thumb too!

Choose a knife that works for you. The ultimate knife for your best friend may not be the right knife for you. If possible, cut with a knife before you buy it to see how it feels in your hands.

Don't use a knife for anything other than cutting food. As a general rule, if you wouldn't bite into it with your teeth, don't touch it with your chef's knife.

Don't use a steak knife for food preparation. Use a chef's knife or paring knife, even if these are the only two knives you own. In many households, the serrated steak knives are often the only sharp knives capable of cutting at all. (That's not a good thing.)

A serrated knife is not a saw. Most items can be cut in a nice slice with a single long draw of a serrated knife.

Keep your cutting area clear. Don't place any item on your cutting board that you don't want to be cut.

Don't toss knives into a sink. Sharp knives + bowls full of soapy water + unsuspecting hands = nasty surprise. Wash your knives after using, dry, and put away in a knife block, knife drawer insert, or secure magnetic rack.

A falling knife has no handle. Don't grab for it. Just let it go and watch your feet. Also, don't cook barefoot.

Skip the huge gift sets. You are better off buying a couple of really good knives than a huge block set of mediocre knives.

Safety first. Brace your cutting board with a kitchen towel for more stability.

The blade is for cutting, not corralling. Many people use the blade edge of a knife to corral the food to the edge of the board. Avoid that. Instead, turn it over and use the spine of the knife, which will keep the working edge sharp.

SOURCES: Adam Marr of Marr Knives; Christopher Miller, owner of Industri Café; Mark Richmond, owner, Chefknivestogo.com; Sebastians; Tom Bolton; Kenny Chan; and Mike Zollner of Zollners.blogspot.com.

WHAT **DEAL SITES** WON'T TELL YOU

Attention shoppers: You'll get the best bargains on daily deal sites by following these insider tips.

1. Sometimes the site will pay you. For example, you can get $10 for every friend you refer to a Groupon deal, for a maximum of $100 in Groupon Bucks.

2. Don't expect the best service. Restaurant staffs, for example, might treat you differently when you come in toting a deal, since they expect smaller tips or none at all.

3. The best deals may be outside your area. Scoping out bargains in other cities and states can pay off. Quite a few "local" deals from national chains (say, Starbucks) are valid all over the United States—just read the fine print to double-check.

4. Beware of overselling. If you see a great deal for a haircut but the site says thousands are available and the coupon expires in a month, it could be tough to redeem. No single salon can cut that much hair!

5. Keep track of expiration dates. No matter how great a deal is, it's not worth anything once it expires. As soon as you purchase a coupon, set a reminder alarm on your phone or computer calendar to go off a week before it expires.

6. Consider secondary markets. CoupRecoup and others like it provide a marketplace where buyers and sellers can trade coupons from various sites.

7. Do your homework. Some vouchers, particularly for travel packages, may be available for comparable prices—or even less!—on the vendor's own website.

TOP SECRET! Outlet stores likely sell special outlet merchandise, and it's not the deal you expect.

8. To get the best deals for you, personalize your account. On Groupon and similar sites, updating profile preferences gets you offers more suited to your interests. If you see a deal you like, click the heart icon, and similar options will be added to your mix.

9. You don't have to pay for vouchers in advance. Sites like Scoutmob offer 50-percent-off vouchers—free. You just have to "collect" the deal offered each day and have it sent to your phone or e-mail address.

10. You don't need to join all the sites to find the best deals. Save time with Yipit, which amasses more than 30,000 offers per month from over 800 sites, then filters them based on your location and interests.

11. Some sites are more discreet than others. At newcomer Savored, make a free reservation online and get special pricing (typically 30 percent off, alcohol included) at top restaurants across the nation. When the bill comes, no need to be embarrassed by coupons; the deductions are automatic. Just show your reservation receipt.

12. You can see the world on a shoestring budget. Sites like Priceline and hotels.com have excellent seasonal deals, but for nearly free travel accommodations, try house-swapping sites like Digsville, which serves over 55 countries.

13. You can save big on everyday items. For a small handling fee (about 5 to 50 cents per coupon), choose from thousands of deals on sites like Coupon Clippers. Reader's Digest tested the site, and our total outlay came to $6.64, including the cost of coupons, postage, and a 50-cent fee. The savings came to $61.75 when we redeemed the coupons at face value!

6 THINGS YOU SHOULD NEVER BUY USED

1. Bike or Motorcycle Helmets

Helmets are meant to protect you from one accident. Sometimes damage isn't visible, so you need to buy a new helmet to make sure you're getting all the protection you need.

2. Child Car Seats

A car seat that has been in an accident may not protect your child in another. Damaged car seats are common; about one in ten have been in an accident, found one survey conducted in England. Brand-new car seats can cost as little as $50, and safety technology improves each year. Don't risk your child's life.

3. Tires

If they've been in an accident, tires are likely to be unstable and unreliable.

4. Mattresses

With bedbugs infesting homes in record numbers, chances are the critters could lurk in any used mattress. You might also end up sleeping with other people's mold, mites, bacteria, and bodily fluids (yuck!).

5. Cribs

Scores of crib recalls, as well as changing safety standards, make it hard to verify the safety of a used crib.

6. Laptops

Laptops are more likely to be dropped, knocked around, and spilled on simply because they're out in the world, while a desktop computer sits (mostly) safe at home.

Insider Expertise

WHAT TO NEVER, EVER POST ON SOCIAL MEDIA

Personal information.

You're identity isn't as safe as you'd think.

1. Boarding pass. Bragging about your upcoming trip online might seem harmless, but snapping a photo of your boarding pass is a definite don't. Sure, your followers already know your name—and they might even know your destination—but according to Brian Krebs, author and founder of Krebsonsecurity.com, which specializes in investigative stories on cyber crime and computer security, other personal data is at risk. Your frequent flyer card and passenger name record (PNR) could be jeopardized with a social post. With a little finagling, hackers can access your earned miles, phone number, date of birth, and even passport data. Based on your booking number, criminals can also find out when you leave and return. Knowing that no one is home could entice burglars to break in while you're away.

2. Money. Posting photos of paychecks, credit cards, and wads of cash is just asking for trouble. Aside from being in poor taste, doing so increases the chances of you getting mugged. Also steer clear of photos (or captions) that give away financial information, such as the name of your bank.

3. Winning lotto tickets. If you're lucky enough to snag a winning lottery ticket, be smart enough not to brag. Sharing betting slips isn't a huge liability for small amounts, but, if they want to put in the effort, criminals can replicate the scannable bar code and steal your winnings.

4. Confidential work e-mails. It's a good rule of thumb to keep work off your social media, especially when it comes to confidential documents. While the National Labor Relations Act protect employees by allowing them to exercise your First Amendment rights and engage in speaking freely and truthfully about the workplace (even when their feedback is negative) there are limitations. If your company sent an exciting e-mail about a new development or branding idea, the last thing you want to do is let the competition know. Airing complaints—or posting photos of "venting" conversations between you and coworkers—isn't smart either. In fact, it's a sure way to get sacked.

5. Birth certificate. Posting identifying information on social media is equivalent to losing it—or giving it away. While snapshot of the birth certificate of your new bouncing baby might seem like a heart-warming announcement about a major life change, it can put your little one at risk for identity theft. According to the Identity Theft Resource Center, allowing this government document to fall into the hands of a stranger could do permanent damage. A birth certificate is considered the "bedrock identifying document" and can get you a new Social Security card, passport, and driver's license. Once someone has control of it, proactively preventing fraud is near impossible.

6. Work that isn't copyrighted. You might be proud of your writing, but posting a snap of the poem or short story you've written before publishing isn't the best idea—especially if you're looking to submit to a journal or enter a competition. Someone stealing your award-winning line might lead to a case of he-said, she-said when it comes to who originally created the work. Even if your writing only has sentimental value—and isn't exactly Pulitzer worthy—posting it online makes it easy for people to copy, paste, and claim. Keep your wise words to yourself until they've been copyrighted and then have your fans buy the book instead.

Your children.

What's so risky about posting smiling, finger-painting photos of your kids on social media? Surprisingly, a lot. Here's what not to post to keep your kids safe.

1. Your location. It might just be a picture of your child saying "cheese" in front of your home, but posting photos of your private property can make privileged information public. Street signs, house numbers, and apartment addresses might seem like harmless background scenery, but once you post that picture, it could get around, making your child vulnerable to identity theft, digital kidnapping, where strangers lift the images and pretend the children are their own, or even actual kidnapping.

2. Personal identifiers. Your kid is holding up a hand-written sign on her birthday that says "I'm 6 today" in adorable letters. No big deal, right? Actually, giving away information such as your child's birth date or place of birth and full name isn't ideal, as those identifiers are used to reference many private accounts. You might think that a well-taken passport photo really capture your kiddo's smile and baby curls, or be so filled with exuberance that your new driver passed the road test that you snap a congratulatory photo of his or her license. Before you post to social, take a step back and think of the information you're giving away.

3. Any state of undress. Babies splashing around during bath time are definitely adorable, but posting photos of your children in any state of undress—even a teeny bikini—isn't smart. As sad as it is to imagine, these photos could fall into the wrong hands and be accessible to online predators. "Think of your kids as autonomous people who are entitled to protection not only from physical harm but intangible harm as well," says Stacey Steinberg, a legal skills professor at the University of Florida Levin College of Law in Gainesville, Florida, and associate director for the Center on Children and Families. Definitely avoid posting photos of other people's kids without their permission.

4. Vulnerability and embarrassing moments. Posting a photo of your sick child might garner comments and compassion on social media, but consider how it could affect your child. What you consider a moment to cherish—and post—might be embarrassing to them. The next time your kid's in bed with a runny nose, being brave while getting a shot at the doctor's office, or sitting in a hospital gown, consider this question before you snap: "Would your child want to see this photo of themselves online in the future?" Same goes for "milestones" like using the potty for the first time, getting her period, or having a first kiss. Keep moments that might make your child blush from embarrassment offline and in the family scrapbook.

5. Behavior struggles. Social media isn't for child shaming. Whether it's an issue of wetting the bed or trouble learning to read, taking a photo and captioning it in a way that highlights your child's difficulties can be problematic. Exposing their weakness could open the door to teasing and bullying—and introduce labels that could stick. "It's important we invite older children into the conversation of what should or shouldn't be shared," Steinberg says. "We should ask them if something might be embarrassing."

6. Poor grades. Shaming your child online by posting that report card "F" is not smart. While it's understandable to reach out and ask for help, social media is not the place to do it. Not only will you be crowdsourcing advice—much of which might not be sound and is better reserved for a parent-teacher conference—but it could potentially come back to hurt your child. According to the online recruitment site Career Builder, roughly a fifth of employers use social networking sites to research job candidates. More importantly, nearly 59 percent say they would be influenced by a candidate's online presence. Don't start your child off in the red.

Yourself.

But it's your page, right? Wrong. The Internet is ultimately an open tundra and your page is a platform for you to be judged, examined, and criticized. Always tread lightly.

1. Gifts you've received, but didn't like. Whether it's your birthday or a holiday, it's important to exercise gratitude instead of rolling your eyes or complaining when you don't like your present. Even if you had hoped your partner would have bought you something different or you're annoyed your mom knitted you yet another sweater you'll never wear, it's better to keep it offline and remember the value of family instead of the value of what was under the tree. "Do not post petty comments about gifts you didn't like or who was cheap in your family," says author and family and couple therapist, Deb Castaldo, PhD. "Those types of comments, even if you don't name names, can be very hurtful and provide the fuel for more family conflicts."

2. Bragging. While it might have been cool to compare notes about your latest Barbie Dreamhouse or rad bicycle you got when you were a kid, as an adult, sharing your extravagance and thus, privilege, with the world isn't flattering. In fact, it could make you appear to be selfish and ungrateful for the blessings you've been bestowed or the luxuries you can afford to give to your family. "It can be fun to talk about what you're going to buy your kids, partner or friends, especially when it's extravagant, but remember others are not as fortunate as you and it can be a reminder of the overdue mortgage, living paycheck to paycheck, and what won't be under the tree this year. Be grateful and enjoy what you have, yet be sensitive to others lack of," says Sarah Mandel, RN, LCSW. Another reason to keep those gifts off online? You run the risk of grabbing the attention of criminals, Mandel adds. "Tweeting or posting photos of your extravagant gifts can be an invitation for robbery. This is the time of year when crime is up and thieves look for that new 55-inch flat screen TV or new loaded laptop to steal," she says.

3. Drama within your family. All families have secrets and you're bound to not like every single person you're related to. But if you want to bash your cousin or reveal some drama about an estranged great aunt, you might only create a giant elephant that'll be felt across the dinner table. "Social media is not a place to resolve family conflict. In fact, social media could create more conflict or hurt feelings. It may create a divide among other family members or friends who know your family members. It may also ruin an enjoyable family event since a majority of your other family is also on social media. Even if you make a message private, remember that others could see it if a mutual friend is tagged in the post or if a mutual friend shows someone else your post," Geter says.

4. Your political viewpoints during the holidays. Regardless of who you voted for, try to let political viewpoints and discussions pause during the holiday season. As it's a time to celebrate, focus on your families and being of service to those in need, instead. "The holidays can be a time of peace for all, to bring our country together in celebration, and create a celebration toward our futures," says Dawn Michael. "So if you are wanting to continue the negative feeling about the election, take a break and keep the holiday spirit positive and joyful," she advises.

5. Anything that puts down other religions. With constant religious celebrations around the world, it might be tough to keep up with which of your friends celebrates which special day. And vice versa: those you might not know so well could wish you the wrong "happy" or "merry," but this isn't the time to dismiss their likely well-intentioned gesture. "Don't get offended if someone wishes you a 'Happy Hanukkah' and you keep 'Christ in Christmas,'" Mandel says. "The bottom line is that these are all well wishes with good intentions unless someone tries to proselytize and pressure you into believing their religious beliefs. It can be difficult to keep up with the many holidays we celebrate in this country but don't let the pressure of being PC keep you from enjoying your traditions."

6. Anything you wouldn't want your boss to see. Even if you keep your profiles on strict lockdown and have privacy settings, friends-of-friends could still see and possibly say something to your employer. Learning to censor yourself when you've had a few too many evening cocktails or want to declare why you deserve a better job is a smart move. "We have become so comfortable with the internet that we often forget that the whole world has access to our posts. And yes, photos can be copied before you know what hit you," Dr. Castaldo says. "You may want to be a viral social media superstar, but do you really want to end up there because your photo was captured while you were in a drunken stupor?"

7. A bunch of selfies. What's way more attractive than filtering away that zit on your chin from one-too-many peanut butter cookies or posing with your hand on your hip in front of your tree? Taking a photo with those you love the most and capturing the magic, love in the air between your family. Dr. Castaldo says we should focus on sharing more group shots in general, but especially in a time when gathering together is celebrated and made a priority. "Although many people are now addicted to posting their best staged selfies and photos of perfect meals and home decor, relieve yourself of the pressure of keeping up. How about switching it up and posting what really matters: a group shot of you and your loved ones enjoying each other's company," she says.

8. Always being online. Less than a decade ago, having your phone handy while sitting at the dinner table would have seemed the height of rudeness. As much as you can, stay focused on the moment so you can truly experience time with cherished company. "Yes it is fun to share the excitement of social gatherings on social media. So go ahead and post your fun times and meals. But keep it to a minimum and just remember your social media posts are now part of your permanent personal and professional 'resume' and a snapshot into you values, morals, and relationships," Dr. Castaldo says. She suggests an experiment: Put your device away at your next shindig and see what fun you can have connecting in real time with your loved ones!

Your relationship.

A relationship is between two people for a reason. Not for your 1,000 Facebook friends or 600 Instagram followers.

1. A fight with your significant other. OK, OK, so your husband had one job and one job only—to pick up the dry cleaning—and he forgot, and now you're scrambling to find another alternative before your event. As tempting as it is to update your status with a snide meme about husbands or a sarcastic post that degrades men, Courtney Geter, marriage, sex and family therapist, says to take a deep breath and refrain for the sake of both your relationship and your community. "Oftentimes, we go to social media to get support from our friends or family. However, the fight you had with your significant other was not witnessed by anyone else. When you reach out, your friends are going to be biased toward you and want to support you. Although their intentions are to help you and make things better, it could create more tension in your relationship. Also, if your friends are mutual friends with your significant other, they may feel divided in wanting to support you but not ruin a relationship with your SO," she says.

2. Your breakup. Spare everyone the gory details, which are more than likely to be TMI or sour grapes. If you and your partner break up, the emotional mess is enough to clean up without having to field comments and advice from the online peanut gallery. "Keep it simple. If it's over, it's over," Spira says. "Posting about how you got dumped shouldn't be public knowledge. Just change your relationship status to 'Single' when and if you call it quits to signal that you're on the market again. Keep the vicious details to yourself."

3. Scandalous pics of your partner. Sexting can be a fun way to entice your partner when they've been stressed out at work or you've both been too busy for intimacy, but those images are never meant to go beyond your shared blue bubbles. As psychotherapist and relationship expert, Sarah Mandel, RN, LCSW notes, there's a lot of trust built between couples who share racy photos, and breaking that is dangerous for the longevity of your relationship. Not to mention that your friends would likely want you to keep it to yourself. "Your partner may be hot, but that doesn't give you the permission to post private pics of him or her for the world to see," Mandel says. "Keep this part of your relationship between the two of you and in the bedroom."

4. Photos of others without checking first. While it's definitely the age of sharing each and every little thing that we do, from selfies in bed with coffee to what you ate for brunch, the only person you truly have permission to share a photo of is yourself. More often than not, your family members and hometown friends won't mind if you share a (ahem, flattering) photo of them, it's always a good idea to check first. "Just like some parents prefer not to post pictures of their children online or prefer to monitor which photos are posted online, some adults also don't want their lives made public," Geter says. "Although you might want to share the memories of your family event with others, check first with others in the photo before tagging them or even posting the picture. If someone knows the picture will be posted online and made public, they may choose to opt out and take a private photo with you later."

5. Your ultrasound. First comes love, then comes marriage, then comes the creative, new way you'll announce your pregnancy on Facebook. While OB-GYNs often suggest waiting until your second trimester to share the happy news with friends and relatives because your risk of miscarriage is lower, updating your social media accounts with an ultrasound might be taking your photo albums too far. The blurry, almost-alien like photo might be the cutest, most amazing image you've ever seen, but your followers might find it awkward. "It's great that you're announcing you're pregnant, but do you have to post a photo of your unborn baby on social media? It violates my 'Rules of Netiquette' as something that makes some people uncomfortable," says Julia Spira, cyber dating expert and author of *The Rules of Netiquette: How to Mind Your Digital Manners*. "While many will toast to your new relationship status, we don't need to see every detail of your doctor's appointments."

Part Seven

WHAT YOU DON'T KNOW ABOUT
YOUR MONEY

Get rich quicker? Be a smarter saver? There are tons of tricks that will help you hold onto your money and even multiply it when you're on the insider track. Find out why your bank is pushing you to open new accounts and what to turn down when your cell phone sales rep is pressuring you. Arm yourself to outsmart identity thieves—which we've made easier to do by interviewing people who've been convicted for that very thing. Absorb all this advice, and you'll get more of what you never have enough of: time and money.

In this part, you'll discover everything from the secrets of debt collectors all the way to what rich people know about saving money. Finances will be a snap once you discover everything they do!

WHAT YOUR BANKER WON'T TELL YOU

What you don't know about your bank can result in extra fees, extra hassles, and less protection against identity theft. We got bankers to open the vault and share their secrets.

1. It takes us three days to post checks to your account. Just because you deposited a check today doesn't mean you can start living it up tomorrow. (And why should we hurry? If you bounce a check, we collect around $40.)

TOP SECRET! Banks don't always promote the accounts that have the highest interest rates. Why tell you about those when you're already willing to sign up for an account that pays less?

2. Call or visit in person to resolve a problem. Filling out online forms will usually get you the by-the-book reply, but with a rep, you can get practically any fee waived if you ask.

3. Small business loans are hard to get. Unless you're Wolfgang Puck, our loan officers have pretty much decided before you walk in that you're not getting a loan for your dream bistro. But they'll let you apply for one anyway. We're not crazy about lending to nonprofits and houses of worship, either. We don't want the bad publicity when we go after them.

4. Our tellers routinely press you into opening new accounts. Their jobs depend on it. Banks hire "mystery" customers who secretly test whether a teller is cross-selling services.

5. There are times when we help you out. Many banks will permit you to withdraw more money than you have on deposit at the ATM, but they'll charge you about $34 for the privilege.

6. Postdating a check rarely works. With stacks to process, we don't look at dates. If the check bounces, you're liable.

7. Please don't haul in plastic bags of loose change. We really don't have the time or manpower to count it.

8. Keep receipts for every ATM transaction. And please don't feed cash directly into the machine without first putting it into an envelope unless you are sure the ATM can handle it.

9. We know you hate itemized penalties, such as a bounced-check fee, but don't leave money in your checking at the expense of your savings account. Personal-finance writer Jason Zweig says, "Banks make a ton of money off this mental quirk since they would have to pay interest on the money if we left it in our savings accounts."

10. A bank has the right to pay itself back. Any fees that you owe can be deducted from your next deposit.

11. Online banking is pretty safe. But it could be better, according to researchers at the University of Michigan. They found design flaws such as banks redirecting users to less-secure sites.

12. Your ATM card isn't as secure as your credit card. If you're using your ATM card for debit transactions, ask your bank what kind of protection it offers if the card is stolen or lost.

13. Don't swallow the poison. If a bank-issued credit card has a universal default clause, run for the nearest exit. It allows the bank to look through all your credit accounts, and if it sees that you're late paying a bill on another card, it gets to jack up the interest rate on its card.

SOURCES: David Bach, author of *Fight for Your Money*; Jean Ann Fox, director of financial services, Consumer Federation of America; Jason Zweig, author of *Your Money & Your Brain*; anonymous bank employees in New York, Ohio, and Texas.

Great Advice
5 COMMON MISTAKES PEOPLE MAKE WITH THEIR MONEY

....

Even the savviest of savers sometimes overlook ways to keep and protect more of what they earn each year. Here are a few common errors from money.cnn.com and *Money* magazine that you can steer clear of so you're not one of the clueless.

1. Failing to Check Credit

Everyone is entitled to one free credit report a year from each of the three major bureaus (Experian, TransUnion, and Equifax), yet John Ulzheimer of smartcredit.com tells *Money* that only 4 percent of those reports are claimed. Discovering errors could prevent you from paying too much for a loan or being denied a credit card or even a job.

2. Missing College Aid

According to Mark Kantrowitz, publisher of finaid.org, a lot of people don't realize that if they applied for financial aid and were denied it for their first child, they can reapply and perhaps qualify once their second is ready for college. Missing the boat for aid and scholarships is another common mistake—different schools have different deadlines. To make sure you leave nothing on the table, reapply for aid annually, and start researching scholarships in the fall before your child enters college.

3. Avoiding a Trust

If you assume that trusts are only for the wealthy, you assume wrong. Even if you don't have millions to bequeath, you can benefit from a revocable living trust, which will save your heirs time and money by keeping your assets out of probate. Once your lawyer sets up a trust, don't forget to transfer title of assets into it, says Justin Fulton, a financial advisor with Signature in Norfolk, Virginia.

4. Skipping Tax Implications

Investment gains are great, but they'll be reduced by the amount of your tax bracket, so they should be managed carefully, says Frank Armstrong, CEO and founder of advisory firm Investor Solutions. You can also offset capital gains by reviewing your portfolio in the fall and dumping any losers before year's end. By selling them for less than you paid, you can then deduct the loss from your capital gains to lower your taxable earnings.

5. Investing with Insurance

Beware of buying cash-value life insurance policies for retirement funding. While the tax-deferred saving feature might be tempting, the steep fees can eat away at so much of your returns that it may make more sense to invest the money on your own, says insurance consultant Glenn Daily.

WHAT YOUR CREDIT CARD COMPANIES WON'T TELL YOU

Those terms and conditions don't say it all.

1. You can charge your way to a better credit score. A person with no history is often considered the same as someone with poor credit, says Jacob MacDonald from Consolidated Credit Counseling Services of Canada.

2. Many companies offer extended warranties on merchandise—such as that new flat screen—for up to a year beyond the manufacturer's guarantee. Restrictions may apply, so call your card provider to find out about exclusions.

3. Keep an eye on sales. Your provider might offer a price protection policy: if you buy an item at full ticket value and it goes on sale within 60 days, you may get reimbursed for the difference by your credit card company. You'll need proof of purchase and a record of the new price.

4. Put your negotiation skills to use. If you're having trouble making payments, ask about having your interest rate reduced. But do your homework first: compare your card with others so that you're armed with a bargaining chip.

5. The key to sitting front row at Cher's next farewell tour might be in your wallet. Credit card companies often have pre-sale deals on tickets to events—from concerts to sports matches. You might have to upgrade to a higher limit or status (along with an annual fee), but the savings could be worth it.

6. Swipe cautiously. In 2008, an American study revealed that buyers were more likely to spend—or overspend—on luxuries when using credit or gift cards rather than cash. Shoppers have a harder time perceiving purchases on plastic as real money spent.

7. Access to credit gives our brains a buzz. Peter C. Whybrow, the director of the Semel Institute for Neuroscience and Human Behavior at UCLA, suggests thinking about the reasons why you're shopping—and ensuring you're not doing it just because it feels good—to avoid spending impulses.

8 Frequently missing payment deadlines? Avoid late penalties by arranging to have your balance settled automatically every month. Call your bank or check online to set up the service.

9. Each company offers different benefits, so you may get perks—like preferred rates or rewards—by switching from one provider to another.

10. That said, loyalty matters. Unless there's a reason you need to switch, stick with what you know. Your credit score is partly based on the length of time you've had your card—the longer, the better.

11. Work in smaller increments. Paying your fees weekly may help you keep better track of funds and facilitate reaching a zero balance every month, MacDonald says.

12. A minimum payment should be just that. It's the amount you must pay in order to avoid having your credit score harmed or interest rate spike. With some cards imposing a rate of almost 30 percent, you might want to consider a credit line (with rates around 2.7 percent) for your next big purchase.

13. If you find yourself in debt, there's help—and advice is often free. Non-profit organizations, like the Credit Counseling Society, can offer tips on how to pay it off or manage your creditors.

WHAT IDENTITY THIEVES DON'T WANT YOU TO KNOW

It's easier than you think to steal an identity. At least according to these real thieves who coughed up their secrets. Here's how it happens—but not to you.

1. Watch your back. In line at the grocery store, I'll hold my phone like I'm looking at the screen and snap your card as you're using it. Next thing you know, I'm ordering things online—on your dime.

2. That red flag tells the mail carrier—and me—that you have outgoing mail. And that can mean credit card numbers and checks I can reproduce. And if a bill doesn't show up when it's supposed to, don't breathe a sigh of relief. Start to wonder if your mail has been stolen. Stealing mail is easy. Sometimes, I act like I'm delivering flyers. Other times, I just stand there and riffle through it. If I don't look suspicious, your neighbors just think I'm a friend picking up your mail.

3. Check your bank and credit card balances at least once a week. I can do a lot of damage in the 30 days between statements.

4. If you see something that looks like it doesn't belong on the ATM or sticks out from the card slot, walk away. That's the skimmer I attached to capture your card information and PIN. If you use the same ATM every time, you're a lot more likely to notice if something changes on the machine.

5. I use your credit cards all the time, and I never get asked for ID. A helpful hint: I'd never use a credit card with a picture on it.

6. Thanks for using your debit card instead of your credit card. Hackers are constantly breaking into retail databases, and debit cards give me direct access to your banking account.

> 🔒 **TOP SECRET! How much is your information worth? I can buy stolen account information— your name, address, credit card number, and more—for $10 to $50 per account from hackers who advertise on more than a dozen black market websites.**

7. Sometimes I pose as a salesman and go into a small office. After I make my pitch, I ask the secretary to make me a copy of something. Since most women leave their purses on the floor by their chairs, as soon as she leaves the room, I can grab her wallet. I also check the top and bottom right-hand drawers of their desks, where I often find company checks.

8. Even with all the new technology, most of us still steal your information the old-fashioned way: by swiping your wallet or purse (thanks for writing your PIN number on that little slip of paper in your wallet), going through your mail, or Dumpster diving. I can dig through Dumpsters in broad daylight, and if anyone asks (but no one does), I just say my girlfriend lost her ring or that I may have thrown my keys away by mistake.

9. That's me driving through your neighborhood at 3 a.m. on trash day. I fill my trunk with bags of garbage from different houses and sort later, because you throw away the darnedest things—preapproved credit card applications, old bills, expired credit cards, checking account deposit slips, and crumpled-up job or loan applications with all your personal information.

10. One time I was on the run and needed a new identity so I went through a hospital Dumpster and found a statement with a Puerto Rican Social Security number for a Manuel Rivera. For a good two years after that, I was Manuel Rivera. I had his name on my apartment, on my paychecks, and, of course, on my credit cards.

11. Why don't more of you call 888-5-OPTOUT to stop banks from sending you preapproved credit offers? You're making it way too easy for me.

12. Is your Social Security number on your driver's license or your checks, or is it your account number for your health insurance? Dumb move.

13. When I send out e-mails "phishing" for personal information by posing as a bank or online merchant, I often target AOL customers. They just seem less computer literate—and more likely (I hope) to fall for my schemes.

SOURCES: Former identity thieves in Kentucky, Florida, Indiana, Virginia, and New York.

Great Advice

4 ONLINE SCAMS AND HOW TO AVOID THEM

1. Free Trial Offer! (Just Pay Forever)

How it works: You see an Internet offer for a free one-month trial of some amazing product—often a teeth whitener or a weight-loss program. All you pay is $5.95 for shipping and handling.

What's really going on: Buried in fine print are terms that obligate you to pay $79 to $99 a month in fees, forever.

Stay away: Read the fine print on offers, and don't believe every testimonial. Reputable companies will allow you to cancel, but if you can't get out of a "contract," cancel your card immediately, then negotiate a refund; if that doesn't work, appeal to your credit card company.

2. The Hot Spot Imposter (He's Close—Really Close!)

How it works: You're sitting in an airport or a coffee shop and you log into the local Wi-Fi zone. It could be free, or it could resemble a pay service like Boingo Wireless. You get connected, and everything seems fine.

What's really going on: The site only looks legitimate. It's actually run by a nearby criminal from a laptop. If it's a "free" site, the crook is mining your computer for banking, credit card, and other password information. If it's a fake pay site, he gets your purchase payment, then sells your card number to other crooks.

Stay away: Make sure you're not set up to automatically connect to nonpreferred networks. Before traveling, buy a $20 Visa or MasterCard gift card to purchase airport Wi-Fi access (enough for two days) so you won't broadcast your credit or debit card information. And don't do any banking or Internet shopping from public hot spots unless you're certain the network is secure. (Look for https in the URL, or check the lower right-hand corner of your browser for a small padlock icon.)

3. Your Computer Is Infected! (and We Can Help)

How it works: A window pops up about a legitimate-sounding antivirus software program like "Antivirus XP 2010" or "SecurityTool," alerting you that your machine has been infected with a dangerous bug. You're prompted to click on a link that will run a scan. Of course, the virus is found—and for a fee, typically about $50, the company promises to clean up your computer.

What's really going on: When you click on the link, the bogus company installs malware—malicious software—on your computer. No surprise, there will be no cleanup. But the thieves have your credit card number, you're out the money, and your computer is left on life support.

Stay away: If you get a pop-up virus warning, close the window without clicking on any links. Then run a full system scan using legitimate, updated antivirus software like free editions of AVG Anti-Virus or ThreatFire AntiVirus.

4. Dialing for Dollars (with a Ring of Fraud)

How it works: You get a text message on your cell phone from your bank or credit card issuer: There's been a problem, and you need to call right away with some account information. Or the message says you've won a gift certificate to a chain store—just call the toll-free number to get yours now.

What's really going on: The "bank" is a scammer hoping you'll reveal your account information. The gift certificate is equally bogus; when you call the number, you'll be told you need to subscribe to magazines or pay shipping fees to collect your prize. If you bite, you will have surrendered your credit card information to "black hat" marketers who will ring up phony charges.

Stay away: Real banks and stores might send you notices via text message (if you've signed up for the service), but they never ask for account information. If you're unsure, call the bank or store directly. You can also try the Better Business Bureau, or Google the phone number to see if any scam reports turn up.

WHAT YOUR FINANCIAL ADVISOR WON'T TELL YOU

Is your financial planner making money for you—or for himself?

1. Do some digging before you hand me the keys to your future. Use BrokerCheck at brokercheck.finra.org to see if I've been in trouble.

2. If I work on commission, I typically make money whenever you buy a new product, and I've probably got monthly quotas to meet. That's why I always seem to call with something to purchase at the end of the month.

3. You aren't qualified. Let's face it—you pay a carpenter to redo your kitchen. You pay a plumber to fix your toilet and a tutor to help your kid get into college. Yet when it comes to the most important area of your life—your financial future— suddenly you think you're qualified for a do-it-yourself project?

4. Certified financial planners and NAPFA-registered (National Association of Professional Financial Advisors) advisors take a pledge to put their clients' interests ahead of their own, but traditional stockbrokers aren't held to the same standard, even if they've given themselves the title "financial advisor."

5. Be careful with annuities. They pay me big commissions, but they're not a good fit for many clients. And stay away from investments that have a fee to get back out. If you get married, get divorced, change jobs, or move, it can come back to bite you.

6. There have been ten recessions since 1953. I have no clue where the market is going, and neither does anyone else. So if someone promises a certain amount of growth, walk away.

7. Some of us can give discounts, but you may not get one if you don't ask.

8. Haven't heard from me in a while? Not a good sign. I don't like to be the bearer of bad news.

> 🔒 **TOP SECRET!** If you ask me, "How are you getting paid?" and I say, "Don't worry about that. My company pays me," that's not a good sign.

9. Sure, I can help you buy 100 shares of IBM. But why pay me, when you can do it on E*Trade for less than you'd pay for a large pizza?

10. I am your inside source. If you're getting your stock tips from Jim Cramer's *Mad Money* and CNBC, you're waaaay late.

11. Paying off your mortgage may be a great idea. But I'd rather get paid to manage that money for you.

12. You're paying me for financial advice. Please come to me before you invest a bunch of money in something you don't understand. I had a client last year who put $80,000 in a currency trading investment that was supposed to pay him $4,000 a month. Of course it was a Ponzi scheme that stopped paying after three months. If he had asked me up front, I could have told him it wasn't legit.

13. Despite what you've read about Bernie Madoff, I am not going to steal your money. Frankly, you just don't have enough. If I were going to risk my entire career and life, you'd need to have $100 million, not $500,000.

SOURCES: Dana Anspach, principal, Wealth Management Solutions, Scottsdale, Arizona; John Gugle, CFP, Charlotte, North Carolina; Geoffrey Hakim, founder, Marin Capital Management, San Rafael, California; Terri Hickman, financial consultant, Grand Junction, Colorado; Jim Joseph, certified financial planner, Rockville, Maryland; Mark Stein, CFP, president, AeGIS Financial Advisors, Phoenix, Arizona.

Great Advice

6 THINGS THAT ARE NEVER WORTH THE MONEY

1. Credit Card Payment Insurance

For a monthly fee, many credit card companies offer an optional insurance policy: They'll cover your payments if you become disabled or unemployed. Financial advisors explain that most of these programs are rife with complex rules and restrictions and recommend using the money you would have spent on insurance to pay down your balance instead.

2. Premium Gas

You may think that filling your tank with premium rather than regular will help your car run better and longer, but according to *Car and Driver* magazine, you'd be wrong. A recent study by the magazine revealed that high-octane gasoline had no effect, except on ultra-high-performance vehicles.

3. Unlimited Cell-Phone Minutes

You may think you need a cell phone plan with unlimited minutes, so you have the freedom to talk as much as you like without incurring extra fees. But most people don't exceed the number of minutes offered in even the least expensive plans from most carriers (about 700 per month for a family plan). Check your usage amount on bills for the past several months before choosing a pricier plan.

4. Automobile Service Warranties

The manufacturer warranty you get when you purchase or lease your car is legit. The one you're offered via a postcard in the mail, in all likelihood, is not. According to an investigation by the Better Business Bureau of St. Louis (home to several warranty companies), nearly $3 million in repairs that should have been covered according to contracts were not. What's more, more than 90 percent of those who purchased such insurance found the process to be "misleading or improper."

5. Bottled Water

Contrary to what most bottled water producers would like you to think, much of what they're bottling came straight from a tap rather than a spring or well. Using a water filter will give you similar results for a fraction of the price. It's also kinder to the planet—most plastic water bottles end up in landfills, rather than at recycling facilities.

6. Lottery Tickets

Yes, $10 million probably will make your life wonderful, but almost anything is more likely to happen than you winning the lottery. The chance of winning most big-ticket lottery jackpots is well over 100 million to one, according to Moneyland.

WHAT **YOUR TAX ACCOUNTANT WON'T TELL YOU**

Reduce your tax bill? We can do that.
Sometimes. But you need to read this first.

1. We see many disastrous returns prepared by ill-trained preparers. Shop experience, not price. You get what you pay for. Some companies put their newly hired preparers through a six-week, evenings-only tax course and then turn them loose to prepare returns with very little oversight. In other words, the person preparing your return might have been styling hair or selling appliances six weeks ago.

2. A box full of receipts pretty much horrifies us. Nothing is more frustrating than when clients show up with a stack of receipts and forms and say "prepare my tax return." Organize your tax items into something we can use—like a spreadsheet. At the very least, write everything down so we know what is included.

3. Keep track of your donations. People often lose out on non-cash charitable contributions. If you make several trips to your local Goodwill or Salvation Army in a given year, keep good records of these donations.

4. When it comes to an audit, hire your CPA to go with you, as opposed to going yourself. I've had a few clients who went to the audit themselves, and they're now facing a huge liability because the auditor found their documentation to be insufficient. If you go yourself, you're probably more vulnerable. You can even authorize your accountant to go on your behalf.

5. When in doubt, throw the receipt in the tax file, and we can discuss it.

6. If you're self-employed, you need to set aside big money for taxes so you're not slapped with a massive tax liability at the end of the year. Independent contractors should be setting aside money for taxes equal to 35 percent to 45 percent of their gross pay and should be paying quarterly estimated tax payments for federal and state taxes. The self-employment tax is computed at 15.3 percent of your net income.

7. Please don't try to bargain down our fees based on the fact that you or your business had a bad year. The time and effort it takes to complete a tax return does not change in relation to your annual income or loss.

🔒 **TOP SECRET!** Better records often mean lower taxes. Use Mint.com or Quicken to track everything you spend, and you'll maximize your eligible deductions, thus reducing your taxable income, which will lead to less tax due.

8. You don't need to spend $200 on a CPA if your return isn't complex. By "isn't complex" we mean you receive a W-2, you receive a couple of 1099s, you don't work in multiple states, you have no partnership income or other flow-through income, and maybe you itemize. If you have just a few issues, those can be easily researched on the Web.

9. But don't overestimate your abilities. If you have complex returns, trying to save by doing the return yourself may cost you more in the long run, through missed deductions or dealing with subsequent IRS tax notices about missed income or misapplied deductions.

10. Just because they say it is deductible on TV or the radio doesn't make it so. Nearly every deduction or tax credit has limitations, exemptions, and exceptions.

11. If you show up after April 10 asking us to prepare your return, in all likelihood, you'll be going on extension. We rarely drop what we're doing for just anyone. If you wait until the last minute and come unprepared, don't even bother asking for it to get finished by the deadline.

12. If you get an extension, you still have to pay now. If you cannot file your return by the April 15 tax-filing deadline, you can file for an automatic six-month extension. However, the extension only extends the time to file your returns—not to pay your taxes!

13. If you pay too much with your extension payment, you can have the excess refunded or applied to the following tax year.

SOURCES: Dennis Coomes, CPA, Kansas City, Missouri, coomescpa.com; Anil Melwani, CPA, New York, New York, armeltax.com; Caleb Newquist, CPA and editor of the accounting blog goingconcern.com.

WHAT THE IRS WON'T TELL YOU

April 15, easy: Follow these insider tips for income tax help and stress-free filing.

1. If you earn less than $64,000 annually, many major tax-prep companies will give you their online filing guides. For information, go to irs.gov/uac/free-filedo-your-federal-taxesfor-free. Also, H&R Block offers free online support for people ages 17 to 50 who earn less than $62,000.

2. The holy trinity of quick refunds: File early, opt to receive your check through direct deposit, and file online. Some e-filing companies report getting refunds to customers in less than three weeks.

3. That said, refunds aren't as exciting as they may seem. When you receive a check from the government, you're getting money back that was yours to begin with—which has effectively been given as an interest-free loan to the government. Some argue that it's better to receive more money month-to-month than one lump sum via your refund. When you do receive your refund check, consider investing it for a long-term goal rather than splurging all at once.

4. Another common pitfall is excessive business deductions. The best defense: accurate records. If you travel for work, the MileIQ app will track your travel mileage. Meanwhile, apps such as Shoeboxed allow you to take photos of your receipts or scan your e-mail inbox to instantly log business expenses throughout the year. (Their services start at $9.95 a month, but free alternatives are available.) Shoeboxed even provides prepaid envelopes if you prefer sending receipts by snail mail.

5. Your weekend side projects might count as self-employment, which means you'll have to make quarterly estimated tax payments in addition to filing your annual return. Don't forget that you can write off expenses for a home office, though the rules are very specific. For more information, go to irs.gov/businesses/small-businessesself-employed/simplified-option-forhome-office-deduction.

6. Green home improvements can earn you tax credits. If you're a homeowner who's dedicated to energy efficiency, you can earn a tax credit of up to 30 percent on select projects—like for installing a nonsolar water heater, for example.

7. Did you get a sign-up bonus for, say, opening a bank account or a credit card? You may have to pay taxes on that. While the IRS treats some rewards as nontaxable discounts (such as most frequent-flier rewards), other payouts are considered income. A rule of thumb: If a company sends you a 1099 form reporting a reward, you should report it.

8. Filing late in itself won't hurt your credit rating, but it could lead to penalties that will ratchet up the amount you owe the government. If you don't pay that debt, the IRS may file a federal tax lien—a public, legal claim against your property that can impact your ability to get credit.

9. File even if you can't pay. While both failure-to-file and failure to-pay penalties exist, the first is generally harsher. And don't panic if you can't pay what you owe the IRS. You'll have to fill out some forms and provide documentation, but you may be able to compromise on a lower amount if you meet certain requirements. (In 2014, the IRS settled with about 40 percent of the people who applied for reductions, with an average decrease of about $6,600.)

10. Itemizing can yield a bigger return, but be careful: Too many deductions may increase your chances of being audited. One red flag: charitable donations that seem disproportionate to your income. Don't make the IRS wonder how you covered your basic needs because of how generous you were!

11. Even if you didn't put pretax money into a flexible spending account (FSA), you can still recoup some child-care expenses. Depending on your income, the government will give you back up to 35 percent of the cost of day care, with a cap of $3,000 per child or $6,000 per family. The catch: You must be employed or actively looking for a job to qualify.

12. Want to avoid an audit? Don't use round numbers, as the IRS may assume you're guessing on expenditures. The government audited 1.2 million people at random in 2015, so there's no guarantee, but you can cut down on your chances by being precise. That said, don't freak out if you realize you forgot to sign your return—that alone almost certainly won't trigger an audit.

13. If you do get audited (gulp!), don't go it alone. Hire an accountant, an enrolled agent, or a tax attorney who has experience dealing with the IRS. Sometimes it can be as simple as providing additional documents or filing an amended return, but it's best to work with a professional who knows the ropes.

SOURCES: IRS.gov, cnn.com, usnews.com, turbotax.intuit.com, howardlevyirslawyer.com, aarp.org, H & R Block, energystar.gov, and David Barral, CPA/PFS, CFP.

Great Advice

4 HELPFUL TIPS FOR TAX TIME

Here's how to make at least one painful moment in life a little easier to take.

1. Make No Mistake. Every year the IRS sends thousands of notices to taxpayers nationwide because of easily preventable errors including these:

* Social Security numbers—wrong number, no number, and misplaced digits could really ruin everything.

* Despite the use of computers, math can still be a source for errors. Especially if you're adding numbers on the side and inputting only the total on the return.

* If you're filing electronically, you'll be signing your return electronically, too. But if you're not filing electronically, make sure you sign that return.

* If you're paying by check, make sure you sign that, too.

* Make sure you're using the right form. Using a simple form like an EZ might be fast, but be sure you wouldn't get a bigger refund with a 1040A or 1040.

2. Paying for a Pro? Use Them. When you decide against do-it-yourself software and enlist the service of a pro, you may not be accomplishing much other than creating a bigger bill. If you're going to pay a pro, ask as many questions as you can about strategies to minimize your taxes and get enough sensible, specific, actionable advice to offset the additional cost.

3. Don't Agree to a Tax Refund Anticipation Loan.

Every year Americans take out loans on their tax refunds . . . and every year tax preparation companies rake in millions in interest and fees. Need your money fast? Use this simple system to get it: 1) File electronically, it's much faster than paper. 2) Use direct deposit. Combining those two things can get you your return within eight to fifteen days. If everybody did this, refund loans would be obsolete. If you're getting big refunds, amend your W-4 to have less withheld on your paychecks.

4. Start Early.

Every year some of us wait until December 24 to do our Christmas shopping or the day before our anniversary to rush out and get a gift. Even though we knew of the occasion well in advance, we procrastinate. While that may seem acceptable, traditional, even cute when it comes to shopping, don't adopt that attitude when it comes to taxes.

Waiting until the last minute and rushing through your taxes is more than just stressful. It's dumb. Because if you miss potential breaks and deductions due to haste, what you might waste is thousands of dollars. Start early, take your time, do a little research, and see how much less taxing your life can be.

SOURCE: Stacy W. Johnson, CPA and financial expert.

WHAT PEOPLE WITH MONEY WON'T TELL YOU

They might not be making more; they may just be saving more. We got their best insider tips on how to save smartly.

1. Many department managers at stores can cut the price of goods you want—if there's a defect or the price is higher than you planned to spend. When one shopper told a manager about her budget for a side-by-side refrigerator, he sold her the $1,400 model she wanted for $1,000.

2. Stores often place coupons in newspaper circulars and magazines you may not get to see. Ask the cashier if there's a coupon you missed and whether you can have the same discount.

3. Sales are usually held at the same time each year. Mark up a calendar so you know in advance when they're coming up. If you buy too early at full price, you may be able to bring back the merchandise and your receipt and get the discount.

4. Make friends with helpful salespeople by taking their business cards and stopping by to see them when you're shopping. Eventually they'll call you to tell you about upcoming sales and specials, or they'll hold items for you.

5. The bigger the cart, the more you buy. If you're going to the supermarket to buy one item, refrain from getting a basket. If you're only buying three items, get a basket, not a cart. When you venture into the store knowing you're going to have to carry your purchases up to the counter, you probably won't make impulse buys.

6. Discount card scanners sound like they're working, even when they're not. If your discount card is on your key chain, be careful when you hand it to the clerk if more than one store's discount card is attached to it. If the clerk scans the wrong card, the machine may still beep as if it's going to give you the discount—but it never does.

7. Buy wine from not-so-famous regions—like Paso Robles, California, instead of Napa—and choose lesser-known grape varieties. Wine from warmer climates, like Spain, will be cheaper because the grape harvests are more reliable there, keeping prices down.

8. From medicines to bleach to spices, hundreds of generic items are just like their higher-priced cousins, except for packaging and price. If you ever buy a name brand when there's a cheaper and identical generic substitute available, you're wasting cash.

9. Saving is as easy as typing what you're looking for into a deals search engine, and plenty of times, a coupon comes up. Shopping without taking a few seconds to do that is silly.

10. Form a neighborhood co-op and split the cost of things like lawn mowers, ladders, chainsaws, and other rarely used items with one or more neighbors. You'll reduce both your cost and clutter by at least 50 percent.

11. Stop paying for things you don't use. Do you pay for premium cable channels you never watch? Health clubs you rarely visit? Magazines you don't have time to read? Do you still really need your telephone landline? Really pay attention to where your money is going and see if there's something you can live without.

12. If you leave the house with only enough cash to buy what you're shopping for, you're automatically unable to succumb to impulse buys, which often bust your budget. We're more likely to overspend with pieces of plastic than real money.

13. For 30 days, promise yourself that you won't make a single big-ticket purchase without waiting a full day. If you still want it 24 hours later, then it's yours to buy. Whether your weakness is shoes, gadgets, or candy bars at noon, this rule can save you big bucks.

SOURCES: Renee Barnett, a mystery shopper in Tennessee; Stacy W. Johnson, CPA and author of *Life or Debt 2010*; Beth Kobliner, author of *Get a Financial Life: Personal Finance in Your Twenties and Thirties* and BethKobliner.com; Anne Obarski, author of *Surprising Secrets of Mystery Shoppers*.

Who Knew?
BUY IT ONCE, KEEP IT FOREVER

. . . .

These items may cost a little more up front, but if you spend good money on good products, you'll save a lot of money by not having to buy them over and over. Plus, they'll be a pleasure to have and use.

Cast-Iron Pan
On a new cast-iron pan, the surface should be uniformly dull gray inside and out and uniformly rough in texture with small grains or "pores." Avoid pans with seams, cracks, or uneven sharp edges. Buy one that is all one piece—not one with a wooden handle. Avoid a ridged bottom; a flat surface conducts heat best.

Kitchen Knife
If you buy a good chef's knife and care for it properly, you should never have to replace it. Avoid knives that have a serrated cutting edge or those that claim to "never need sharpening." Good knives do need sharpening. Buy one that you feel comfortable handling. Also buy a honing steel and use it regularly to keep your knife honed.

Hand Tools
Good quality hand tools should last not just one lifetime, but for a couple of generations. Look for forged rather than cast metal, and plastic, fiberglass, or metal handles rather than wood.

Albums
Look for a baby book, photo album, or scrapbook with pages made from dye-free, pH-balanced archival paper. Affix your photos and memorabilia with picture corners or small mounting squares. Avoid plastic sheets and sticky-backed pages, and don't use regular tape.

WHAT YOUR CELL PHONE SALES REP WON'T TELL YOU

We got cell phone salespeople to spill the beans about how companies get you to pay more, so you don't ever have to overpay again.

1. Resist the temptation to get a new phone the moment your contract expires. Wait a few weeks, and we'll start dangling all sorts of discounts and incentives in front of you.

2. Always come in at the end of the month when we're scrambling to make our quotas.

3. Don't let us gouge you with our ridiculously high 411 fees. Use a free service like 800-FREE411 or 800-CALL411.

4. That phone advertised for $29? You'll have to pay $129 for it, then fill out a bunch of paperwork to get a $100 rebate mailed to you. We make money because many of you won't go through the hassle.

5. Leaving your phone in the bathroom while you take a steamy shower is almost as bad as dropping it in the bathtub.

6. We've got all sorts of discounts—some as big as 28 percent off your monthly bills—that we can offer to employees of large companies and government agencies, credit union members, and more.

7. Trust me: You do want all the accessories and the unlimited-texts package. I make a lot of money off those, so I'll be much more likely to give you a discount on your phone or service plan if you get them. Then, if you don't want them, bring back the accessories the next day and call to cancel the text package.

8. Want out of your contract? Tell us you're moving somewhere we don't have service. Most of us don't require proof.

9. Another way out: Watch your bill. If we raise your nonregulatory taxes and fees without notifying you, we have to let you out. Maybe we sent you a notification by mail, but you didn't open it, or there was a text message you didn't read. Raise enough stink, and we'll let you go.

> **TOP SECRET!** Are you way over on minutes or text messages? If the billing cycle hasn't closed yet, call us and upgrade to the next plan. It can mean the difference between paying a whopping 35 to 45 cents for each extra minute or $5 to $10 for the higher plan.

10. Thanks for buying our fancy rhinestone case for $25. You can get the same one at a flea market for $5.

11. When you see those commercials on TV urging you to "text now!" to get a free ring tone or your daily horoscope, don't do it. You're almost always subscribing to a service with monthly fees ranging from $2.99 to $29.99. And we can't get you out of it.

12. If your phone gets a lot of static and seems about to drop the call, don't hang up! We track dropped calls to identify and fix dead spots. If you hang up, we won't know there was a problem.

13. You don't have to be related to take advantage of a family plan. You can team up with a group of trustworthy friends to get one. As an added bonus, most networks have free in-network calling, so if you sign up with the people you talk to most, you'll never go over your minutes.

SOURCES: Cell phone salespeople in North Carolina, Mississippi, and Michigan; and Jeff Brown, a "digital lifestyle coach" in Nashville.

Great Advice

IMPORTANT TECHNOLOGY AND PHONE ETIQUETTE

· ·

These are the new rules for being polite in a world full of rude devices.

Long "@" conversations on Twitter bore other followers. Take them to Twitter's Direct Message (DM) or send an e-mail.

Don't use cell phones in a waiting room, checkout line, restaurant, train, or (heaven forbid!) bathroom stall.

When instant-messaging, always ask if now is a good time to chat.

It's OK to piggyback on a neighbor's free Wi-Fi as long as you don't hog it and realize it's not secure.

RSVP to legitimate online invitations promptly.

Things not to do when e-mailing: "shout" in all caps, use colored fonts or clip-art emoticons, attach large files, forward an e-mail (unless appropriate).

You can e-mail thank-yous for party invitations and birthday gifts given in person as long as you send each of them separately. (No cc's.) For mailed gifts, letters of recommendation, and wedding presents, a written note is still preferable.

Work e-mails can be sent anytime, but business texts should be restricted to one hour before the start of the workday to two hours after it ends, according to *The Modern Gentleman*.

It's OK (and even advisable) to follow your boss on Twitter, but you shouldn't try to friend him on Facebook. Friends implies equivalency; followers, not so.

WHAT YOUR SALES CLERK WON'T TELL YOU

Learn how to get a deal—and what guarantees that you won't get—at all your favorite retail stores.

1. Many retailers count the shoppers who come in, then calculate the percentage who actually buy something. If I don't "convert" enough browsers to buyers, I hear from my district manager.

2. New merchandise goes at the front of the store, bargains at the back. The endcaps on the backside of aisles at Target, for instance, usually have items 15 to 75 percent off. If you want a deal, try to figure out when your favorite retailer does its markdowns. Some do them on Thursdays or Fridays, others at the end of the month.

3. Plenty of stores have great prices on Black Friday. Even if mine isn't one of them, you still line up and wait for us to open.

4. After you buy something, keep your receipt and pay attention. Most mainstream retailers promise a refund if the item goes on sale within a certain number of days after you buy it.

5. With savings clubs, e-mail deals, coupons, Internet discount codes, and other incentives, fewer and fewer people are paying full price.

6. This is not a garage sale. I can't give you a lower price just because you haggle.

7. If you start to throw a fit in front of other customers because I won't take a return, I'll probably give in and offer your money back. But I really want to kick your tush.

8. Most shoplifters aren't the people you'd expect. They're great customers who come in all the time, buy a lot of stuff, and are really nice to you. I guess they're thinking, *I'm a good customer, I deserve a little something.*

9. Our store sends out a birthday coupon to customers on our mailing list. When people redeem it, I often say, "Happy Birthday" as they walk away. Sometimes the customer will say, "you too." I know it's because they aren't really listening, but that cracks me up.

10. Everything gets marked down eventually. Watch and wait for the discount, then pounce.

11. Some of us will tell you anything to make the sale. Especially if you haven't been nice.

12. If I'm $200 from my sales goal and having a tough day, and you ask me if it's going to be cheaper tomorrow, I may lie.

13. If you want some extra attention or you need something special, call ahead and see if the store will let you make an appointment for a private visit. In a lot of stores, especially upscale ones, clerks are willing to open a little early or stay there a little late for a loyal customer.

SOURCES: Retail sales associates in North Carolina, Massachusetts, New Hampshire, Texas, and Florida, and a clerk in the Pacific Northwest who blogs at blametheclerk.blogspot.com.

14 WAYS TO DRESS FOR LESS

Follow these top tips from financial expert and CPA Stacy Johnson of MoneyTalksNews.com to save big on what you wear.

1. Buy out of season: shorts and bikinis in January, coats and sweaters in July.

2. Always check a coupon search engine first before you shop. Think of it as an instant savings dispenser attached to your computer.

3. Find it cheaper in the boy's or men's department. If you're a woman shopping in a department store for something unisex like a T-shirt or sweatshirt, you might be able to spend less by shopping in the men's section. Apparently the sexist pigs who price clothing believe women will pay more for comparable clothes than men. Call 'em on it.

4. Don't overwash your clothes. It wears them out faster. Avoid dry-cleaning if possible, and when you do wash your clothes, avoid dryers. That lint in your dryer screen is made of little pieces of your clothes that get rubbed off. Hanging them on a rack or clothesline is better for them and your electric bill.

5. Develop a hang-up. How many times have you had to wash otherwise unsoiled clothing just because you threw it in a wad on the floor?

6. Learn to sew. My mother wouldn't let me leave for college until I'd mastered simple stitchery, like button-sewing. Next time you're in a fancy hotel, take the sewing kit.

7. Use a budget. This is a tip that works for everything. If you plan what you're going to spend, you'll spend what you plan.

8. Use cash. Cash, along with budgets, is the ultimate way to avoid impulse buys. Remember all that stuff in your closet that you never wear? That's where it came from.

9. Use a list. This applies to everything you shop for and is also effective at preventing impulse buys.

10. Swap with your friends. Have a small party and ask everyone to bring stuff they're not wearing. What doesn't get taken can be given to charity. Besides, your friends are going to borrow your clothes and not return them anyway . . . might as well get something back.

11. Buy outfits, not items. It doesn't do you any good to buy a shirt that doesn't go with any of your pants. Plan ahead. Build a wardrobe around a few key things and make sure new additions build on that foundation.

12. Don't buy clothes to change your mood. Don't shop for the high, to build your self-esteem, or to fight off depression or boredom. The good feeling you get by buying new clothes (and most other things) is temporary, ineffective, and expensive. Physical solutions have no effect on emotional problems.

13. Shop alone. If you really need someone's input, fine. But be aware that friends, especially when combined with our own ego, often result in purchases that we might not otherwise make.

14. Buy the right size. This almost sounds too obvious to mention, but even I've done it: "It's a little too small, but that's OK because I'm about to lose a few pounds." Who am I kidding? If I'm really about to change sizes, what the heck am I doing shopping now?

WHAT YOUR DEBT COLLECTOR WON'T TELL YOU

Here are the hard-knock and straightforward strategies they use to get you to part with your money and pay up.

1. The more money I get out of you, the bigger my bonus will be. Every month, we watch top performers get bonus checks of $10,000 or more.

2. We also have an astounding power to wipe out thousands of dollars of your debt. Most accounts have a one-time settlement rate that's preapproved.

3. They teach us that all debtors are compulsive liars, and no matter what you tell us, we're supposed to keep pushing. So we ask, "Can you take money out of your 401(k)? Can you pay it with another credit card?" All are horrible ideas that would make a good financial planner cringe.

4. We've heard every tale of woe. We may listen and act sympathetic, but in our notes, all those excuses are summed up as *HLS*, for "hard-luck story." You're wasting our time, and time is money.

5. A lot of agencies buy debt for pennies on the dollar, so always start your settlement offer low, maybe 25 cents on the dollar. Say something like "I have $200 that I can apply toward this debt. Will you accept that as payment in full?"

6. **Sometimes when we're negotiating, I'll say I have to get a manager involved,** and then I'll have another collector be the "bad cop." The theory is that just having another voice on the line will open up your wallet.

7. **Like us or not, we're a vital part of keeping the cash flow going in this country.** In 2010, more than 10,000 collection agencies collected more than $8 billion.

8. **Always check whether the debt has passed the statute of limitations in your state** (see a list at creditcards.com). If it has, we can't sue you or put it in your credit report. However, if you make any kind of payment or even acknowledge the debt, that usually starts the clock over.

> **TOP SECRET!** We love calling you at work because of the extra pressure it puts on you. If you specifically ask us not to, by law we have to stop, but we're not going to tell you that.

9. **If you decide to settle, I am trained to "take your application."** In a bored voice, I ask for your cell number, your spouse's work phone, and so on, as if I'm filling out a form. But it's just a way to get the information we need to find you in case the settlement falls through.

10. **Many times when we leave a message on your phone,** it's just a recording of a made-up person. Our office uses the name Jim Taylor. When you call back and ask for him, we say he's out to lunch and offer to help you instead.

11. **Don't ask for a manager.** He or she will not help you.

12. **If you are having a really bad time with one collector,** you're better off just calling back and getting another person.

13. **If I threaten to have you arrested,** use profanity, or call before 8 a.m. or after 9 p.m., report me to your state attorney general's office and the Federal Trade Commission. Those are violations of the Fair Debt Collection Practices Act.

SOURCES: Michelle Dunn, former owner of a debt-collection agency and author of *The Guide to Getting Paid*; Fred Williams, who worked as a debt collector for three months to write *Fight Back Against Unfair Debt Collection Practices*; and debt collectors in Florida, New Jersey, and Pennsylvania.

Who Knew?

HOW TO TELL IF YOU'RE A SMART SPENDER

Concerned about how much you're spending, how much you should be saving, and how much house you can afford? Use these easy equations to determine how fiscally healthy you are.

1. The price of your home should not be more than 2.5 times your annual gross household income.

2. Your total monthly debt payments (including mortgage, student loans, car, and credit card payments) should not be more than 35 percent of your monthly gross income. Some mortgage brokers will stretch this ratio up to 40 percent, but that leaves you very little budgetary wiggle room.

3. Your nest egg, if you want to retire comfortably, should be about 20 times what you want your annual income to be. If you anticipate needing about $75,000 a year to live on when you retire, you'll need a nest egg of about $1.5 million. Of course, this will vary if you retire early or continue to work longer than usual.

Insider Expertise

SMART, SIMPLE WAYS TO SAVE MORE MONEY FOR LIFE

No matter what the market does, you should know how to shore up your resources so you won't have to worry about every little hiccup. Here are time-tested strategies you can master—how to spend less, reduce your debt, make the most of your tax breaks, invest wisely, and finance your retirement. The idea, says William Speciale, a Boston-based advisor with the financial planning firm Calibre, is to focus on what you can control: "Little steps can really make a huge difference."

Taxes

Forget the short form. Most taxpayers—65 percent of us, to be specific—just take the standard deduction. But you may save money by itemizing your deductible expenses. It doesn't matter if you use an online program, a current tax guide, or a storefront preparer. Out-of-pocket health care charges, business expenses (including some for job searches), and charitable donations are just a few of the items you may be able to deduct. Fill out the long form, known as the 1040, and compare numbers. If your total deductions are greater than the standard deduction, you'll save money by itemizing when you file.

Your kids should file a tax return. The IRS doesn't care how old they are. If they earn more than $5,450 in a given year (in wages and/or interest income), they have to file—even if you claim them as dependents. And if they make less than that, they should still file because they'll get back all the money their employer withheld. Help them fill out the paperwork. It's a great learning experience that may earn them some extra cash.

Avoid a tax refund. You may feel giddy knowing you'll get a check from the IRS this spring, but you shouldn't. Getting money back means you're essentially lending money, interest free, to the government for the year. Better to have that cash in your account than lend it to Uncle Sam. So if you've been getting big refunds or have had a big life change (a marriage, a baby, a divorce, a radical increase or decrease in income), adjust the withholding allowances on your W-4 form. You can do that at irs.gov. Use the withholding calculator to determine the correct figure for you. Then print a new W-4, fill it out, and give it to your payroll department.

Avoid "rapid refund" programs. Sure, they sound great. After all, what can be better than getting your money fast? A tax-prep chain might try to get you to agree to one of these "instant" or "anticipation" options. Don't take the bait. This is not your refund. It's a loan—and a very high-interest loan at that. Some have been higher than 120 percent. If you file electronically, even if it's through a tax chain, the IRS will deposit your refund directly into your bank account within a week or two.

Checking and Savings

Make sure your free checking is really free. A lot of banks advertise it, but read the fine print. If the minimum balance is steep—thousands of dollars, in some cases—look for a bank with no minimum requirement. This could save $100 a year or more. Bankrate.com is a good site for comparing accounts. (And don't waste $2 on ATM withdrawals at another bank's machines.)

Bank online. You'll be surprised how easy it is to pay bills, transfer funds, save automatically, and keep track of it all. In fact, gathering records at tax time will be a cinch. And by setting up the automatic bill-payment option, you'll help protect your credit score. Banking online is actually safer than banking at a brick-and-mortar institution. Banks have spent a fortune to make sure their sites are among the most secure on the Internet.

Keep your money in super-safe places. Aim to amass at least six months of emergency expenses, in case you lose your job or become disabled. Where's the best place to keep it?

FDIC-insured bank savings, CD, and money market accounts are still three of the most secure places. Money market funds that invest in Treasury bills are super-safe, too, but low yielding. Internet banks and credit unions tend to pay higher interest rates, but go to fdic.gov and check to make sure they offer the same government-insured guarantee. Look into Series I bonds, or I bonds, which are just as safe and are guaranteed to keep up with inflation. They're also free from state and local taxes (and possibly federal tax, if you use them for college costs). The downside? You can't redeem them for at least a year. And if you cash them in before five years, there's a small penalty. Other savings options, including corporate and tax-exempt money market funds, are a bit riskier. Compare yields at cranedata.us.

Debt

Cut up your extra credit cards. But don't close the accounts. Yes, it's smart to reduce your temptation to splurge by destroying your cards. But if you actually cancel them, it could hurt your credit rating. Here's why: Lenders worry about how close you are to using all the credit available to you. If you close an account, you lose its credit line. As a result, you are using a greater portion of the reduced amount you can now borrow. How many cards do you need? While the average American household has nine, two or three active cards should be plenty.

Pay your bills on time. A single late payment means that you could pay a much higher interest rate on any future loans and on your existing credit card accounts. That's because even one missed payment can lower your credit score by as much as 100 points. That plunge means that lenders view you as a risky customer. If you're shopping around for a mortgage, you could end up paying as much as a full percentage point more. That's an increase that could ultimately cost you tens of thousands of dollars in interest. Set up automatic payments to make sure you're never late on your major bills. The sooner you can show lenders you're back on track, the better.

Pay $10 more each month. Most American households keep their credit balances at around $2,000, but about 10 to 15 percent carry balances that are $9,000 or higher. If you paid the minimum $224 required on that $9,000 balance each month, it would take you 31 years and more than $13,000 in interest to pay it off. Increasing your payment by just $10 a month, to $234, until you've paid off the balance would save you $8,900. And you'd get rid of the debt in five years. (To check your own balances, try the calculator at bankrate.com.)

Put your savings to work. Many people who are deep in debt usually have some savings stashed in a bank account. They argue that they don't want to use their hard-earned savings to pay off debt. But do the math: It would make sense to keep the money in savings only if the bank is paying you an interest rate higher than the one your credit cards charge. Paying off a card with an interest rate of 13 percent is the equivalent of earning 13 percent interest on your money after taxes. There are no savings or investment options with that kind of guarantee. Experts caution that you still want to keep emergency cash on hand. A good rule is to take 5 percent of your paycheck to pay off debt and put an additional 5 percent into savings.

Pay more on your mortgage. You may have heard that because the interest is tax deductible, a mortgage is a good debt. But even if you're getting a tax break, you're still paying interest—and the longer you've had the mortgage, the smaller the tax break (because you pay less interest each year). As with all debt, paying it off sooner is better. So once you've paid off your credit cards and other high-rate debt, go ahead and add an extra payment each year (or spread it out over 12 months). If you do that over the life of a 30-year fixed loan with a rate of 6 percent, you'll shave roughly 20 percent off the total interest you pay. On a $150,000 mortgage, that means saving about $26,000.

Reduce your credit card interest rate. It may be time to get nervy with the credit card companies. If you pay your bill on time and your credit card company still raises your rates or lowers your limits, call the company's toll-free number (ask for the retention department) and explain that you're thinking of taking your business elsewhere. You may reap a rate reduction. And credit crunch or not, banks are still motivated to keep good customers. And check your accounts often. These days, banks are increasing rates even on good customers.

Get your credit report for free. You're entitled to one free report from each of the three credit bureaus (Experian, TransUnion, and Equifax) every year. Beware, though. Many sites advertising "free credit reports" are actually fronts for companies trying to sell you services—credit monitoring, debt consolidation, credit repair—most of which you don't need. The reports are free, but you'll be automatically signed up and billed for these products. Get your reports from annualcreditreport.com, which is sponsored by the three bureaus and the Federal Trade Commission. You can purchase extras on this site, too, but just stick with the free reports. If you want to see your credit scores (a numerical representation of how good a credit risk you are), you'll have to pay around $50 all in at myfico.com.

Insurance

Shop around for car insurance. An online search and a few phone calls can turn up vastly different rates in the same area. You'll also want to ask about lesser-known breaks. For example, even if your kids are grown and out of the house, they might be able to get a substantial discount if they insure their cars through the company you use.

Sign up for an FSA. Many employers offer flexible spending accounts as a way to set aside part of your salary for health care and child-care costs. You can pay for everything from Band-Aids to orthodontic work with pretax money, which translates into a discount of about 30 percent or more, depending on your tax bracket. But plan carefully. If you don't use all the money in your account within the year (at many companies, you have until March 15 of the following year to submit receipts), you lose whatever's left.

Keep grown kids on your health insurance policy. If you're going to end up lending (or giving) your children money for coverage, it's much cheaper to keep them on your policy as long as possible. In some states, you can do this until they are 26, whether they're still in school or not. (New Jersey will give you until they turn 30.) Some states require proof that they are single, without children, and that they live in the same state as you. Even if your state doesn't mandate extended coverage, your plan might, so call your human resources department for details.

Hold off on that long-term-care insurance. The soaring cost of extended nursing care has prompted many people in their forties and fifties to sign up for long-term-care insurance in order to lock in a rate. It's true that the premiums go up as you get older, but not by the huge amount you might expect. According to data collected by America's Health Insurance Plans, a 65-year-old may end up paying just $126 more a year than someone who bought a policy at age 55. During those ten years, that person would spend close to $19,000 on coverage, even though he or she probably won't need it until age 83 or so (if at all). Depending on your health, the best time to buy is between 60 and 65. Until then, make retirement savings the priority, not long-term-care insurance.

Sign up for disability insurance. It helps protect your income in the event you become unable to work for a long period. Ideally, you should have enough to replace 60 to 70 percent of your salary. If your company plan doesn't provide this much coverage, consider buying more on your own. It can be costly, but it's worth it. Visit affordableinsuranceprotection.com or unum.com for quotes.

Think twice about life insurance. If you don't have dependents, you may not need it. If you do have kids or other dependents, you're probably better off with term life insurance until, say, your children are grown and can take care of themselves. It's generally less expensive than whole-life or other types of policies that build up value until you die or cash them in. Agents will tell you that whole-life insurance is a good investment because your money builds up tax-free, but these policies often have very high fees. You're better off putting that money toward your 401(k) and IRA instead. To comparison shop for term life policies, try term4sale.com.

Write your will. Although no one likes to think about dying, you need to. A will doesn't have to be a fancy contract that teams of lawyers slave over. It's just a written record of whom you want to entrust your kids and assets to when you die. You can write one using a simple boilerplate form and then sign it in the presence of witnesses (usually two people who aren't named in the will). You'll also want to make sure all the beneficiaries on your life insurance policies and bank and retirement accounts are up-to-date.

Investments

Stay away from individual stocks. In spite of what you may hear from your cousin the broker, buying the stock of a single company is generally not wise. It's essentially putting all your eggs in one basket—and paying broker fees that could eat up your earnings. In fact, you don't really need a broker. Instead of buying individual stocks, invest directly in mutual funds, which spread your dollars among a group of stocks. It's usually safer, cheaper, and simpler. But remember, you should do this only with money you can invest long term and can afford to lose in the short term.

Stick with index funds. You'll want to go with a special type of mutual fund called an index fund, which buys a little piece of each of the companies that make up established market benchmarks like the S&P 500. One of the best-kept secrets of investing is that in the long run, index funds perform at least as well as the funds that charge high fees and have a professional stock picker making the choices. For a list of low-cost index funds, go to vanguard.com or fidelity.com.

Don't buy investment products from your bank. Banks sell a wide range of mutual funds, annuities, and individual stocks and bonds. These aren't FDIC-insured, and they tend to be more expensive than what you could get elsewhere because banks usually charge high sales commissions. Buy directly from mutual fund companies instead. Go with companies like Vanguard or Fidelity, which charge low fees and no commissions.

Build a portfolio. The rule of thumb is to put 50 percent of your long-term savings in stocks and 30 percent in bonds and keep 20 percent available in cash (that means in a savings or money market account where you can withdraw it at a moment's notice). In tough times especially, getting the right mix will depend on the risk you're willing to take and how soon you'll need your money. Stocks are generally more risky than bonds, but there are exceptions. For example, bonds issued by companies that are in questionable financial health—called junk bonds or, more euphemistically, high-yield bonds—are a lot riskier than, say, stock in utility companies.

Retirement

Contribute to your company's 401(k). If your company matches funds, sign up. This will be the best investment you can possibly make. Typically, a company will kick in 50 cents for every dollar you save, up to 6 percent of your salary. That's the equivalent of earning an immediate 50 percent return— a rate you can't get anywhere. Yet incredibly, one in three American workers who are eligible isn't taking full advantage of it. With the matching funds, you can more than double the size of your 401(k) in 20 years, even if the stock market remains flat. For a family making $44,000, your contribution may cost you as little as $30 a week, money you won't even miss after a while.

Put retirement savings ahead of college savings. This sounds crazy to parents who need to come up with tuition money well before it's time to retire. But because of the tax breaks and the flexibility of retirement accounts, you're much better off contributing to a 401(k) or an IRA and taking out loans for college. Many people don't realize that the contributions you put in Roth IRAs can be withdrawn free of penalties at any time. That's very different from the college savings plans, called 529s, that smack you with a significant penalty if the money is not used for college. Another plus: Most schools don't count money in your retirement accounts when assessing how much financial aid they'll offer you.

Say no to company stock. Think of Lehman Brothers, Bear Stearns, and Enron. All were once on top, but when they went under, many employees were left without jobs and with retirement accounts that were overloaded with worthless company stock. You already have a huge stake in the company because you depend on it for your paycheck. Don't risk your retirement money as well. If your employer offers company stock as a 401(k) option, don't take it. If you get company stock as part of your matching-funds plan, sell it as soon as you're allowed to, and switch that money into some other type of investment. Ask your HR representative for details.

Don't worry about Social Security. You've probably heard the dire predictions that anyone younger than 35 can't expect to collect Social Security. Even in bleak economic scenarios, though, Social Security will probably pay you 65 to 80 percent of your currently promised benefits. And with some fairly modest changes—like raising the retirement age or increasing payroll taxes for anyone earning more than $250,000 annually—the system can be shored up for decades to come. Make sure you're saving enough so you don't have to count on the program for your entire retirement income.

Part Eight

WHAT YOU DON'T KNOW ABOUT
YOUR JOB

What takes you from wannabee to gainfully employed and moving up the ladder? We pulled back the curtain and got headhunters and HR professionals to reveal the best and worst of what they see (and believe us, they've seen it all). Your coworkers told us what you're doing to annoy them, and your company spilled about how people wrangle higher salaries.

From first impressions that get you hired to bad moves that get you fired, the pros get frank about where you stand at the office. It's not always where you think.

WHAT YOUR HEADHUNTER WON'T TELL YOU

Here's what they're really saying about your résumé.

1. You're considered pretty much unemployable once you've been unemployed more than six months. We assume that other people have already passed you over, so we don't want anything to do with you.

2. Who you know really does matter. No matter how nice your résumé is or how great your experience may be, it's all about connections.

3. Often the best thing to do is to avoid HR entirely if you're trying to get a job at a specific company. Find someone at the company you know, or go straight to the hiring manager.

4. People assume someone's reading their cover letter. I haven't read one in 11 years.

5. We will judge you based on your e-mail address, especially if it's something inappropriate like kinkyboots101@hotmail.com or johnnylikestodrink@gmail.com.

6. Don't put the year you graduated on your résumé if you're in your fifties or sixties.

7. Children and hobbies do not belong on a résumé. And never, ever say, "Now that my kids are in college, I'm ready to get back in the workforce."

8. There's a myth out there that a résumé has to be one page. So people send their résumé in a two-point font. Nobody is going to read that.

9. I always read résumés from the bottom up. And I have no problem with a two-page résumé, but three pages is pushing it.

10. We get résumés on fancy schmantzy papers. We get them with gold-pressed lettering. We get them in binders and in document protectors with ribbons. None of that sways me.

11. I had somebody list their prison time as a job. And once an exotic dancer called herself a "customer service representative."

12. Most of us use applicant-tracking systems that scan résumés for key words. The secret to getting your résumé through the system is to pull key words directly from the job description and put them on. The more matches you have, the more likely your résumé will get seen by a real person.

13. About 98 percent of the résumés we receive when we post a position on a big jobs site like Monster or Careerbuilder are junk that come from people who are nowhere near qualified. That's why we like posting jobs on websites that target specific industries.

SOURCES: Chris Ferdinandi, HR professional in the Boston area; HR director at a financial services firm; HR director at a health-care facility; HR manager in St. Cloud, Minnesota; HR professional at a midsize firm in North Carolina; Rich DeMatteo, a recruiting consultant in Philadelphia, Pennsylvania; Sharlyn Lauby, HR consultant in Fort Lauderdale, Florida; Shauna Moerke, an HR administrator in Alabama who blogs at hrminion.com; Cynthia Shapiro, former human resources executive and author of *Corporate Confidential: 50 Secrets Your Company Doesn't Want You to Know*; Michael Slade, HR director at Eric Mower and Associates, an integrated marketing communications agency.

Great Advice

7 THINGS CAREER CHANGERS NEED ON THEIR RÉSUMÉS

....

1. Broader Skills

Reanalyze your skills and include every area of the business that you've been able to impact, says Jill Smart, chief human resources officer at Accenture, a management consulting and technology firm. "People changing careers need to make sure their résumé shows the full breadth of their skills—operations, leadership, management, communication," explains Smart.

2. Summary Paragraph

Experts' opinions are mixed on the need for a résumé summary or objective if you're staying in your field, but it's an important feature for a career changer, says Bonnie Marcus, a New York-based business coach and founder of Women's Success Coaching. In the summary paragraph, tie "everything in the job description with everything you've accomplished in the past," she says.

3. Relatable Job Title Descriptions

Adding a short descriptor after the official job title can help hiring managers easily identify your transferable skills. "For example, if your job title was 'software engineer,' but you want to transition to project management, consider writing the job title as 'Software Engineer (with a heavy emphasis on Project Management),'" résumé writer Robyn Feldberg explains. But, she adds, "You only want to use this approach if you can do it honestly."

4. A Mixed Format

When working with career switchers, Feldberg creates a functional-style résumé on the first page and includes the traditional chronological format on the second page. "In other words, the first page looks like a glorified profile," says Dallas-based Feldberg, who runs Abundant Success Coach, a career coaching and résumé writing service.

5. A Little Name Dropping

Showing that you've been able to succeed and work with established industry leaders in your previous career shouldn't be saved for the interview, says Theresa Szczurek, chief executive of Radish Systems, a Boulder-based software firm.

6. Non-Work Related Experience

Include activities that relate to your desired role, like professional association memberships, volunteering, internships, or part-time consulting.

7. Natural Alignments

"Look for things about your current position that would have meaning to the person considering you for the new position," says Luke Tanen, who left the music industry to work as the director of the Chicago Innovation Awards. For example, Tanen's mention of closing sponsorship deals was similarly impressive in both fields.

WHAT YOUR HIRING MANAGER WON'T TELL YOU

Avoid these top mistakes on your next job interview, and you'll be as good as hired!

1. It's amazing when people come in for an interview and say, "Can you tell me about your business?" Seriously, people. There's an Internet. Look it up.

2. A lot of managers don't want to hire people with young kids, and they use all sorts of tricks to find that out, illegally. One woman kept a picture of two really cute children on her desk even though she didn't have children (hoping job candidates would ask about them).

3. Is it harder to get the job if you're fat? Absolutely. Hiring managers make quick judgments based on stereotypes. They're just following George Clooney's character in *Up in the Air*, who said "I stereotype. It's faster."

4. I once had a hiring manager who refused to hire someone because the manager was worried that the car the applicant drove wasn't nice enough.

5. I've seen managers not hire a woman because the environment is mostly male, and they're worried that no matter how smart or talented she is, she won't fit in.

6. If you've got a weak handshake, I make a note of it.

7. Someone might tell you to "Be yourself" in the interview. Don't be yourself. That's the worst advice ever. We don't want people who are neurotic and quirky and whatever else. All we care about is your skill and experience.

8. I once had someone send me forget-me-not seeds with their thank-you note. Yes, thank me for taking the time, that's great. But sending me seeds? That's weird.

9. One time a candidate sent—I love this—a thank-you card with a professional picture of herself, which quite honestly became the running joke for weeks. The picture was blown up and posted in my office with hearts drawn around it.

10. Don't ever tell me that you have to have this job because you're going to lose your house, your kids have nothing to eat, your mother has cancer. Companies aren't a charity.

TOP SECRET! I know a lot more about you when you walk in the door than you realize. I'll search for you on the Web and often use my own personal network to do a pre-interview reference check.

11. In interviews, everyone works well with others, and everyone learns quickly. Please tell me something else.

12. If you're a candidate and the hiring manager spends 45 minutes talking about himself, the company, or his Harley, let him. He's going to come out of the interview saying you're a great candidate.

13. Don't just silence your phone for the interview. Turn it all the way off.

SOURCES: HR director at a financial services firm; HR manager at a medical-equipment sales firm; HR professional at a midsize firm in North Carolina; HR manager in St. Cloud, Minnesota; HR professional in New York, New York; Senior HR Executive in New York City; Sharlyn Lauby, HR consultant in Fort Lauderdale, Florida; Suzanne Lucas, a former HR executive and the Evil HR Lady on bnet.com; Cynthia Shapiro, former human resources executive and author of *Corporate Confidential: 50 Secrets Your Company Doesn't Want You to Know*; Laurie Ruettimann, HR consultant and speaker in Raleigh, North Carolina.

Great Advice

THE COVER LETTER YOU SHOULDN'T USE

. . . .

Templates are useful as ways to know what should be in a cover letter. But don't use the template outright. Frank Risalvato, a recruiting officer for Inter-Regional Executive Search Inc., is deluged with cover letters from different candidates that all obviously use the same template from the same career coaches.

"Some of these [cover letters] we see are very obviously not written by the individual," says Risalvato. "We get fifteen to twenty of these a month, and it sounds disingenuous and insincere, seeing these cover letters from Seattle one week, Chicago another, and it's all the same style."

Some career experts also warn against the tired stand-by opening lines in a cover letter. "Opening a letter with a passive and clichéd statement such as 'Enclosed please find my résumé highlighting my experience and skills that would help your company to grow and succeed,'" is a no-no, says Ann Baehr, certified professional résumé writer and president of New York–based Best Résumés. "It's best to use something catchy and more specific such as, 'If your company could benefit from the expertise of a hard-charging sales producer with a flawless record of success . . .'"

If you're uncomfortable with that approach, make your cover letter unique to you with insights about the company you're applying to, advises Darrell Gurney, Los Angeles–based founder of career coaching site Careerguy.com and author of *Backdoor Job Search: Never Apply for a Job Again!* Prove you understand their business.

"Put in a note saying something like, 'I've been following your company's progress in the last year and in February I noticed your company was mentioned in the journal of such and such,'" Gurney says.

WHAT YOUR HR PERSON WON'T TELL YOU

The truth about who really gets hired—and who stays happily employed—may surprise you.

1. I have better things to do than deal with who slept with who, or who's talking about you behind your back. Sometimes I feel like a high school guidance counselor.

2. Even in jobs where you test applicants and those with the top scores are supposed to get the job, I've seen hiring managers fix scores to get the people they like.

3. I was asked by one CEO to hire the long-legged girl with the long dark hair even though she didn't have the right skills. Another time, I was instructed not to hire anyone with children because the company had too many people leaving for soccer games. That kind of thing happens all the time.

4. Networking does not mean using Facebook or LinkedIn. It means going to events, getting your face in front of people, and setting up informational interviews.

5. My LinkedIn profile is for myself, a way for me to find another job. It's not a way to find a job with me.

6. If it's been a week or two and I tell you "I don't have an update yet," that often means there's a better candidate we're talking to, but we can't tell you that in case they decide not to take the job.

7. If you call to check on the status of your résumé and I ask, "What job did you apply for?" and you don't know, you're done.

8. If we ask you to travel for your job or attend a conference, it's not really a question. Say no, and it can be career-ending.

9. When we had someone go out on disability and we knew he was faking it, we didn't want to go to court to prove it. So we put him on an assembly line in a job where we knew he wouldn't succeed. Eventually, we were able to fire him.

10. I know many of you met your spouse at the company. But the thing is, for every one of you, there are five people it doesn't work out as well for. And your office romance can and will be held against you.

11. Many people think, *If I work extra hard, I'm going to get noticed.* But it doesn't work that way. If you want to advance, some of the responsibility falls on you to toot your own horn. Make sure your supervisor and your supervisor's supervisor are well of aware of what you're contributing.

12. Don't stalk me. If you have a question, come to my office. Don't corner me in the bathroom.

13. You're right to be paranoid. The company is always watching you, and there's a record of everything you do: every phone call, every text, every tweet and instant message. At most companies, they save that data forever.

> 🔒 **TOP SECRET!** The number one thing in job security is your relationship with your boss. Even if he says, "I'm sorry I really wanted to keep you, but they made me lay you off," that's almost never true. He probably made that decision.

SOURCES: Kris Dunn, chief human resources officer at Atlanta-based Kinetix who also blogs at HRcapitalist.com; HR pro at a mid-level staffing firm; HR professional at a midsize firm in North Carolina; a human resources professional in New York, New York; HR representative at a Fortune 500 financial services firm; HR representative in the manufacturing industry; recruiting consultant Rich DeMatteo, Philadelphia, Pennsylvania; Laurie Ruettimann, HR consultant and speaker in Raleigh, North Carolina; Cynthia Shapiro, former human resource executive and author of *Corporate Confidential: 50 Secrets Your Company Doesn't Want You to Know*; Michael Slade, HR director at Eric Mower and Associates, an integrated marketing communications agency.

Who Knew?
SCARY BUT TRUE OFFICE ANTICS

Sometimes, you'd really rather not keep your job. *Please Fire Me*, by Jill Morris and Adam Chromy, collects dozens of hilarious vents from anonymous clock punchers forced to put up with various forms of crazy nine-to-five. Some doozies:

Last week a coworker asked me, "What day is Black History Month?"

Our HR girl overheard me describing the plot of *The Road* to a coworker, you know, the book about survivors of nuclear Armageddon who are being chased across a deserted America by anarchist cannibals. She asked, "Was that based on a true story?"

I just caught my old boss copying down my goals from last year's review and noting them as his own for this year.

My team leader took a digital picture of everyone's face and pasted it to an animal cutout. Now each employee is a different animal on the "productivity" board. Whoever does the most work each week gets one step closer to the piece of meat that person's animal likes to eat, which is glued to the other end of the poster. I'm the bison.

WHAT YOUR IT DEPARTMENT WON'T TELL YOU

Ever wonder what the computer whizzes really think about solving other people's problems all day long? Find out what it's like to be on call all the time and how you can rise to the top of their priority list.

1. Just because we're "buddies" at work, don't expect me to come running every time you've got a problem. I've got a slew of IT problems to fix.

2. We use the word "corruption" when we don't have a real answer. Occasionally, when trying to fix a problem, something goes wrong and some part of the system breaks or stops working, or more damage happens. I was helping a customer a couple weeks ago move e-mail over from one system to another and accidentally lost all of his calendar items. Of course I didn't tell him it was my fault.

3. It drives me crazy when you just ignore the work I've done to explain something. People will ask me how to do simple tasks that I have spent time documenting for them. Read the document. I'm taking screenshots and writing instructions to make things easier for you.

4. E-mail me. I would love to talk to you on the phone, but it's not efficient. E-mail me a list of your problems and questions, and it's a lot easier for me to respond to them all.

5. If you travel with your laptop, get a lock. One survey by the Computer Security Institute found that 50 percent of respondents had a laptop or other mobile device stolen in the past year. A simple cable lock (starting at about $20) lets you physically secure your laptop anywhere you go.

6. If your company owns the computer, they own what's on it, too—even your e-mail in some cases. Act accordingly.

7. You can't hide anything from us. Think trashing cookies and clearing your Web history are keeping you invisible? Think again. Everything still goes through my firewall, which sees all traffic when you connect to the Internet. It goes from your computer to a device that directs the traffic out. That's why we can use things like content filters that block sites like Facebook, YouTube, and pornography.

> **🔒 TOP SECRET!** Sometimes we talk about you—in code. If you hear **"HKI error"** (for human-keyboard interface) or **"PEBCAK"** (problem exists between chair and keyboard), we're insulting you.

8. Sometimes we're asked to get dirt on employees a company wants to fire. I was once asked to sniff out all of an employee's traffic and show what sites she went to and how much time she spent surfing.

9. You're right. Sometimes we make five-minute jobs last an hour.

10. If you don't understand me, I'm not doing my job. Confusing tech jargon is a sign of insecurity, not intelligence.

11. We're like Santa: We know if you've been bad or good. Fessing up to what really happened right before the system crashed is going to save time—and I'm going to figure it out anyway.

12. Urgency is based on priority. Just because you say your problem's urgent doesn't really mean it's urgent to me. Your e-mail not working is not as important as another customer's server being down.

13. We didn't create the problem; we're just trying to help you fix it.

Who Knew?

TOP IRRITATING PHRASES TO AVOID IN E-MAIL

When Lifehacker.com asked readers which e-mail phrases they'd like to see banished—or at least improved—they got a flood of responses. Here's a choice selection of the best:

1. "We need to . . . " Translation: "XYZ needs to be done, but . . . I'm not actually going to come out and directly tell any of you to do it."

2. "Cheers"—especially when used outside British pubs or the U.K. in general.

3. "Thanks in advance"—as opposed to thanks from the past?

4. "Touch base."

5. "Circle back."

6. "To be honest."

7. The worst: "Please consider the environment before printing this e-mail." I'll print it if I need to, whether you nag me or not!

WHAT YOUR COWORKERS WON'T TELL YOU

Are you hearing office snickers but don't know why? Here's how to guarantee they won't be about you.

1. Using a speakerphone at full volume to go through your voice mailbox is the definition of annoying. Don't use a speakerphone unless you're in your office and holding a meeting that's being attended by someone remotely.

2. Popping up and "prairie dogging" above someone's cubicle is just weird. Don't hold a conversation as a disembodied head.

3. Stop microwaving stinky foods in the lunchroom.

4. "Hello" is the word that greases many squeaky wheels. Get into the habit of smiling and greeting your colleagues. It's really amazing how fast this little courtesy can thaw chilly workplace relations.

5. Many helpful alliances are born at the office bowling league or softball games. These are great ways to get exercise while you get to know your coworkers in an informal setting.

6. Keep your cell phone out of the conversation. When talking to someone in person, don't glance down at your cell phone to see who's trying to reach you.

7. People love to be asked their opinion, so go out of your way to ask, "What do you think belongs in this report?" or "How do you think I should handle this situation with client X?"

8. Office gossip can stop with you. When a coworker sidles up to you bearing a juicy tidbit of gossip about Betty's office romance or Bill's impending firing, respond with, "Really?" and then change the subject or get back to work. If you don't respond, the gossiper will move on—and you'll retain the trust and respect of your colleagues.

9. If you're dealing with a difficult coworker, pretend your kids are watching. This neat little visualization will help you keep a cool head. After all, you've taught your children to be mannerly. With them "watching" you, it will be difficult to stoop to the level of your infuriating colleague.

10. You're saying "you're unimportant to me" if you ignore people's e-mails and phone messages. Return them promptly.

11. Make it clear that you would never ask anyone to do a level of work you wouldn't be willing to take on yourself. Always work at least as hard as anyone working with or for you.

12. When you don't end e-mails with a suggestion or a request for action, nothing is likely to happen. You might end with something like, "I will call you on Monday at 10 a.m. to discuss this" or "When can we get this done?"

> 🔒 **TOP SECRET!** If you want to annoy people, make them read three paragraphs into your e-mail before you get to the point. If you want to rise in the company, state your purpose in the first sentence or two and then get to the why and how of the matter.

13. Some companies are well managed; some are managed by idiots. On the outside chance executive management is not a bunch of idiots, did you ever think that maybe, just maybe, they know more than you do? Try a little experiment: If you experience an issue or two and it changes when you jump companies or groups, then you were probably in a dysfunctional workplace. But if it doesn't change, if it's always the same, then it's probably you. You might want to see somebody about that.

Great Advice

HOW TO RUN A MEETING PEOPLE WON'T DREAD

....

"If you had to identify, in one word, the reason the human race has not achieved, and never will achieve, its full potential, that word would be meetings." So said humorist Dave Barry, and many of us would agree. But it doesn't have to be this way. Some tips for having a good one:

Start and end strongly. Running a productive meeting isn't rocket science. As Denver-based consultant Teri Schwartz notes, much of it boils down to opening and conducting every meeting with a purpose and closing it with a plan for "going forward." Problems arise when people forget this. "It's like flying a plane," says Schwartz. "Most crashes happen at takeoff and landing."

Pick a leader. Cleveland's KeyCorp bank adopted this principle for meetings: Always assign someone to lead. "The worst thing you can do is go into a meeting with no one in charge," says the bank's senior EVP and chief risk officer, Charles Hyle. "It turns into a shouting match."

Think small. Be realistic about what you can accomplish. "You can't solve world hunger in an hour," Schwartz says. By the same token, keep the number of attendees manageable to stimulate discussion. "When you have too many people in the room," says Hyle, "everyone clams up."

Direct, don't dominate. "People hate it when they can't get their work done because they have to go to somebody else's meeting," says Michael Feiner of Irving Place Capital. So encourage others to speak up and get involved, especially junior staffers. "They need to believe it's not his meeting or her meeting, but 'our' meeting," Feiner says.

WHAT YOUR PAYROLL MANAGER WON'T TELL YOU

Don't negotiate for a salary or raise without these insider tips.

1. There's one website that will drive you and the company crazy: salary.com. It supposedly lists average salaries but if you look up any job, the salary it gives you always seems to be $10,000 to $20,000 higher than it actually is.

2. On salary, some companies try to lock you in early. At the first interview, they'll tell the HR person to say, "The budget for this position is 40K to 45K. Is that acceptable to you?" If the candidate accepts, they'll know they've got him or her stuck.

3. You think you're all wonderful and deserve a higher salary, but here in HR, we know the truth. And the truth is, a lot of you aren't very good at your jobs, and you're definitely not as good as you think you are.

4. Be careful if a headhunter is negotiating for you. You may want extra time off and be willing to sacrifice salary, but he is negotiating hardest for what hits his commission.

5. I once hired someone, and her mother didn't think the salary we were offering was high enough, so she called me to negotiate. There are two problems with that: 1) I can't negotiate with someone who's not you. 2) It's your mother. Seriously,

I was like, "Did that woman's mother just call me, or was that my imagination?" I immediately withdrew the offer.

6. Never accept the job immediately. Think about it overnight. Once you sign on the dotted line there's no room for negotiation.

7. Some companies do everybody's raises on their anniversary dates. I'm not a fan of that because if the budget comes out in January, those poor people hired in December get, "Oh sorry, we'd like to give you more, but we gave a huge increase to Bob so you're just going to get 2 percent."

8. Yes, the HR person has access to everyone's salary, but, says one, "I don't look unless I have to. There's nothing worse than having to reprimand someone, and then seeing they make $60,000 more than me."

9. Unlimited sick days usually benefit the company. When people are told they have a set number of sick days, they end up taking them all because they don't want to lose a day off. If given unlimited sick days, they may take none at all.

10. Protocol is still important. When introducing people, name the person of greater status first: "Mrs. CEO, I'd like you to meet the mail guy, Ron."

TOP SECRET! If we ask "What salary are you looking for?" say you're flexible or it depends on the responsibilities of the job. Try not to name a salary unless it's required, because that gives us a leg up in the negotiating.

11. Your group gets no respect. IT is always getting dumped on. Sales and marketing has it easy. Guess what? The other group probably feels the same way.

12. Being on time shows you respect other people's time. Being late over and over again will definitely get noticed.

13. If you're accused of sexual harassment, even if you're found to be not guilty, people will always look at you funny afterward. It can kill your career.

SOURCES: Ben Eubanks, HR professional in Alabama; HR director at a public relations agency; HR professional in New York, New York; HR professional at a midsize firm in North Carolina; Suzanne Lucas, a former HR executive and the Evil HR Lady on bnet.com.

Great Advice

THE BEST WAY TO ASK FOR A RAISE

....

1. Do your homework. Do some market research to determine what others in your industry currently earn at your position and poll your friends and colleagues in similar positions—as long as you work for different companies.

2. Know your employer. Many companies have official policies for discussing salary increases. If your employer offers salary reviews once a year, that's probably the best time for you to negotiate a raise. If the company's practices are more flexible, take the pulse of the financial situation of your department and the corporation as a whole when considering the timing of your discussion.

3. Show them what you're worth. Keep a journal, list, or spreadsheet of your daily tasks and accomplishments. Use this documentation as evidence to support your assertion that you're worthy of a salary increase.

4. Have a number in mind. Based on your industry research, your responsibilities, and your accomplishments, determine the salary you feel you deserve in advance of a meeting with your boss.

5. Come prepared. When you meet with your boss, be ready to back up your request with specifics about your performance and accomplishments, as well as goals for the future and additional responsibilities you're willing to take on. Keep the meeting professional and avoid discussing any personal reasons you feel you need a higher salary. Beware of using tactics such as a competitive job offer to get a raise—they may backfire on you.

WHAT PRODUCTIVITY EXPERTS WANT YOU TO KNOW

Your company's food service would love you to come in for a cookie or three when the afternoon slump hits, but there are better ways to perk back up.

1. Ten minutes outdoors is practically prescription-strength. When the slump hits, head outside and sit in the daylight for 10 minutes. Better still, have your lunch outside and divide your break between eating and a walk. It will help reset your biological clock, keep down the amount of melatonin (the sleep hormone) your body produces during this circadian dip, and give you a valuable boost of beneficial vitamin D, reducing your risk of osteoporosis, as well as various cancers.

2. A green salad sprinkled with low-fat cheese, a hard-boiled egg, and some sliced turkey wins over a pasta salad. Basically, protein will give you energy, while carbs may sap it. So a tuna salad without the bread is a better choice than a tuna sandwich. The change can really make a difference.

3. Teatime can soothe and energize. A mid-afternoon cup of tea is a good step toward beating the afternoon doldrums thanks to that little bit of a caffeine burst and the few quiet minutes it entails. Keep a selection of exotic flavored teas (preferably caffeinated) in your office and an aesthetically pleasing cup just for tea.

4. Your desk and e-mail inbox can pick you up—if you clean them out. Cleaning them out is a relatively mindless task that doesn't require great amounts of concentration or clear thinking, and both will leave you feeling more energized because you'll have accomplished something visible, as well as having reduced energy-sapping clutter.

5. Put a drop of peppermint oil in your hand and briskly rub your hands together, then rub them over your face (avoid your eyes). Peppermint is a known energy-enhancing scent.

6. You don't even have to leave your desk to gain energy. Simply roll your shoulders forward, then backward, timing each roll with a deep breath in and out. Repeat for 2 minutes.

🔒 **TOP SECRET!** An "I was thinking of you" phone call works wonders. A five-minute keep-in-touch call to your wife, child, siblings, parents, a friend, or a retired colleague will lift your spirits for hours and reinvigorate you to get your work done.

7. Consider a morsel of dark chocolate. Unlike milk chocolate, dark chocolate is truly a healthy food, closer to the category of nuts than sweets given the high levels of healthy fat and antioxidants it contains. Plus, it has abundant fiber and magnesium. Additionally, it provides a little caffeine, as well as a satisfyingly decadent feeling. Just stop at one square.

8. Chewing gums with strong minty flavors are stimulating, and the mere act of chewing is something of a tonic to a brain succumbing to lethargy. Plus, chewing stimulates saliva, which helps to clear out bacteria responsible for cavities and gum disease from lunch. Just be sure to choose sugar-free gum.

9. If you often work on your own, try to organize work involving others at the time of day when your concentration might otherwise be waning. We are social animals, and interactions always rev us up. But make sure it's an interesting, interactive activity. Sitting in a room listening to someone else drone on and on will just send you snoozing.

10. You can get your blood moving and feel more energized even in a meeting. Isometric exercises involve nothing more than tensing a muscle and holding it. For instance, with your arm held out, tense your biceps and triceps at the same time and hold for 5 to 10 seconds. You can do this with your calf muscles, thigh muscles (front and back), chest, abdomen, buttocks, shoulders, and back.

11. Not only will sharing your space with a plant—a live, growing thing—provide its own mood boost, but also studies find the scent of rosemary to be energizing. Whenever you need a boost, just rub a sprig between your fingers to release the fragrance. Or, if you're really wiped out, rub a sprig on your hands, face, and neck.

12. Have an afternoon snack designed to get the blood flowing. That's one that combines protein, fiber, and complex carbohydrates (such as whole-grain crackers or raw vegetables) to raise your blood sugar levels steadily and keep them up.

13. Keeping manageable items on your to-do list will keep you motivated. Checking off tasks you've completed makes you feel productive and ready for the next job. Be sure to keep routine items that you are always accomplishing on your list so you can have the satisfaction of checking them off.

Insider Expertise

THE BEST WAYS TO MANAGE A STRESSFUL DAY AT WORK

Sometimes work can be tough and we react by getting stressed out. We don't always have control over what happens to us, says Allen Elkin, PhD, director of the Stress Management Counseling Center in New York City. Yet that doesn't mean we have to react to a difficult, challenging situation by becoming frazzled or feeling overwhelmed or distraught. Instead, use these easy, natural methods to overcoming anxiety when it hits.

Mental Relaxation Techniques

Visualize calm. It sounds New Age-y, but at least one study, done at the Cleveland Clinic Foundation, has found that it's highly effective in reducing stress. Dr. Cooper recommends imagining you're in a hot shower and a wave of relaxation is washing your stress down the drain. Or try this routine, recommended by Gerald Epstein, MD, the author of *Healing Visualizations*: Close your eyes, take three long, slow breaths, and spend a few seconds picturing a relaxing scene, such as walking in a meadow, kneeling by a brook, or lying on the beach. Focus on the details—the sights, the sounds, the smells.

Do some math. Using a scale of one to ten, with one being the equivalent of a minor hassle and ten being a true catastrophe, assign a number to whatever it is that's making you feel anxious. "You'll find that most problems we encounter rate somewhere in the two to five range—in other words, they're really not such a big deal," says Dr. Elkin.

Be a fighter. "At the first sign of stress, you often hear people complain, 'What did I do to deserve this?'" says Dr. Cooper. The trouble is, feeling like a victim only increases feelings of stress and helplessness. Instead, focus on being proactive. If your flight gets canceled, don't wallow in self-pity. Find another one. If your office is too hot or too cold, don't suffer in silence. Call the building manager and ask what can be done to make things more comfortable.

Put it on paper. Writing provides perspective, says Paul J. Rosch, MD, president of the American Institute of Stress in Yonkers, New York. Divide a piece of paper into two parts. On the left side, list the stressors you may be able to change, and on the right, list the ones you can't. "Change what you can," Dr. Rosch suggests, "and stop fretting over what you can't."

Count to ten. Before you say or do something you'll regret, step away from the stressor and collect yourself, advises Dr. Cooper. You can also look away for a moment or put the caller on hold. Use your time-out to take a few deep breaths, stretch, or recite an affirmation.

Just say no. Trying to do everything is a one-way ticket to serious stress. Be clear about your limits, and stop trying to please everyone all the time.

Admit it. Each of us has uniquely individual stress signals—neck or shoulder pain, shallow breathing, stammering, teeth gritting, queasiness, loss of temper. Learn to identify yours, then say out loud, "I'm feeling stressed," when they crop up, recommends Dr. Rosch. Recognizing your personal stress signals helps slow the buildup of negativity and anxiety.

Schedule worry time. Some stressors demand immediate attention—a smoke alarm siren or a police car's whirling blue light. But many low-grade stressors can be dealt with at a later time, when it's more convenient. "File them away in a little mental compartment, or make a note," Dr. Elkin says, "then deal with them when the time is right. Don't let them control you."

Time-Outs That Help You Focus Later

Space out. Look out the window and find something natural that captures your imagination, advises Dr. Sobel. Notice the clouds rolling by or the wind in the trees.

Take a walk. It forces you to breathe more deeply and improves circulation, says Dr. Cooper. Step outside if you can; if that's not possible, you can gain many of the same benefits simply by walking to the bathroom or water cooler, or by pacing back and forth. "The key is to get up and move," Dr. Cooper says.

Soak it up. "When I have the time, nothing is more stress relieving for me than a hot bath," Dr. Weston says. "But when I don't have time, I do the next-best thing: I wash my face or even just my hands and arms with hot water. The key is to imagine that I'm taking a hot bath. It's basically a visualization exercise, but the hot water makes it feel real."

Dial a friend. Sharing your troubles can give you perspective, help you feel cared for, and relieve your burden.

Make plans. "Looking forward to something provides calming perspective," Dr. Elkin says. Buy concert tickets, schedule a weekend getaway, or make an appointment for a massage.

Goof off. It temporarily removes you from a potentially stressful situations. Esther Orioli, president of Essi Systems—a San Francisco–based consulting company that organizes stress-management programs—keeps a harmonica in the drawer for when she's feeling stressed out. Bonus: Playing it promotes deep breathing.

Part Nine

WHAT YOU DON'T KNOW ABOUT
YOUR
VACATION

Life isn't a day at the beach for the people who get you to the shore (or the slopes or the plains) and check you in when you arrive. But if you know what they're up against, you can use a little compassion and some insider info to turn even tough travel situations to your advantage.

Knowing how the systems work lets you take advantage of huge travel deals, avoid lines, and save big bucks at your destination without feeling like you're pinching every single penny. Sometimes it's knowing where to go, and sometimes it's knowing when. Veteran globetrotters, travel agents, pilots, cruise lines, and many others all have unique information that will round out your expertise to make you a travel-savvy vacationer, so read this before you hit the road!

WHAT TRAVEL AGENTS WON'T TELL YOU

Use these tricks and your next trip may add up to a lot less money—and seriously better stories—than you thought it would.

1. It's a rare day when a $20 bid on priceline.com won't get you an economy rental car anywhere.

2. Sometimes airlines really are playing tricks on you. But there are ways to get around it. You're shopping for a flight on the Web, and the flight prices seem to keep going up, not down. Why is that? Many Internet sites install "cookies" on your computer when you visit. A "cookie" is a collection of information that will include your user name and the date and time you visited the site. Sometimes travel websites use this information to increase their prices if you repeatedly run the same searches for airlines or hotels. If you price a flight, and go back to the site a few hours later only to find that the price has increased, it's probably a cookie at work. Before you buy a ticket, erase the cookies from your computer.

3. Not all islands are hurricane prone. Hurricanes not only do major damage, but they also scare the heck out of tourists. So what to do? The best places for a Caribbean vacation are the ABC islands: namely, Aruba, Bonaire, and Curaçao. They all lie outside the path that hurricanes have been following for hundreds of years. So next time you book that summer getaway, be sure to sneak a peek at these less-traveled gems.

4. Nobody uses traveler's checks anymore. If you have been faithfully ordering traveler's checks every time you hit the road, give up the habit. These days, the most economical way to manage money in a foreign country will probably be withdrawing currency from local ATMs as needed with a bank card.

5. But be sure to ask your bank in advance what fees are charged for international transactions and whether there are any no-fee ATM withdrawal arrangements with any banks at your destination. To lower the impact of a significant flat fee, make larger, less frequent withdrawals during your trip.

6. Advance tickets to Disney World can pay off. A seven-day parkhopper pass costs up to $485 (or about $70 a day) and expires after two weeks. This is a good idea because it allows you to get some of your travel arrangements out of the way now; you can work on the scheduling later. Buy the tickets at the gate and just one day will cost around $160.

7. There's a way around exorbitant hotel dry-cleaning bills. A product called Wrinkle Releaser spray is an inexpensive solution to hotel laundering. You just hang up your clothing, spray it, smooth out the wrinkles with your hands, and let it air dry. Or you can try making your own by mixing 1 tablespoon of fabric softener and ¼ cup of unscented rubbing alcohol with 1 cup of distilled water. Put it in a travel spray bottle and gently mist the garment about a hand's length away.

8. There are secret words that can get you upgrades. If you're willing to spend a little extra money, it's worth asking the agent to "split the difference" on the price of the first-class ticket. If first class isn't booked, which usually happens on less-traveled routes on off-peak travel days, the agent has some discretion when it comes to moving people into first class. Some airlines also let you use your frequent-flier miles to "purchase" an upgrade.

9. Sometimes we can get resort fees waived. The extra $10 to $15 per day they try to charge you as a "resort fee," supposedly to cover such amenities as the swimming pool and fitness club, is nothing but a ruse to make a hotel's rates appear lower at the time you are scouting for a room, say industry insiders. At the time of booking, scan the fine print of your agreement and ask the hotel about any fees that are not included in the quote. If you're surprised by such fees at the registration counter, call your credit card company after checking in and ask it to get the fee waived.

🔒 **TOP SECRET!** Cruise lines love repeat customers. All cruise lines have loyalty programs, and the more you vacation with one company, the better the perks will get—they could be anything from $100 cruise vouchers to private cocktail parties or free bottles of wine.

10. Cab drivers are our best friends. "I always depend on the taxi drivers," says Mark Zwick, one of the partners of PhillyTrips.com. "They always know the places to go, the things to see."

11. Many times a taxi driver works in tandem with bars and restaurants and will have special coupons for his favorite places. He'll be more than happy to let you have them. Why? Because he gets a kickback from the establishments. So let those taxi drivers take you to some places where they get a little something extra, because most of the time you'll be getting something extra as well, in the form of discounted meals or drinks.

12. We pretend we're traveling solo. Airline search engines mess with your head a little when it comes to booking your family's travel. The truth is, sometimes you'll get a cheaper rate by booking seats individually, because single seats can easily go unsold (especially middle seats in the back of the plane). Airlines jump at the chance to get rid of them. See what happens when you book seats individually.

13. We think trains, not planes. While traveling by train in North America is not the most popular choice, it's the way to go when traveling abroad, especially in Europe. If you really want to become an expert at this type of travel, you must go to www.seat61.com. It's the most comprehensive site out there when it comes to trains the world over.

Great Advice

8 TIPS FOR AFFORDABLE VACATIONS—NO PENNY PINCHING NEEDED

Here's how to shop online and get the best prices with the fewest clicks.

1. Become an expert well in advance. Sign up for e-mail alerts and online newsletters, recommends George Hobica of airfarewatchdog.com. It's the best way to familiarize yourself with destinations and prices. In other words, for now, keep your mind open and your wallet closed. And don't forget to ask friends on Twitter and Facebook for their tips.

2. Decide on a few destinations. Now that you have a better sense of what's out there, you want to work backward. Barbara Messing of travel-ticker.com explains, "Don't fixate on one place. Let the deal be your inspiration."

3. Reassure yourself. Before committing, play detective. For videos of hotels, restaurants, activities, and attractions, go to tripfilms.com and insiderperks.com. Tripfilms depends on travelers for their observations, while the videos on InsiderPerks are created by the site's staff. Watch both to get a good overview of your destination. Browse through other families' vacation photos on flickr.com (it's OK—really), and read candid reviews by travelers on tripadvisor.com.

4. Search for the lowest airfare. Experts consider kayak.com the best first step in searching for low-cost airline deals (it doesn't include Southwest, so you'll have to check that airline separately). You'll almost always get a better deal if you're flexible—you can fly out on one carrier and return on another, for example, or fly to an offbeat airport like Bob Hope Airport in Burbank, California

(15 miles outside L.A.), or Midway in Chicago. Lock in your rate, but don't pull the trigger yet. (Depending on the airline, you may have 10 minutes to 24 hours to commit, so do the next steps—fees and hotels—quickly.)

5. Find the hidden fees. If you want to know the real price of the ticket, check "Airline Fees: The Ultimate Guide" at smartertravel.com. Will you have to pay for that blanket, the soda, and the pretzels? Some airlines charge up to $100 extra for a seat with more legroom. To find out what your airline charges, go to its website or check the Guide. Then compare bag fees with FedEx, UPS, and U.S. Postal Service rates. "Depending on the route and method," says Hobica, "the cost savings from shipping versus schlepping can range from little or nothing to dramatic."

6. Get a room, then book your flight. Hotels.com features more than 70,000 properties—from small bed-and-breakfasts to all-inclusive luxury resorts—and flags special deals. For unbiased shots of lobbies, rooms, and neighborhoods, go to tvtrip.com. At oyster.com, you get photos, plus the pros and cons. Once you've booked your room, book your flight.

7. Rent a car before you leave. If you don't care which car-rental company you use, head to hotwire.com for deep discounts on rentals, says Anne Banas of smartertravel.com. Check rates for both airport and off-site pickup. (But if there's no free shuttle service, factor in the cost of a cab. Off-site hours may be limited.)

8. Once you've landed, "check in" with Foursquare, a free app for iPhones, BlackBerrys, Palms, and Android phones. Tell your friends where you are, and get their recommendations on the hot spots in town. If they're in the area, they just might join you.

WHAT YOUR PILOT WON'T TELL YOU

Most of us never get the chance to talk the pilot, but who hasn't wondered what's going on in the cockpit during all those hours of flight time?

1. We miss the peanuts, too.

2. I'm constantly under pressure to carry less fuel than I'm comfortable with. Airlines are always looking at the bottom line, and you burn fuel carrying fuel. Sometimes if you carry just enough fuel and you hit thunderstorms or delays, then suddenly you're running out of gas and you have to go to an alternate airport.

3. We tell you what you need to know. But we don't tell you things that are going to scare the pants off of you. So you'll never hear me say, "Ladies and gentlemen, we just had an engine failure," even if that's true.

4. We'd like to wait, but we can't. The Department of Transportation has put such an emphasis on on-time performance that we pretty much aren't allowed to delay a flight anymore, even if there are 20 people on a connecting flight that's coming in just a little late.

5. The truth is, we're exhausted. Our work rules allow us to be on duty 16 hours without a break. That's many more hours than a truck driver. And unlike a truck driver, who can pull over at the next rest stop, we can't pull over at the next cloud.

6. Some FAA rules don't make sense to us either. Like the fact that when we're at 39,000 feet going 400 miles an hour, in a plane that could hit turbulence at any minute, flight attendants can walk around and serve hot coffee and Chateaubriand. But when we're on the ground on a flat piece of asphalt going five to ten miles an hour, they've got to be buckled in like they're at NASCAR.

7. The two worst airports for us: Reagan National in Washington, D.C., and John Wayne in Orange County, California. You're flying by the seat of your pants trying to get in and out of those airports. John Wayne is especially bad because the rich folks who live near the airport don't like jet noise, so they have this noise abatement procedure where you basically have to turn the plane into a ballistic missile as soon as you're airborne.

8. I'm not the best person to ask for directions to the airport. We're in so many airports that we usually have no idea.

TOP SECRET! At some airports with really short runways, you're not going to have a smooth landing no matter how good we are: John Wayne Airport; Jackson Hole, Wyoming; Chicago Midway; and Reagan National.

9. We really do know the weather. This happens all the time: We'll be in Pittsburgh going to Philly, and there will be a weather delay. The weather in Pittsburgh is beautiful. Then I'll hear passengers saying, "You know, I just called my friend in Philly, and it's beautiful there, too," like there's some kind of conspiracy or something. But in the airspace between Pittsburgh and Philly there's a huge thunderstorm.

10. Your plane isn't truthfully labeled. You may go to an airline website and buy a ticket, pull up to its desk at the curb, and get onto an airplane that has a similar name painted on it, but half the time, you're really on a regional airline.

11. The regionals aren't held to the same safety standards as the majors. Their pilots aren't required to have as much training and experience, and the public doesn't know that.

12. How you land is a good indicator of a pilot's skill. So if you want to say something nice to a pilot as you're getting off the plane, say "Nice landing." We do appreciate that.

13. You really are getting there "early" more often. No, it's not your imagination. Airlines really have adjusted their flight arrival times so they can have a better record of on-time arrivals. So they might say a flight takes two hours when it really takes an hour and 45 minutes.

SOURCES: 17 pilots from across the country, including an AirTran Airways captain from Atlanta; Joe D'Eon, a pilot at a major airline who produces a podcast at flywithjoe.com; a US Airways pilot from South Carolina; Jack Stephan, US Airways captain based in Annapolis, Maryland, who has been flying since 1984; Jim Tilmon, a retired American Airlines pilot from Phoenix, Arizona.

Great Advice
TOP WAYS TO AVOID JET LAG

· ·

Acclimate. If you're going to be gone longer than a couple of days, begin acclimating your body to the new time zone by altering your eating schedule three days before your plane takes off. If you're heading west to San Diego from Boston, for example, three days before you leave, eat an hour earlier each day. Flying from San Diego back to Boston? Help reverse the acclimation and get back on home time by eating an hour later each day for three days.

Chug. Stay hydrated with bottled water. Avoid alcohol during your flight. It can dehydrate your body, mess up your internal clock, and exaggerate jet lag symptoms.

Hit the linguine. Or any other carb-dense food at dinner on the night before your flight. Scientists have been arguing for some time about whether or not this decreases jet lag and increases your potential for normal sleep, but recent research on has uncovered subtle effects that indicate carbs boost your ability to sleep— particularly when you fly westward. No one's quite figured out how they help, but they do know that carbs provide your brain with a source of tryptophan, from which it can make the sleep-inducing neurotransmitter serotonin.

Refrigerate. If you're flying during what would be night hours at your destination, try to get some sleep on the plane. Use ear-plugs to eliminate noise, an eyeshade to kill the light, and turn the air-conditioning valve on high. Another cue your body uses to set its internal clock is temperature. A lower temperature lowers your body's core temperature and signals it's time for sleep. To keep from getting too chilled, bring along one of those silk blanket-and-pillow sets that are sold through airline and online travel catalogs.

Avoid airline food. Your body also uses food to set its internal clock. Since airline food is served onboard according to the time at your home base, eating it can sabotage efforts to reset your clock to the time zone to which you're traveling.

Consider melatonin. No, you don't need a prescription. But since it has the ability to really mess with your brain chemicals, consult with a doctor anyway—especially if you're taking another medication. It's not as strong as a sleeping pill, but it directly affects your body's internal clock and nudges it toward sleep. But the safety profile of melatonin has not been seriously investigated, so it's not, experts agree, for long-term use until studies verifying its safety over the long haul have been done.

Have the eggs benedict. A protein-rich meal the morning after you arrive will give your brain what it needs to produce neurochemicals to increase your alertness throughout the day.

Stay on home time. If you're going to be away from home for only a couple of days, stay on the same eating and sleeping schedule while you're away as you would at home.

Or switch immediately. If you're away for more than just a couple of days, don't just set your watch to local time when you arrive—help reset your internal clock by eating, going to bed, and waking at the local time as well.

Bring your workout gear. Schedule a 30-minute workout each day you're on the road. You'll feel and sleep better.

WHAT YOUR FLIGHT ATTENDANT WON'T TELL YOU

The bathrooms really *are* that gross, your over-sized suitcase isn't helping anyone, and other insights from the travel experts who've seen—and dealt with—it all.

1. Want to start off on the wrong foot with me? Put your carry-on in a full overhead bin, leave it sticking out six inches, then take your seat at the window and wait for someone else (me!) to come along and solve the problem you just created.

2. We're not just being lazy. Our rules really say we aren't allowed to lift your luggage into the overhead bin for you, though we can "assist."

3. Yes, passengers are incredibly rude. But stealing a beer, cursing out passengers, and jumping out of a plane is not the way to handle it. You disarm an unruly passenger by introducing yourself, asking his name, and saying something like "I've been incredibly nice to you for three hours. Why are you treating me like this?" Generally that gets the other passengers on your side—and sometimes they'll even applaud.

4. Don't ask us if it's OK to use the lavatories on the ground. The answer is always yes. Do you think what goes into the toilet just dumps out onto the tarmac?

5. Do not poke or grab me. I mean it. No one likes to be poked, but it's even worse on the plane because you're sitting down and we're not, so it's usually in a very personal area. You would never grab a waitress if you wanted ketchup or a fork, would you?

6. I hate working flights to destinations like Vail and West Palm Beach. The passengers all think they're in first class even if they're not. They don't do what we ask. And the overhead bins are full of their mink coats.

7. If you're traveling with a small child and you keep hearing bells, bells, and more bells, please look to see if it's your child playing with the flight attendant call bell.

8. The lavatory door is not rocket science. Just push.

> 🔒 TOP SECRET! If you're traveling overseas, do yourself a favor and bring a pen. You would not believe how many people travel without one, and you need one to fill out the immigration form.

9. If you have a baby, bring diapers. If you're diabetic, bring syringes. If you have high blood pressure, don't forget your medication. That way, I'm not trying to make a diaper out of a sanitary pad and a pillowcase or asking over the intercom if someone has a spare inhaler.

10. If you hear us paging for a doctor or see us running around with oxygen, defibrillators, and first aid kits, that's not the right time to ask for a blanket or a Diet Coke.

11. You really expect me to take your soggy Kleenex? Or your kid's fully loaded diaper? I'll be right back with gloves.

12. Just in case you hadn't noticed, there are other people on the airplane besides you. So don't clip your toenails, snore with wild abandon, or do any type of personal business under a blanket!

13. I'm sorry it's taking forever to get you a wheelchair, but that's one thing you can't blame the airline for. The wheelchair service is subcontracted to the cities we fly into, and it's obviously not a top priority for many of them.

Great Advice
HOW TO FLY COMFORTABLY

You can get in and out of the airport faster—and with a lot less stress.

Fly early in the day. At airports scheduled to capacity, any delay in the morning means there will be at least that much of a delay for every flight thereafter.

Leave a day early. Depart a day in advance for crucial trips, such as a key business meeting or a wedding.

Check the delay statistics for your flight. Use websites like bts.gov (Bureau of Transportation Statistics) or flightstats.com to see how often that flight is more than 15 minutes late on a scale of 1 to 9 (the lower the number, the more often it's late)—before you book your tickets. If the number is 5 or below and time is of the essence, consider another flight.

Skip the lines. Sign up for the registered traveler program to take some of the pain out of the preflight experience. Travelers who pass a voluntary background check can use special lanes to whisk through security at certain U.S. airports.

Don't let it drop. If you have a truly terrible experience, write a reasonable letter afterward to the airline CEO, explaining what happened and asking for compensation. Refer to the contract of carriage listed on the airline's website; it explains the compensation policies. It's up to the airline whether to remedy a passenger's bad experience. If you used plastic to buy your ticket, your credit card company can challenge the airline for violating its contract with a customer.

WHAT AIRLINES WON'T TELL YOU

From how to get the best seats to disgusting airplane habits to avoid, get these insider secrets to a safer, cheaper flight.

1. Here's what a safety demo doesn't say: We dim cabin lights at night so your eyes are adjusted to the dark if you need to find a way out. We put up tray tables at takeoff and landing so passengers next to you can escape. And you should open your window shade, so if there's a crash, firefighters can see inside.

2. We're extremely stingy about fuel. It's expensive to carry, so keeping levels low saves us money. But it also means if there's rough weather or an unexpected delay, we're more likely to make an emergency landing because we're running out of gas.

3. If your flight is overbooked, don't accept the first $200 voucher we offer. We typically keep increasing the offer until we have enough volunteers willing to give up their seats. If we don't get enough volunteers and have to bump you involuntarily, insist on cash compensation instead. Department of Transportation rules say you're entitled to as much as $1,300 in cash.

4. If you book a group trip, search for only one ticket at a time. Why? Because if you search for, say, four tickets, and we have only three at the lowest fare, all four are bumped to a higher price bracket.

5. Some airlines don't allow two pilots flying together to eat food from the same source within an hour of each other. Either they have to eat at different restaurants, or one waits at least an hour to make sure the other doesn't get poisoned or sick.

6. Lost your luggage? Don't delay reporting it. Most of us require you to file a report within a very short time period. If you miss the deadline, your claim may be denied.

7. You're not imagining it: Our seats really are getting tinier. In the Boeing 777s used for long-haul international flights, we recently shrank the seats by one inch so we could fit an extra seat in each row.

8. You don't want that pretzel you dropped on the tray table. Most airlines don't clean trays between flights. Before you touch anything, clean it with sanitizing wipes.

9. If your flight is canceled, get in line at the ticket desk or the gate counter—but also get on the phone. You'll probably reach an airline phone agent first.

10. We pay a fee every time you book through price-comparison online sites like TripAdvisor and Orbitz, so we're making it harder for you to use them. Some airlines (Delta, Southwest) don't release fares at all to certain third-party sites.

11. Check the seat map about four days (100 hours) before your flight. That's when we start upgrading fliers from coach to business and some of the best seats open up.

12. We are totally disgusted when we see you walking around barefoot on the plane. That carpet? Everything you can imagine has been spilled on it: vomit, milk, baby pee, and blood, to name a few.

13. If we cancel your flight, we will offer to put you on another one. But you should also know that even if you have a "nonrefundable" fare, we will give you your money back if you ask.

SOURCES: Charlie Leocha, chairman and cofounder of Travelers United, a consumer travel organization; Melisse Hinkle, head of content and social media at cheapflights. com; Chris Lopinto, cofounder and president of expertflyer.com; Rick Ingersoll, author of Frugal Travel Guy Handbook; George Hobica, founder of airfarewatchdog.com; and a captain for a regional airline.

WHAT YOUR HOTEL DESK CLERK WON'T TELL YOU

Here's the real deal on upgrades, lower rates, and what we talk about when you can't hear us.

1. The 1-800 reservations number will probably send you to a central office with set rates. If you call the hotel directly instead, you can negotiate.

2. Hotels can pay a commission of up to 30 percent to online booking sites. So offer me 20 percent less than the online price, and we both come out ahead.

3. Independently owned hotels are far more likely to give you a discount. Some chains balk at dropping the rate.

4. Don't ask me for an upgrade when other guests are within earshot. Want a more spacious room without paying more? Request a corner room or a handicapped one.

5. If you request a king bed, there's no guarantee. No matter how confident the reservations agent sounds, call the hotel directly and make the request again a few days before you travel. Then do it again on the day of. If we still don't have one when you get there and you're nice about it, we may comp your breakfast or upgrade you to a suite.

6. Most of us are happy to help. If you ask us to, we'll tell callers you're not registered at the hotel, or tell you where to park so you can't see your car from the interstate. But we're also talking behind your back about what you might be hiding.

7. Some concierges get kickbacks for sending you to pricey tourist traps. If you want an unbiased recommendation, ask the clerk.

8. Sometimes my boss makes me lie, like when the elevator's not working and I tell you someone is coming to fix it soon. I know it won't be fixed until Monday, because the manager doesn't want to pay the repairman's weekend rate.

> 🔒 TOP SECRET! **Always request clean linens when you check in. We wash the sheets every day, but blankets often only get washed once a week. And the bedspreads? If there's no visible stain, it's maybe once a month.**

9. Everything is negotiable. If your hotel offers a hot breakfast buffet as well as a free continental breakfast, ask if you can get the hot breakfast with your room. Very rarely will we tell you no.

10. Never use the long distance. Unless you want to pay $10 for a five-minute call, it's best to specifically ask for it to be turned off. We've had situations in which housekeepers have made calls from a guest's phone.

11. If you travel to the same place frequently, use the same hotel each time. Get to know the staff. Regulars are recognized and treated as VIPs. You could get free upgrades, discounts, and more.

12. My official job description: errand runner, toilet plunger, bow-tie tier, towel deliverer, and chef (that free continental breakfast doesn't appear from above). I've also sprinkled rooms with rose petals and dealt with dead bodies. All for about $10 an hour.

13. It seems to have gone out of fashion to tip your housekeeper. Most are paid minimum wage with the expectation of tips. Take care of them, and they'll take care of you.

SOURCES: Current and former desk clerks at hotels in Mississippi, Kansas, Colorado, Maryland, Vermont, and Washington.

7 TIPS FOR TOTAL HOTEL SAFETY

Burglars told us you're a target in your home-away-from-home, too. These tips for keeping protected while you're traveling will make sure you can relax to the max.

1. Ask for a room on the third floor or higher. Most thefts occur on the first two floors. Stay below the seventh floor, however; few fire engine ladders can reach above it.

2. Choose a hotel over a motel. Burglaries are easier when your room's door is quickly accessible from the parking lot.

3. Make sure the front-desk person doesn't say your room number aloud when you're registering. They should write it down and hand it to you. If he does say it aloud, ask for another room and ask that he write down the number.

4. Ask who is at your door and verify before opening. If you didn't order room service, or don't know why the "employee" is there, call the front desk and verify that they sent someone.

5. Use the main entrance of the hotel when returning in the evening.

6. Use all locking devices for your door, and lock all windows and sliding glass doors.

7. Don't leave the "Please Make Up Room" sign outside your door unless you want to tell the whole world you're not there. Instead, put the "Do Not Disturb" sign on the door. If you want your room made up while you're out, call housekeeping and let them know.

WHAT WORLD TRAVELERS WON'T TELL YOU

Great deals happen in the off-season—you just have to know how to find them. We got frequent travelers to reveal when and where those money-savers really are.

1. Off-season doesn't mean the wrong season, when no one wants to go or when you won't be able to experience the best of that area. Some of my favorite travel experiences have been during the off-season.

2. It does mean deals and discounts. Huge tourist destinations are the best bet for sharp discounts in the off-season because these economies are completely dependent on tourist income as opposed to business-travel income.

3. You'll save more on hotels than airfare if hotels can fill an otherwise empty room for 25 or 50 percent of what they normally get. That money is just straight to their profit. Airlines just won't fly as many trips. By far the nicest hotels I've stayed in for very small amounts of money have been off-season deals on major chain hotels, like Marriott, which I get on priceline.com.

4. Getting on the phone often gets you deals. I find a specific deal online or something through the hotel's own social-media marketing efforts or through a discount club like jetsetter.com. Then I call the hotel and try to book it directly.

5. Use community-generated review sites like tripadvisor.com to get the real scoop on hotels and locations. You'll see pictures of rooms and facilities posted by guests, instead of the hotel's marketing team. Plus, you'll get the real deal about the staff, the location, and the overall experience of staying in the hotel.

6. Not that children aren't delightful, but I've been in places where there are huge groups of schoolkids running around making it a much less pleasant experience than it would otherwise have been.

7. Cities and major business centers are not as likely to have off-season deals, because there's no off-season for business travelers. It's hard to imagine a season in New York City that's the off-season.

🔒 **TOP SECRET!** Sign up for the city you are traveling to with sites like Groupon and Scout Mob. These discount-finders will send you amazing local deals on spas, restaurants, and entertainment that usually only the locals know about.

8. You'd be surprised at what you can negotiate. I called a place in Barbados. It was the off-season, and I said, "Is that your cheapest room? What if I stayed a few extra days?" She said, "Well, I can offer you the rate for Caribbean citizens." Caricom is the term for the Caribbean community, and there's a rate for native Caribbeans. It was really easy for her, and it would never have come up online. Only by my calling the hotel did she think of saying, "Oh, we can slip you in under this Caricom rate."

9. If you want to get a taste of the real local culture, ask a waiter, the girl giving out pool towels, or the bartender where to hang out. You're sure to find some great spots that aren't overpriced for tourists.

10. Public transportation is the way to go. If you can figure out the bus system, take it. You can literally save hundreds of dollars taking buses instead of flagging down cabs every time you want to go somewhere.

11. In any season, beware of extra fees. If you can't avoid them or talk them down, at least be aware of additional fees such as extra legroom charges, hidden hotel fees, and rental car extras you don't really need.

12. There are great currency-converter apps that you can download to your phone. Use one if you're traveling somewhere that has a much different monetary system than you're used to, and you won't end up paying $12 American for a can of mystery soda.

13. Refundable tickets can really pay off, especially if you're booking a trip months in advance. Spending an extra forty or fifty dollars up front is a lot better than paying hundreds of dollars in change fees, which all major airlines consider mandatory.

SOURCES: Loren Bendele, CEO, savings.com; Seth Kugel, Frugal Traveler blogger, *New York Times*; Nina Willdorf, former editor in chief, *Budget Travel*.

Great Advice

THE 5 EASIEST WAYS TO PREVENT TRAVEL STRESS?

1. Invest in a lightweight, microfiber, rolling carry-on.
You'll be less inclined to overpack and less likely to go over the airline's allowed carry-on dimensions.

2. Pack one pair of shoes. Make the ones you wear onboard slip-ons. The Transportation Security Administration (TSA) and your fellow passengers will thank you when it comes time to remove them.

3. Decant your shampoo. No need to pack whole bottles into your checked luggage. Buy inexpensive 3-ounce plastic bottles at your drugstore, and decant at home.

4. Pack one lightweight sweater suitable for day or night. Unless you're visiting the Arctic, there is no reason to travel with your entire winter wardrobe. Choose carefully, and pack lightweight clothes that can be layered.

5. Stick with one color scheme. Our experts uniformly agree that packing clothes that are black or white is the wisest way to travel. Everything will always match, black can be very dressy (or not), white always looks crisp, and you can brighten up outfits with a simple, lightweight scarf.

WHAT CRUISE LINES WON'T TELL YOU

Here are the perfect times to book a trip, what "all-inclusive" really means, and more secrets you need to know before setting sail.

1. Our "all-inclusive" rate? Typically, that doesn't include alcohol, tips, shore excursions, Internet, dining outside our dining room, and what you spend on casino or bingo play. And please, do come play: Your odds are often even worse than on land.

2. Always look at the ship's deck plan before you choose your cabin. Don't pick one directly under the gym, the pool deck, the disco, or any late-night venue. Know that if you book a cabin at the front of the ship, you're going to feel some up-and-down motion.

3. If your ship permits it, pack a charging station or a power strip. Many cruise ships still have only one or two outlets per cabin—and that's not going to cut it in 2016.

4. If you're arriving by car, do not park in the cruise terminal, which can cost $20 to $30 a day. Off-site lots typically cost half as much, offer shuttle service to port, and have your car waiting with the AC on at trip's end.

5. You're twice as likely to be sexually assaulted on a cruise as you are on land, a 2011 study found, and two thirds of assailants are crew members. Yet cases are hard to prosecute, with alcohol often involved and police often not on board. Stay safe by sticking with a friend.

6. Shhh … here's a secret: You can book many of the same land excursions we offer for a fraction of the cost by arranging them privately with tour companies beforehand.

7. For God's sake, wash your hands. There were 11 outbreaks on cruise ships in the first six months of 2016, almost as many as in all of 2015. Most were norovirus, a highly contagious bug that causes stomach cramps, vomiting, and diarrhea.

8. Thanks to laws that allow us to register our ships in foreign nations, we don't have to comply with U.S. labor regulations, so crew members typically work 12 to 13 hours every day, with no minimum wage, overtime, or benefits. Don't be shocked if your service reflects this.

9. Ever wonder where we get all that freshwater? We make it. That's right—giant onboard desalination systems remove salt and impurities from ocean water so it's safe to drink.

10. Our Wi-Fi prices can be crazy high for subpar performance. So save your surfing for port days, and ask the crew for the nearest free hot spot. (Since they can't afford ship Wi-Fi either, crew members flock to Internet cafés when they disembark.)

11. Sorry, procrastinators: Most cruise lines now favor early booking promotions over last-minute deals, and the least expensive rooms sell out first. For the lowest price, book right when we announce an itinerary, often about 18 months out.

12. We're not required to report thefts of less than $10,000, so no one knows how much petty crime really happens on board. But it's a lot: Leave your valuables at home.

13. We really do train for pirate attacks (even though they're extremely rare). We can't share many details, but let's just say that our ship's fire hoses can fight more than fires.

SOURCES: Sherry Kennedy, founder of cruisemaven.com; Jim Walker, a maritime attorney who specializes in cruise-line law; Brian David Bruns, a former crew member on six cruise lines and the author of *Cruise Confidential;* a former cruise crew member from Thailand; and three current cruise-line employees who asked to remain anonymous.

WHAT AMUSEMENT PARKS WON'T TELL YOU

From how to beat the crowds to the real reasons rides get shut down, former and current amusement park employees dish their biggest secrets.

1. The best way to beat lines? Get there an hour early, walk in the minute it opens, and hit the coasters and other popular rides first. At Disney's Magic Kingdom Park, every minute you arrive after the park opens is two extra minutes of waiting in line.

2. Grab an umbrella and come when the forecast is iffy. Many people skip a visit on those days, so we have some of our shortest lines.

3. Get in the single rider line. Most big attractions have one (although they're not always well marked), and if you don't mind not sitting together, your wait will be 20 or 30 percent of the regular line wait, so 15 to 20 minutes instead of an hour. You and your friends can still hang out in line, and you'll be off the ride within a few minutes of each other.

4. Never, ever buy your ticket at the gate. Nearly every theme park has an online discount.

5. Choose your vacation days wisely. You can cut the cost of your hotel stay by moving your summer vacation by just a few days. Every theme park has different seasons that roughly correspond to school schedules and holidays, and they charge more when school's out. But the season generally ends the first or second week of August. So if you can move your five-night summer trip to mid- or late-August instead of early August, you can save hundreds of dollars.

6. Ready to win one of those big stuffed animals? Watch other customers play first, ideally until you see a few wins. And remember, our prizes are very low quality. Economically speaking, you're always better off saving your money and buying your own stuffed animal in a store.

> 🔒 **TOP SECRET!** Amusement park employees are know to play "guest bingo." To win, they have to find specific types of guests (someone in a cowboy hat, families dressed alike, etc.)

7. Should you pay for the express pass? Only for the busy times. At most parks, prices change based on demand. The cheaper they are, the more likely it is that you won't need them. So if you're going to a theme park on the Fourth of July or over spring break and you don't want to spend two or three hours in line, get the pass.

8. No one really knows if theme park rides are getting safer or more dangerous. This is because no single federal agency is responsible for collecting data or enforcing standards. A 2013 study revealed that more than 93,000 children were treated in ERs for amusement park-related injuries between 1990 and 2010 (about 20 kids a day during the summer months).

9. Don't get frisky on dark rides. Every inch of every ride is monitored by security cameras (including infrared ones that work in the dark). If you decide to get busy with your honey, not only will the person in the control tower see it, but he'll call over all his buddies to watch.

10. Even though some of the character costumes have fans, it can get very hot in there. That's why each mascot is available for only short time periods. So when our handlers say it's time for us to go, please don't ask us to take one more picture with little Johnny. It's a safety issue.

11. Stuck on the tracks? Chances are it's a scared child. We're not allowed to let a train leave the station with a crying child inside, because of the risk that he or she may try to hop out at the last minute. **12. We purposely change our music during the day.** In the morning, when we want to get you deep into the park, we play fast marching-band music. But at the end of the day, we play slower waltz music to encourage you to linger and shop before you leave.

13. Every night, after the crowds are gone, more than 100 feral cats make themselves at home in Disneyland. They're quietly fed, vaccinated, and neutered by Disney because they perform an important job: they help control the rodent population.

SOURCES: Former Walt Disney World cast member Robert Niles, editor of themeparkin-sider.com; Len Testa, programmer for touringplans.com and coauthor of the Unofficial Guides theme park series; and former and current employees of Cedar Point in Sandusky, Ohio; Six Flags Magic Mountain in Valencia, California; and Universal Studios in Orlando, Florida.

Great Advice

HIT THE ROAD EQUIPPED WITH THESE KIDS' GAMES

If you want your vacation to be spent away from the screen—bring along these games and ideas for young kids:

Create your own scavenger hunt, challenging young passengers to spot license plates identifying as many states as possible. For an educational boost, *Kids' Road Atlas* (ages 6–12) from Rand McNally is a colorful U.S. atlas offering a kid-friendly map, state symbols, and games that describe each state's history, geography, or folklore. Young travelers learn how to read a map by using a legend, scale, and coordinates.

Give kids a map and a highlighter, and have them follow the route you take.

Bring along a sketch pad and lots of pencils. If you want to get a little fancier, a laptop coloring desk is a great way for kids to keep occupied and make postcards to send to friends and family.

Play 20 Questions. You think of a person or object, and your opponent(s) asks you 20 yes-or-no questions to try to figure out who or what you're thinking of.

Try the Memory Game. "I'm going to the World's Fair, and in my trunk I packed . . ." Players take turns adding a new item to the list. Beginning with A, the first letter of each new item must start with the next letter of the alphabet.

Hold a Sound Contest in which kids imitate the noises they hear in places such as home, street, farm, or zoo. After 20 minutes of that, you may want to try the Quiet Contest—whoever can be quietest the longest wins a prize.

Pack a deck of cards. Popular games like War, Rummy, or Go Fish can keep kids busy for hours.

Keep a family vacation scrapbook. It doesn't have to be an elaborate production; in fact, the simpler, the better. A spiral-bound sketchbook or individual pages saved in plastic sheet protectors and kept in a loose-leaf binder work well. Bring along some crayons, colored pencils, or washable markers. Along the way, collect mementos of your trip—restaurant menus or placemats, ticket stubs from zoos, parks, and museums (and hopefully not speeding tickets!). Each day have the kids draw a picture of something or someone they saw. Older children can include written memories. The finished journal will make the vacation easy to revisit and share with friends and family.

WHAT PARK RANGERS WANT YOU TO KNOW

From excellent deals to cautionary tales, these tips and tricks will leave you perfectly prepared for a trip to the national parks.

1. Go beyond the overlooks. No matter which park you're visiting, walk at least a quarter mile down a trail. You'll get away from the crowds and experience a completely different perspective.

2. Stay put if you get lost. The more you move around, the harder you are to find. If you can't reach us on your phone, spread out brightly colored clothing.

3. Have a fourth grader in your family? You're in luck: At everykidinapark.gov, fourth graders can sign up for an annual pass that grants them and a carload of passengers free access to all national parks.

4. To avoid crowds during busy summer months, check out Death Valley instead of the Grand Canyon, Kings Canyon instead of Yosemite, or Capitol Reef instead of Zion.

5. We work hard to keep poachers out. Some raid our parks for plant life to sell to the floral industry. Others have used antifreeze to collect moths and butterflies. Some have even killed bears for their gallbladders, which can fetch $3,000 each as a "traditional medicine" in Asia.

6. You're closer to a national park than you think. People associate national parks with the wilderness, but about a third of the 410 National Park Service sites are actually in urban areas.

7. Keep your distance from any animal, whether it's a squirrel or a buffalo. One time at Yellowstone, a bison was eating grass near a parking lot. People tried to take selfies, but the bison got mad and attacked someone. If you must get a close-up, invest in a telephoto lens.

8. Never spend time in a park without talking to a ranger. Our heads are crammed with trivia, interesting facts, and historical information about our locations, and we love sharing it with you. Your tax dollars are paying for us so you might as well take advantage. Here are a few good questions to ask: What's something I wouldn't learn just by looking at exhibits or walking the trails? What is your favorite spot in the park?

9. We aren't just being polite when we ask you these questions: "Where are you hiking today? How much water do you have?" It's part of an effort called "Preventative Search and Rescue" that aims to help visitors be more prepared before they hike. If I suggest a shorter hike or a long break in a shady spot, take my advice. We've seen a dramatic drop in our search-and-rescue calls since we launched the program in the Grand Canyon in 1997.

10. If you've got kids, don't miss our Junior Ranger program. Designed for children ages 5–12, kids pick up a booklet in the visitor's center and complete a specified number of age-appropriate activities, such as finding items in the park, completing a word search, or attending a ranger-led program. Once they finish, a ranger will lead them in a mini-ceremony and give them a coveted Junior Ranger Badge.

11. Visit early morning or evening if you can. That's when the wildlife will be out, the crowds will be thin, and the light is truly beautiful.

12. Don't pay for a tour when you can get one for free. In most parks, we know more than the paid tour guides, and we have regular talks, tours, and programs. In Washington, D.C., for example, we offer tours on the National Mall every day, including a weekend bike tour, an evening lantern walk, and programs for kids. Check nps.gov for a schedule.

13. Staying hydrated is very important, but don't overdo it. Hikers sometimes drink too much water and suffer from water intoxication, which can be just as deadly as being dehydrated. So go for what we call "mellow yellow." Drink just enough water to keep your urine light yellow in color. This is what your urine color says about your health. And, if you get low on water...uh, we don't recommend drinking your own urine.

SOURCES: National Park Service Rangers Kathy Kupper, Brandon Torres, Michael Kelly, Michael Liang and Enimini Ekong; and former rangers Andrea Lankford, author of *Ranger Confidential: Living, Working and Dying in the National Parks* and Bruce Bytnar, author of *A Park Ranger's Life.*

THE SMARTEST WAYS TO TAKE A SPUR-OF-THE-MOMENT VACATION

Sometimes you just need to get out of town, and you really can take a last-minute trip without paying premium prices. But if you just need a break from the office and don't want the hassle of travel, there's always another way to go: home! Use these tips for saving big on a last-minute booking or creating a fabulous "staycation."

How to Book a Last-Minute Vacation

Even if you're a procrastinator, a spontaneous getaway doesn't have to drain your wallet. Here's how to get a great deal when you want to travel quickly.

Troll the travel websites. Sites such as Expedia.com, Priceline.com, and Travelocity.com are treasure troves for last-minute travelers. A few clicks will provide you with the latest transportation and accommodation availability, as well as deals on bundled packages (flight, hotel, car rental) and all-inclusive vacations. Save a few steps by going straight to Kayak.com, which allows you to compare rates, dates, and availability from all of the major travel websites at once.

Register for last-minute travel e-mail blasts. Those same travel websites, and most airlines, offer weekly e-mail newsletters that include up-to-the-minute deals on flights, cruises, hotels, and more. If you're flexible about where and when you travel, finding a great deal to an exciting destination can be as easy as checking your inbox.

Remember the 14-day rule. If they're not fully booked, airlines, hotels, and cruise ships often offer significant discounts two weeks in advance of travel. The key is to get both your transportation and accommodations to line up, so the more flexible you can be about arrival and departure dates, the better.

Go off-peak. Airlines and hotels are less crowded on weekdays, particularly Tuesdays and Wednesdays. If you can book your arrival and departure during the week, you'll have more flights and rooms to choose from. Tuesdays and Wednesdays are also the best days for booking last-minute travel, as prices tend to climb as the weekend approaches. (Remember: When booking your hotel, keep in mind that the best deals on many round-trip flights require a Saturday night stay.)

Try for a last-minute house rental. Despite what real estate brokers might have you believe, vacation rentals can still be found post-Memorial Day. And the good news is, the later the date, the more eager owners are to find renters and the more likely they'll be to offer discounts or accommodate requests, such as flexible arrival or check-out times. Be sure to visit vacation rental sites like vrbo.com as well as contacting realtors, and consider slightly off-the-beaten-path locations and properties that are farther from town or the beach.

Have the Ultimate Staycation

The perfect staycation isn't just another day off. It's a way to set your body and mind into total relaxation mode. It means there is no stress about doing extra housework or tackling those home improvement projects allowed—that's too much work! Staycationing *is* vacationing. Here's how to do it:

Unplug your alarm. Turn off your alarm and let yourself sleep as late as you like. Like vacationing, staycationing doesn't require you to clock-in. Go to bed when you want to and wake up whenever—remember, a good vacation has no set routine.

Play tourist. Whether you live in a big city or a small town, surely you haven't done everything there is to do. Check out the latest gallery opening, grab tickets to a matinee, hop on a tour bus, or take a trip to your local historical centers. You'll see the place you live from a whole new perspective.

Turn off your phone. Pretend that you're half a world away with little access to your phone. Leave a voicemail that says that you're on vacation and will only be checking messages when you get the chance. Forgetting about your phone will keep you focused on your main goal—relaxation.

Don't check e-mails. Set an out-of-office reply or a vacation message on your work and personal e-mail accounts and don't peek until you "return" from your vacation.

Don't tackle your to-dos. It's easy to think that your time spent at home can be used to reorganize, clean, and do a few home improvements, but a vacation is no time to do extra work. If you were on an actual vacation would you be upset that your floors at home weren't being scrubbed? No way. Let things around the house stay as they are. Or, for a real treat, hire a cleaning service to come spruce the place up while you're out on the town.

Order in. Hate to cook? Then don't do it. It's rare that you would be cooking your own food if you were out of town, so enjoy the benefits of ordering in or grabbing your favorite take-out. Added bonus: fewer dishes to clean up.

Go out to dinner. With all of the money you've saved by not going out of town, you can afford to dress up and go out to a fancy dinner. Splurge on the chef's special or the market-priced lobster. Explore some fine dining that you've never tried before, and truly enjoy your night out.

Have a TV/movie marathon. If you've been too busy to catch up on the latest television series or movies, grab some DVDs or go through your DVR list. Missing a few classics on your movie bucket list? Take the opportunity to see some of the greatest movies of all time, all from the comfort of your own home.

INDEX

A

Air travel. *See also* Vacations and travel
  airline tricks and secrets, 330, 343–344
  arrival/departure schedules, 337, 342
  booking family or group trips, 332, 343
  finding lowest fares, 333–334
  flight attendant secrets, 340–341
  flying comfortably, 342
  hidden fees, 334, 349
  international flights, 341
  jet lag, 338–339
  last-minute vacations, 362–363
  nonrefundable fares, 344
  off-season/off-peak, 348, 363
  pilot secrets, 335–337
  refundable tickets, 350
  stress management for, 351
  upgrades, 331
  worst airports, 336
Amusement parks, 354–356
Animals, sensory perceptions of, 168. *See also*
  Cats; Dogs
Ants, controlling, 13–14
Aphids, controlling, 15
Apologies, 151, 172
Apples vs. oranges, 131
ATMs and ATM cards, 257, 262, 331
Attitude, half-empty vs. half-full, 170

B

Baby products, 204–205, 245
Babysitters, 140
Baby wipe containers, 206
Baby wipes, 4, 204
Bacon vs. sausage, 130
Baking soda, for hair care, 194

Banks. *See also* Credit cards; Loans; Money
  banker secrets, 256–257
  checking and savings accounts, 294–295
  investment products, 299
  online banking, 257, 294
Barista secrets, 54–55
Bar Keepers Friend, 36
Bartenders
  secrets of, 57–58
  tipping, 51
Basement boondoggle, 44
Bathrooms. *See also* Plumbing; Toilets
  cleaning tips, 35, 36
  in restaurants, 49
  safety in, 3
Baths
  for better sleep, 111
  for stress relief, 328
Batteries
  car, tips and tricks, 183
  recycling, 31–32
Beer
  stains from, 190
  uses for, 15, 59
  weight control and, 126
Berries, 104, 131
Blinds, cleaning, 35. *See also* Window coverings
Blueberries, 104, 131
Bottled water, 270
Breath and breathing
  bad breath, 99, 101
  visualizing calm and, 326
Broccoli vs. cauliflower, 131
Burglar secrets, 19–20, 21
Butcher secrets, 66–67

C

Caffeine
    in coffee, 49, 55
in pain relievers, 112
    productivity and, 323, 324
Calm, visualizing, 326
Camp
    affordable options, 159
    counselor secrets, 157–158
Cars
    battery tips and tricks, 183
    buying tips, 174–175
    cleaning, 185–187
    cracked light precaution, 184
    dealer secrets, 174–175
    detailer secrets, 184–186
    driving tips, 176–178
    extending life of, 176
    gas- and fuel-saving tips, 177–178, 269
    insurance, 297
    mechanic secrets, 181–182
    paint importance and care, 184
    premium gas for, 269
    renting, 330, 334, 349
    service warranties, 269
    waxing, 185, 187
    windshield repair, 184
Car seats, 245
Cast-iron pans, 282
Cats
    giving pills to, 164
    veterinary secrets, 163–165
Cauliflower vs. broccoli, 131
Cell phones
    accessories for, 284
    etiquette for using, 53, 55, 84, 124, 207, 285, 317
    exceeding minute/text limits, 284
    family plans, 284
    free directory assistance, 283
    getting out of contracts, 284
    moisture precaution, 283
    polarized glasses and, 102
    recycling, 32
    sales rep secrets, 283–284
    scam alert, 266

    unlimited minute plans, 269
    vacation from, 364
    work, privacy and, 312
Cereals, 73
Checking and savings accounts, 294–295. *See also* Banks; Money
Chewing gum
    benefits of, 99, 324
    removing from hair, 7
Children. *See* Kids
Chimney sweep swindle, 45–46
Cleaning
    cars, 185–187
    clothing, 188–189, 190, 331
    furniture, 59
    home and appliances, 7–8, 35–36
    jewelry, 59, 216
Cleaning agents
    beer, 59
    biggest secret weapon, 36
    hazardous, recycling, 32
    vinegar, 35, 187, 190
    WD-40, 7–8
    weird, 187
Closets, organizing, 37–39, 40
Clothing
    buying tip, 211
    dressing for less, 288–289
    dry cleaning, 188–189, 331
    organizing, 37–39
    returning unused, 38
    stain removal for, 190–191
    storing winter, 38, 39
    for travel, 351
    washing, 10, 12, 288
Clutter, organizing, 40
Cobwebs, cleaning, 36
Coffee
    barista secrets, 54–55
    benefits of, 56
    café au lait vs. caffe latte, 132
    decaf, 49, 55
    stains from, 59, 190
    tea vs., 130
    whole bean, 55
Cola stains, 190
Collection agencies, 290–291

College
  financial aid, 258
  saving for, 300
Computers. *See also* E-mail; Internet
  antivirus scam, 266
  backing up, 203
  company-owned, 315
  energy efficiency tips, 11, 203
  IT department secrets, 314–315
  laptops, 245, 315
  maintenance tips, 203
  passwords and security, 202–203
  tech secrets, 202–203
Contractors
  hiring guidelines, 24
  plumbers, 2–3
  tips for working with, 22–23
Convenience foods, 64–65
Cooking spray, cleaning with, 187
Cookware, cast-iron, 282
Cosmetics. *See* Makeup
Credit cards
  ATM cards compared to, 257
  credit reports and, 258, 260
  debt-reduction strategies, 295–296
  identity theft and, 262, 263, 264
  interest rate reduction, 260, 296
  online scams, 266
  payment insurance, 269
  payment issues, 260, 261
  restaurant servers messing with, 49
  shopping with, 261
  text message scam, 266
Credit reports
  car loans and, 175
  checking your own, 258, 297
  credit cards and, 260
Cribs, 245
Crudités platter, 70
Cruises, 332, 352–353
Customer service
  cancellation threats, 222
  customer complaints, 220
  escalating tactics, 221–223
  going public about, 223
  guerrilla guide to, 220–224
  reaching a real person, 221

D

Debt. *See also* Credit cards; Loans
  collection agencies, 290–291
  percentage guidelines, 292
  reduction strategies, 295–297
Dental care
  bad breath, 99, 101
  bleeding gums and gum health, 98
  brushing/flossing, 98, 99
  dentist secrets, 98–100
  insurance issues, 100
  migraine headaches and, 99
  pain issues, 98, 99
  whitening teeth, 100
Deodorant stains, 191
Dermatologist secrets, 105–106
Diamonds, 216. *See also* Jewelry
Dieting. *See* Weight loss
Dietitian secrets, 126–128
Disability insurance, 298
Dishwashers, 11
Disney theme parks, 331, 354, 356
Doctors, hospitals, and doctor visits. *See also*
  Pharmacists and pharmaceuticals
  dermatologist secrets, 105–106
  doctor secrets, 84–85
  emergency rooms, 88, 90–91
  evaluating, choosing, 83, 87, 115
  eye doctor secrets, 102–104
  nurse secrets, 80–82
  pain issues, 80, 81, 92, 93, 98, 99
  patient information for, 83
  pediatrician secrets, 93–95
  podiatrist secrets, 107–109
  preventing medical mistakes, 83
  second opinions, 80, 83
  sleep doctor secrets, 110–112
  surgery tips, 115–117
  therapist secrets, 121–122, 142–143
  tips for doctor visits, 86–87
  trusting your instincts, 83, 95
  urgent care center secrets, 88–89
Doggie-doo, on shoes, 8
Dogs
  security and, 19
  sense of smell, 168
  training dos and don'ts, 166

veterinary secrets, 163–165

Doors
front, security tips, 18
locksmith secrets, 16–17
Drugs. *See* Pharmacists and pharmaceuticals
Dry cleaning, 188–189, 331
Dryer sheets, cleaning with, 187

E

Earwigs, controlling, 15
Eating out. *See* Restaurants
E-mail
address, impact of, 304
clearing inbox, 324
etiquette, 285
getting action from, 318
"phishing," 264
phrases to avoid, 316
public Wi-Fi precaution, 203
responding promptly, 318
travel alerts, 333, 362
vacation from, 364
work-related, 246–247, 285, 318
Emergency funds, 294–295
Emergency rooms, 88, 90–91. *See also* Doctors,
hospitals, and doctor visits
Energy
savings and efficiency tips, 9–10
tax credits and, 275
top 3 questions/answers, 12
Exercise
better sleep and, 114
eye health and, 104
family activities, 96–97
goals for, 125
gym memberships, 200–201
jet lag and, 339
personal trainers, 123–124, 201
for stress relief, 327–328
surprising workout tips, 125
work productivity and, 324–325
Exterminator secrets, 13–14
Eyes and eye health, 102–104

F

Facebook secrets, 232–233
Families. *See also* Kids; Marriage
adult relationships with parents, 149–151
cell phones plans, 284
healthier, more active, 96–97
nanny secrets, 152–153
sibling relationships, 170
traveling together, 332, 343, 357–358
when to take Grandpa's car keys away, 169
Fans, 11
Farmers' market tips, 68–69
Fast food worker secrets, 52–53
Feet, caring for, 107–109
Finances. *See* Banks; Credit cards; Insurance;
Investments; Loans; Money
Fish, 48
Flexible spending accounts, 297
Floors, cleaning, 7, 35
Flowers
choosing and displaying, 214
florist secrets, 212–213
making them last, 212–213
money-saving tips, 212
Food. *See also* Restaurants
choice comparisons, 130–132
convenience foods, 64–65
crudités platter, 70
energy efficient cooking, 9
for eye health, 104
farmers' market tips, 68–69
grocery shopping tips, 62–69
jet lag and, 338–339
kitchen knives, 241–242, 282
losing weight and (*See* Weight loss)
lunches, 129, 130, 323
manufacturer secrets, 71–73
organic, 74–75
TV chef secrets, 239–240
work productivity and, 323, 324, 325
Foot care, 107–109
401(k) accounts, 300
Free trial offers, 265
Friendship
between men and women, 169
mother/daughter, 171
social media and, 235

when to end, 170
Frozen vegetables, 64
Fruit, 75, 104, 131
Fruit juice stains, 190
Funeral director secrets, 218–219
Furniture (wood), cleaning, 59

G

Garbage disposals, 3
Gardening, 96
Gas- and fuel-saving tips, 177–178, 269
Generic products, 118, 119, 280
Glass, cleaning, 35
Glassware, stuck together, 7
Gluing technique, 6
Gold jewelry, cleaning, 59
Grease stains, 190
Grocery shopping tips, 62–69
Gym memberships, 200–201

H

Hair
    as health indicator, 193
    clarifying products, 194
    dye stains, 190
    economical treatments for, 59, 194–195
    hairstylist secrets, 192–193
    layering, 193
    loss, 105
    natural shine for, 195
    protecting drains from, 4
    removing chewing gum from, 7
    satin pillow covers and, 195
    shampooing, 194, 195
Handyman secrets, 5–6
Happiness, 170, 171
Hardware, storing, 5–6
Hazardous materials, recycling, 31–32
Headhunters secrets, 304–305, 320. *See also*
    Job search
Health. *See also* Dental care; Doctors, hospitals,
    and doctor visits
    eye care, 102–104
    foot care, 107–109
    hair as indicator of, 193

healthier, more active families, 96–97
    heart attack response guide, 92
    preventing medical mistakes, 83
    sleep and, 110–112
    trusting your instincts, 83, 95
Health insurance, 297–298
Heart attack response guide, 92
Heating and cooling, 10, 11, 104
Helmets, buying, 245
Hiking, 96
Home
    basement boondoggle, 44
    burglar secrets, 19–20
    chimney sweep swindle, 45–46
    cleaning tips, 7–8, 35–36
    housecleaner secrets, 33–34
    increasing value of, 27–28
    mold scam, 46
    moving tips, 29–30
    organizing, 37–40
    painting exterior, 27–28
    pest control, 7, 8, 13–15, 44–45
    contractor secrets, 22–24
    repair scam alerts, 43–46
    roof repairs and maintenance, 43
    security while vacationing, 21
    selling tips, 25–26
    yard sale tips, 41–42
Hospitals. *See* Doctors, hospitals, and doctor visits
Hotels
    concierge kickback alert, 346
    deal-making tips, 334, 345, 348–350,
    363
    desk clerk secrets, 345–346
    dry-cleaning bills, 331
    hidden fees, 349
    resort fee waivers, 331–332
    safety tips, 347
    tipping in, 346
Hot spot imposters, 265
Housecleaner secrets, 33–34

I

Identity thief secrets, 262–264
"I'm sorry," saying, 151, 172
Insects and pests. *See* Pest control

Insurance
    auto service warranties, 269
    car, 297
    contractor liability, 23
    credit card payment, 269
    dental, 100
    disability, 298
    health, 297–298
    housecleaners and, 34
    investing with, 259, 298
    jewelry, 216
    life, 259, 298
    long-term-care, 298
    money-saving tips, 297–298
    moving and, 30
Internet
    banking online, 257, 294
    coupons and discounts on, 280, 286, 288
    free trial offers, 265
    hot spot imposters, 265
    online safety, 202–203, 246–254
    pharmacies online, 120
    public Wi-Fi precaution, 203
    scams to avoid, 265–266
    shopping online, 243–244
Investments
    banks and, 299
    building portfolio, 299–300
    insurance as, 259, 298
    in stocks and mutual funds, 299–300
    tax implications of, 259
IRS secrets, 274–276
IT department secrets, 314–315

J

Jet lag, avoiding, 338–339
Jewelry
    buying, 215–216
    cleaning, 59, 216
    insurance for, 216
    jeweler secrets, 215–216
    removing stuck rings, 7, 215
    storing, 217
Job search
    following up with prospective employers, 311–312

    headhunter secrets, 304–305, 320
    hiring biases, 308
    hiring manager secrets, 308–309
    HR secrets, 311–312
    interview tips, 308–309
    networking tips, 304, 311
    résumés for, 304–307, 310
    salary/benefits negotiation, 320–321

K

Ketchup stains, 190
Keys and locks, 16–18
Kids
    baby products, 204–205, 245
    babysitters for, 140
    back-to-school stress and, 156
    becoming adults, 170
    camp costs, 159
    camp counselor secrets, 157–158
    child care tax credit, 276
    crayon stains, 191
    family activities with, 96–97
    haircuts, 193
    health insurance for, 297–298
    mother/daughter friendships, 171
    nannies and, 152–153
    parents berating, 172
    pediatrician secrets, 93–95
    road-trip games/activities, 357–358
    Santa (mall) secrets, 160–161
    sibling relationships, 170
    social media and, 247–249
    tax returns for, 293
    teacher secrets, 154–155
    teaching money management to, 162
    vaccinating, 93
Knives, kitchen, 241–242, 282

L

Laptop computers, 245, 315
Lemon oil, cleaning with, 36
Lemons
    for hair care, 195
    for pest control, 14, 15

requesting in restaurants, 48
Libraries, 280
Life insurance, 259, 298
Life's toughest questions, 167–172
Lights
    recycling CFL bulbs, 31
    turning off, 12
Lines, slow-moving, 55, 168, 354
LinkedIn, 229–231, 311
Loans. *See also* Credit cards
    car, 175
    credit reports and, 258
    debt collector secrets, 290–291
    debt guidelines, 292
    debt-reduction strategies, 295–297
    mortgages, 292, 296
    small business, 256
    tax refund anticipation, 278, 294
Locksmith secrets, 16–17
Long-term-care insurance, 298
Lottery tickets, 270

M

Makeup
    industry secrets, 196–197
    for tired faces, 198–199
Marriage. *See also* Families; Kids
    lasting love, 167
    marriage counselor secrets, 142–143
    mothers-in-law and, 146–148
    scheduling time for, 144
    sex and, 139, 140
    signs of failing, 143
    social media and, 252–253
    between spenders and savers, 171
    strengthening relationship, 144–145
    survey results, 145
    surviving betrayal, 167–168
    tips from happily married people, 139–141
    wedding planning, 134–138
    why spouses begin to look alike, 167
    work spillover and, 145
Mattresses, 110–111, 245
Mayonnaise, cleaning with, 187
Meat

buying tips, 65, 66–67
    freezing, 67
    sirloin steak vs. rib-eye, 132
    tenderizing with beer, 59
Media. *See* Social media; Television sets and programs
Mold scam, 46
Money. *See also* Credit cards; Insurance; Investments; Loans; Taxes
    banker secrets, 256–257
    checking and savings accounts, 294–295
    common mistakes with, 258–259
    contractor issues, 22–24
    debt-reduction strategies, 295–297
    emergency funds, 294–295
    financial advisor secrets, 267–268
    foreign currency transactions, 331
    happiness and, 171
    identity thief secrets, 262–264
    nest eggs, 292
    online scams to avoid, 265–266
    paying for things not used, 280
    as root of all evil, 171
    saving strategies, 279–281, 293–301
    six things not worth spending on, 269–270
    smart-spender parameters, 292
    spenders and savers marrying, 171
    teaching kids about, 162
Mortgages, 292, 296
Mothers-in-law, 146–148
Movies, staycation marathon, 364
Moving tips, 29–30
Mr. Clean Magic Eraser, 35

N

Nannies, 152–153
National parks, 359–361
Nest eggs, 292
"No," and stress relief, 327
Nurse secrets, 80–82. *See also* Doctors, hospitals, and doctor visits

O

Olives, 131
Oranges vs. apples, 131
Organic food, 74–75
Organization tips, 37–40
Ovens
    cleaning, 35, 36
    energy efficiency and, 9

P

Pain issues
    dental problems and, 98, 99
    health care providers and, 80, 81
    heart attack symptoms, 92
    vaccinations and, 93
Painting
    drip catcher, 5
    home exterior, 27–28
Parents. *See also* Families; Kids; Marriage
    adult relationship with, 149–151
    advice from, 150
    back-to-school stress management, 156
    berating child, 172
    mother/daughter friendships, 171
    turning into our parents, 170
Pasta, 73
Pediatrician secrets, 93–95
Perf board uses, 6
Personal trainers, 123–124, 201
Pest control
    exterminator secrets, 13–15
    squirrels, 7
    termites, 44–45
    wasps, 8
Pets. *See* Cats; Dogs
Pharmacists and pharmaceuticals
    generic drugs, 118, 119
    newest drugs, 85, 89, 93–94
    online pharmacies, 120
    pain medications, 89, 112
    pharmacist secrets, 118–119
Photo albums, 282
Pizza delivery, 60–61
Plumbing. *See also* Toilets
    avoiding clogged drains, 4
    tips from plumbers, 2–3, 4

water conservation tips, 4
Podiatrist secrets, 107–109
Processed food, 64–65, 71–73
Productivity
    increasing, 323–325
    social media and, 234
Professional organizer secrets, 37–39

R

Real estate tips, 25–26
Refrigerator efficiency, 9–10
Relationships, and social media, 235, 252–253
Resort fee waivers, 331–332
Restaurants
    barista secrets, 54–55
    bartender secrets, 57–58
    fast food, 52–53
    getting great service, 76–77
    pizza delivery, 60–61
    staycation splurge, 364
    tipping, 50, 51, 61, 77
    waiter secrets, 48–50
Résumés
    for career changers, 306–307
    checking on status of, 312
    cover letters for, 310
    headhunter secrets, 304–305
    writing tips, 304–305
Retirement
    investments for, 300
    nest egg for, 292
    Social Security and, 301
Roof repairs and maintenance, 43
Rust stains, 191

S

Safety and security
    burglar secrets, 19–20
    front-door security, 18
    of home while vacationing, 21
    in hotels, 347
    identity thief secrets, 262–264
    locksmith secrets, 16–17
    online safety, 202–203, 246–254
Salad dressings, 132

Salads, 49, 64, 132, 323

Santa (mall) secrets, 160–161

Sausage vs. bacon, 130

Savings and checking accounts, 294–295. *See also* Banks; Money

School

    back-to-school stress, 156

    teacher secrets, 154–155

Scuff marks, removing, 7

Seasons, perceived length of, 168

Secrets, revealing, 172

Security. *See* Safety and security

Seniors, driving, 169

Sensory perception, of animals, 168

Sex, 139, 140

Sexual harassment, 321

Shoes and boots

    best socks for, 109

    foot care and, 108–109

    proper fit, 109, 208

    removing doggie-doo from, 8

    shoe salesmen secrets, 207–208

    shopping for, 207–208

    for travel, 351

    waterproofing, 8

Shopping. *See also* Customer service

    at 99-cent stores, 209

    big-ticket purchases, 281

    buying quality items, 282

    loyalty cards, 210, 280

    men's tip, 211

    money-saving tips, 279–281, 286–287, 288–289

    online daily deals, 243–244

    outlet stores, 244

    retailer marketing strategies, 210–211

    retailer pricing strategies, 209–210

    sales clerk secrets, 286–287

    used items to avoid, 245

Skin care, 105–106

Sleep

    going to bed angry, 142–143

    improving, 110–112, 235

    during staycation, 363

    stress-reducing tips for, 113–114

    time with spouse and, 141

Slugs and snails, controlling, 15

Social media

    benefits of quitting, 234–235

    Facebook secrets, 232–233

    LinkedIn tips, 229–231, 311

    Twitter, 285

    what not to post, 246–254

Social Security benefits, 301

Social Security numbers, 263, 264, 277

Socks

    best materials for, 109

    waxing car with, 187

    wearing to bed, 111

Soups, 48, 129, 132

Sports equipment, storing, 40

Stain removal

    clothing, 190–191

    countertops, 8

    rugs, 59

Staycations, 363–364

Stock investments, 299–300

Stock options, 300–301

Storage tips

    hardware, 5–6

    household items, 40, 206

    jewelry, 217

    tools, 6

    winter clothing, 38, 39

Strawberries, 131

Stress management

    for back-to-school stress, 156

    for better sleep, 113–114

    counting to ten for, 327

    exercise for, 327–328

    mental relaxation techniques, 326–327

    saying "No" and, 327

    scheduling worry time for, 327

    social media and, 235

    time-outs, 327–328

    for travel stress, 351

    for workplace stress, 326–328

Suede, cleaning, 190

Sugar

    natural vs. white, 131

    in processed foods, 72

    in restaurant food, 48

Sunscreen, 196, 197

Surgery tips, 115–117

T

Taxes
    accountant secrets, 271–273
    audits, 271–272, 276
    avoiding preventable errors, 277
    deductions and credits, 272, 274–275, 276
    filing extensions, 273
    on investments, 259
    IRS secrets, 274–276
    kids filing returns, 293
    long vs. short form, 293
    money-saving tips, 293–294
    paying pros to prepare, 272, 277
    preparation tips, 271, 277–278
    receipts and records for, 271, 272
    refunds, 274, 278, 294
    self-employment and, 272, 275
Taxis, taxi drivers, 58, 332
Tea
    benefits of, 130, 323
    coffee vs., 130
    for foot odor, 107
    iced, powdered, 64
    stains from, 8, 59, 190
Teacher secrets, 154–155
Teeth and oral health. *See* Dental care
Television sets and programs
    ads, noise level of, 228
    reality TV shows, 236–238
    staycation marathon, 364
    TV chef secrets, 239–240
    weatherman secrets, 226–227
Termites, 44–45
Text messages. *See also* Cell phones
    scams, 266, 284
    work, privacy and, 312
Therapist secrets, 121–122, 142–143
Thermostat efficiency, 10
Tile, cleaning, 36
Time-outs, for stress relief, 327–328
Tipping etiquette
    in hotels, 346
    for pizza delivery, 61
    in restaurants, 50, 51, 77
Tires
    buying used, 245
    inflation pressure, 178, 179, 180
    life-extending tips, 179–180
    rotating, 180
    storing "snakes" in, 6
    tread levels, 179–180, 182
Toast, falling buttered-side down, 172
Toilets
    cleaning, 8, 36
    clogged, 4
    running continuously, 4
    seat replacement, 3
Tomatoes vs. tomato sauce, 132
Tools
    preventing rust on, 5
    quality of, 282
    storing, 6
Traffic jams, origin of, 168–169
Trail mix, 64
Train travel, 332
Travel. *See* Air travel; Vacations and travel
Trusts, avoiding, 258–259

U

Urgent care centers, 88–89. *See also* Doctors, hospitals, and doctor visits

V

Vacations and travel. *See also* Air travel; Hotels
    affordable vacation tips, 333–334
    amusement park secrets, 354–356
    car rentals, 334
    cruises, 332, 352–353
    Disney theme parks, 331, 354, 356
    dry-cleaning and, 331
    foreign currency and, 331
    home security while away, 21
    laptop precaution, 315
    last-minute vacations, 362–363
    off-season/off-peak, 348, 349, 363
    park ranger secrets, 359–361
    public transportation, 349
    road-trip games/activities, 357–358
    staycations, 363–364
    stress management for, 351
    taxi drivers and, 332
    train travel, 332

travel agent secrets, 330–332
turning water off while away, 4
work travel, 312, 315
world traveler secrets, 348–350
Vegetables
frozen, 64
organic, 75
Veterinary secrets, 163–165
Vinegar
as ant-repellent, 14
cleaning with, 35, 187
for hair care, 194, 195
for stain removal, 190–191
Vision and eye care, 102–104
Visualization, 326
Vitamins, for pets, 164

W

Washing machines, 4
Wasp nests, preventing, 8
Water
avoiding damage in home, 3, 4
bottled, 270
conservation tips, 4
hydration/dehydration, 106, 124, 361
ordering in restaurants, 49
sparkling vs. club soda, 131
temperature and energy efficiency, 10
turning supply off, 2, 4
WD-40 uses, 7–8
Weatherman secrets, 226–227
Weatherproofing, 10
Wedding planning
cost-cutting tips, 137–138
wedding planner secrets, 134–136
Weight loss
big meal of the day and, 129
clothes shopping and, 289
resisting food temptations, 126–128
worldwide tips for, 129
Wills, 298–299
Window coverings

for better sleep, 111
cleaning blinds, 35
energy efficiency and, 10
Windows
preventing snow buildup on, 8
security issues, 16, 19–20
Wine
buying, 280
stains from, 190
Work. *See also* Computers; Job search
asking for raise, 322
collection agencies calling at, 291
company stock, 300–301
coworker secrets, 317–318
e-mail, 246–247, 285, 318
401(k) plans, 300
HR secrets, 311–312
interacting with coworkers, 314–315, 317–318
IT department secrets, 314–315
knowing what you want to do, 168
marriage and, 145
meetings people won't dread, 319
office antics, 313
paranoia alert, 312
payroll manager secrets, 320–321
productivity enhancers, 234, 323–325
protocol importance, 321
salary issues, 320–322
satisfaction in, 169
sexual harassment charges, 321
stress management and, 113, 326–328
top job security factor, 312
unlimited sick days, 321
Wrinkle Releaser spray, 331

X

X-Rays, 99

Y

Yard sale tips, 41–42

Keep discovering new secrets all year long with

America's Favorite Magazine

featuring the ever-popular
13 Things They Won't Tell You column
and so much more!